FORGIVENESS AND OTHER ACTS OF LOVE

Stephanie Dowrick was born in New Zealand, worked in Europe for many years, and now lives in Sydney with her family. She worked in publishing during the 1970s, but since 1982 writing has been her principal occupation. She is currently Chairwoman of The Women's Press, London, which she co-founded in 1977. She is actively engaged with the concerns of modern life, and has experience in a range of psychotherapeutic approaches, including Psychosynthesis, analytic therapy and Jungian analysis. Her novels and nonfiction works, as well as her regular contributions to ABC Radio National's 'Life Matters' and *New Woman*, have gained her a wide following. Her published works include the much-loved international bestsellers *Intimacy and Solitude* and *The Intimacy and Solitude Workbook*.

Also by Stephanie Dowrick

NON-FICTION

Land of Zeus

Intimacy and Solitude

The Intimacy and Solitude Workbook

FICTION

Running Backwards Over Sand (Viking, 1985)

Tasting Salt (Viking, late 1997)

CHILDREN'S FICTION

Katherine Rose Says No

AUDIOTAPES

Intimacy and Solitude

Living with Change

The Humane Virtues

Forgiveness and Other Acts of Love

STEPHANIE DOWRICK

W. W. Norton & Company

New York • London

For information about permission to reproduce selections from this book, write to
Permissions, W. W. Norton & Company, Inc., 500 Fifth Avenue, New York, NY 10110.

The text of this book is composed in Bembo
Manufacturing by The Haddon Craftsmen, Inc.
Book design by Sandy Cull, Penguin Design Studio
Calligraphy by Ingrid Garbenis

Library of Congress Cataloging-in-Publication Data

Dworick, Stephanie.
Forgiveness and other acts of lonve / Stephanie Dowrick. —1st American ed.
p. cm.
Includes bibliographical references.
ISBN 0-393-04545-5
1. Virtues. 2. Conduct of life. 3. Dowrick, Stephanie. I. Title
BJ1521.D68   1997
248.4—dc21   97-17814
CIP

ISBN 0-393-31820-6 pbk.

W. W. Norton & Company, Inc., 500 Fifth Avenue, New York, N. Y. 10110
http://www.wwnorton.com

W. W. Norton & Company Ltd., 10 Coptic Street, London CW1A 1PU

1 2 3 4 5 6 7 8 9 0

Contents

FOR JANE MOORE,
AND FOR GABRIEL AND KEZIA

Cultivate Virtue in your own person,

And it becomes a genuine part of you.

Cultivate it in the family,

And it will abide.

Cultivate it in the community,

And it will live and grow.

Cultivate it in the state,

And it will flourish abundantly.

Cultivate it in the world,

And it will become universal.

TAO TEH CHING

Introduction

*T*he one thing that a writer should never be short of is words. Yet when it comes to explaining how I had the temerity to write about six of the greatest qualities humankind has ever named – and to try to make sense of their personal and social meaning at this point in our shared history – I find myself searching for something beyond words.

First some facts. In 1995 I was diagnosed with breast cancer. That experience, which finds many silent echoes within this book, has been life-changing. Yet it took me months even to be able to speak of it beyond my group of closest friends. I was not filled with courage or fortitude in the wake of the diagnosis. What arose in me was devastating fear that my children would be left, as I had been, without a mother.

Then there was more. At the beginning of 1996 I was faced with a court case I had been dreading and hoping to avoid for three years. Negotiations to find a settlement had failed. The time had arrived when the matter would go to trial.

I had to find whatever strength it would take to endure that. A bone weariness that seemed to have settled within me and aged me twice over was my constant companion.

It was in this extreme situation that I remembered what I had learned twenty years before when I first encountered Psychosynthesis, an approach to psychotherapy that is as attentive to spiritual and social concerns as it is to personal awareness and healing. It was Psychosynthesis founder Roberto Assagioli's view that there are qualities that we can call on, almost like entities. He also taught that *what we pay attention to, reverberates in our lives.*

I had spent three years paying attention to a legal case, having to return repeatedly and in debilitating detail to the past. During that time I was also writing, occasionally teaching, seeing clients, enjoying my friends and loving and being loved by my children. Yet I felt the case was also always present: or perhaps what was present was my anxiety about its emotional and physical costs, which seemed all too gruesomely mirrored by the financial costs.

It was at that time of grim uncertainty that I suggested to Geraldine Doogue, presenter of 'Life Matters' on the Australian Broadcasting Corporation's Radio National, that I would like to embark on a series of fortnightly talks with her on what I was then calling 'the humane virtues'. I chose the word 'humane' for its silken, civilising quality; for its promise of kindness, decency, truthfulness and order; and because it is through our 'humanity' that we recognise our connections with one another. And I chose these six virtues for what they could teach me about honour, strength, humility, steadfastness and endurance and, above all, for what they could teach me about love: that sublime ideal that comes to life only when it moves from intention to action.

For a year, Geraldine and I had been talking to each other on radio each fortnight. In the strange, refracted intimacy of those public broadcasts, we had covered a whole range of topics of concern to people trying to make sense of their lives and to live them with increasing awareness, self-responsibility and choice. With a breadth of social, psychological and spiritual concerns established between us, we 'took on' the virtues.

The court proceedings lasted for five days but those days were spread over several months. Throughout that time, I worked closely and intensely on the virtues, meeting each of them – courage, fidelity, restraint, generosity, tolerance and forgiveness – in turn, and experiencing how each did, indeed, endow me with its unique grace and blessing.

ROBERTO ASSAGIOLI HAS not been the only psychological or spiritual teacher to know that one's circumstances are in part created by the quality of one's attention to meaning. Each of the world's major religions has taught its followers to pay as close attention to the companions within their minds – their own thoughts – as they would to their companions in the world outside.

From his knowledge of Hindu philosophy and Western science, endocrinologist and writer Deepak Chopra explains the process in more detail: 'You can consciously change the energy and informational content of your *own* quantum mechanical body, and therefore influence the energy and informational content of your extended body – your environment, your world – and cause things to manifest in it.

'This conscious change is brought about by the two qualities inherent in consciousness: attention and intention. Attention energizes, and intention transforms. *Whatever you put your attention on will grow stronger in your life* [my italics]. Whatever you take your attention away from will wither, disintegrate, and disappear. Intention, on the other hand, triggers transformation of energy and information. Intention organizes its own fulfilment.'

THE ACUTE PHASE of my crisis passed. But aftershocks remained, and I continued to need the virtues. The more I had come to know them, the more convinced I had become that these ancient 'entities' – which are among the most profound expressions of compassionate love known to humankind – offer something that is surely as urgently and universally needed now as at any other time in human history.

We have never been more deluged with information about how to live. We have never been richer or better educated. Yet there is despair everywhere. How do we meet that? How do we salvage wisdom, resilience and even meaning out of meaningless suffering? How do we cultivate love in a climate of selfishness, petulance and greed? How do we remain alert to what we share with people whose rage and negativity cost us our homes, our happiness and perhaps our lives? How should we meet the blindness and arrogance that threaten the planet on which we depend for our most transformative experiences of wonder and beauty, as well as for our very existence?

Individual solutions have come to seem increasingly hollow. No matter how sincere or hard won, personal insight or even spiritual enlightenment that has no roots in a commitment to social responsibility and planetary justice offers paltry salvation. But experience has taught us that we should equally be extremely wary of any attempts to save the outer world that fail also to look at the relationships closest to home; that fail to develop subtle, constant self-responsibility, maturity, awareness and compassion.

The brilliance of the humane virtues is that they are big enough to embrace all the spheres of human existence: inner and outer; personal and social; psychological and spiritual. They are humble as well as awe-inspiring. They can teach us as much about beauty as survival; and as much through silence as through words.

It has been exceptionally moving to discover time and again, sitting in my office in a wooden house in an ordinary street in suburban Australia, that many of our most urgent questions about how to live, how to love, how to endure and relieve suffering, were answered thousands of years ago. And to discover how, in cultures as diverse as those of India, China, Tibet, Persia, Greece and the Middle East, we are returned repeatedly to the unifying principles of love, as well as to a sobering gratitude for life itself.

One of the most stunning privileges of late-twentieth-century life is that we do now have Eastern spiritual and psychological teachings easily available to us, as well as the freshly reclaimed teachings of Christian mysticism. In writing this book, I have plucked jewels as freely from the East as from the West, gathering as I went psychological insight, wisdom and inspiration, as well as moments of awesome splendour and relieving hilarity.

Yet what I learned from the virtues returns me to the limitation of words. There are words in this book that can readily inspire fresh thinking and action, but for these ideas to become tools for transformation and healing, they need to reach into an opened heart, perhaps even a cracked heart. From five thousand years ago, this voice calls to us from *The Egyptian Book of the Dead*:

My heart, my mother;
my heart, my mother!
My heart of transformations.

Listening through the heart is not something you must learn to do. It is something you need only reclaim, and remember.

Forgiveness
and Other Acts
of Love

Courage

It isn't for the moment that you are struck that you

need courage, but for the long uphill climb back

to sanity and faith and security.

ANNE MORROW LINDBERGH

C ourage comes out of and expresses love. This love may be intensely personal or individual, but it is just as likely to express a commitment to the belief that life itself is something marvellous, precious, worth having, worth living fully and, in ten thousand ways, worth fighting for.

Psychological and spiritual teachings increasingly suggest that the opposite of love is fear. Courage, as an expression of love, does not put an end to fear. Nothing can do that. Fear is part of the human condition. But courage offers something that can balance fear, draw the sting from it, put it in its place, open us to life, and set us free.

BEING COURAGEOUS IS not quite the same thing as being brave. Being brave is easier to think about somehow; more literal, more linear. I move towards this topic tentatively.

'What is your first memory ever of being brave?' I ask ten people. Mostly they smile, remembering. This is what they say.

'School. Definitely the first day of school.'
'My mother went away somewhere for a few days. I was told to be brave and I was.'

'Preschool.'

'Having my tonsils out. Going to hospital and feeling I was
  completely by myself.'

'Waking up in a dark room. I must have been less than two.
  I was in a cot. It was cold and dark. Or is that my first
  memory of being afraid?'

'I can't remember anything before I was ten . . . Maybe I am
  not brave enough to remember! But when I was ten
  I learned to swim. That was really brave.'

'Starting school. I thought the day would never arrive. When
  it did, I thought it would never end.'

'Can I tell you about my most recent memory instead? I was
  able to stay with my mother through her several weeks
  of agonising dying. That really took me into a new realm
  of braveness.'

'I broke my arm when I was about two. I've always been told
  how brave I was when that happened and I can still preen!'

'Being thrown into the air. It terrified me and I wanted to
  cry. Somehow, I didn't. I asked for more.'

'WHAT DO YOU think courage is?' I ask my friend Sally. She's
a writer and a dream therapist. Both those areas of work are
confronting. In neither of them is there much hiding. In her
personal life, too, Sally pursues a path of knowledge rather than
ease. She surely knows a great deal about courage. I want
something from her, something illuminating. I can feel my
teeth getting ready to bite.

  She laughs. Her own teeth flash. 'Writing about it. It takes
courage to write about courage.'

We sit in silence. And think the same thought: *but it takes much more courage to live it.*

LISTENING TO PEOPLE talk, I hear repeated stories of what it is like to step from the known into the unknown – or to be pushed. Leaving one's mother; going to school; becoming an adult; entering a new relationship; becoming a parent; a marriage collapsing; the loss of paid work; the loss of a breast or the use of limbs; an unexpected failure or success; the death of someone loved; the loss of certainty; the darkness of self-doubt; discovering middle age, old age; living through illness and facing death: these are all voyages into the new.

Courage is more than voyaging, though. It is voyaging *and* reflecting. It is an engagement with the complexity of life through the body, the powers of the intellect *and* what some would call heart or soul. 'I don't want to do this, but I choose to.' 'I will go with this even though it is hard.' 'I will face this with my eyes open.' 'I am ready to move on.'

Sometimes the reflecting is done on the run. But it's there.

WITHOUT COURAGE THERE can be little consciousness. Increasing our consciousness or awareness of who and what we individually and collectively are – and may be – demands courage and allows it. It takes courage to wake up to how mysterious and profound life is, and not to avoid, deny, scorn, repress or contain what doesn't fit easily with our world view. It takes courage to know how wrong we can be, and allow our minds to be changed as well as broadened. It takes courage to live wholeheartedly through the range of all our emotions: to be as thoroughly sad and uncertain as we are sometimes buoyant and sure. It takes courage to dive into the murky complexities, ambiguities and contradictions that make up each life, to think about what lies beneath the surface of things that are available to the rational mind. To bring up what is usually revealed only indirectly through dreams, symbols, slips of the tongue, jokes; the way we react when someone speaks to us; the way we breathe, walk, make gestures, sit, smile; the way we dress, cook meals, pick our hobbies, our friends; the way we care for the earth, create our homes. None of us has the courage to face the meaning of all of that, all of the time. It is not even desirable that we should. Life is for living, as well as for contemplating. But when we can and do live our life with some commitment to discovering *what is* – what is open and free in ourselves, as well as what is shadowy and unpalatable – then we are, inevitably, equipping ourselves also to face the unknown.

'THE PURPOSE OF life is to be happy,' says the Dalai Lama. It's a huge claim and, as an unambiguous statement, somewhat provocative, especially when Buddhism urges us to pay close enough attention to suffering to know, eventually, how to free ourselves from it. But given that happiness is what most human beings want, how should any of us achieve it? The Dalai Lama goes on: 'As a Buddhist I have found that one's own mental attitude is the most influential factor in working towards that goal.'

Courage is a mental attitude that finds its expression through words, gestures, feelings and deeds. It can be cultivated and enhanced, but it is not, itself, an emotion. It involves emotions and it can certainly change our emotions, yet it arises from thought, and is supported by 'right thinking'. That is, it is supported in part by what we pay attention to; what we allow ourselves to see, experience, feel, absorb and express; how we liberate the potentials of consciousness.

This notion – that courage is, or arises from, a mental attitude – brings courage into reach. We can't choose our feelings. They are like the elements: wind, rain, fog, cloud, snow, heat. They come and go. But attitudes are something else entirely. We can choose them, even when they seem a little reluctant to choose us.

Courage is a way of living in the world. It arises out of the cultivation of an attitude that you can then bring to any situation, even when you feel at your worst. It is courage that is needed when a crisis has long ceased to be exciting and has become instead a new version of your old life to which you must adjust; when the person who was in intensive care now needs hourly turning in a clean bed into an indefinite future; when your intellectually disabled child turns twelve and needs sanitary towels as well as nappies; when you have been unemployed for three years and face the possibility of never being employed again; when you are thirty-nine and have neither the partner nor the child you had always hoped for; when you must spend your days in a nursing home to save the health and energy of your aged partner whom you still passionately love.

Courage is what allows you to learn that even when life has apparently betrayed you *life itself is still present*. In the presence of life, it is impossible to be totally diminished by events that are outside you, or are outside your control, no matter how deeply and permanently they affect you. It is possible – with time, self-love, compassion and some creativity – to again find some pleasure, some joy. A neighbour calls by to relieve you for an hour and tells you a story that has you both helpless with laughter. Your disabled child sings, in perfect tune, the entire first verse of 'Jesu, Joy of Man's Desiring'. You give a day to writing letters on behalf of your neighbourhood, which you could never have spared while you were working. You wake up in the morning to a quiet house; the phone rings, and you are asked to drop everything and take part in a marvellous event, which you can accept only because you do not have ties. You return to your own apartment from the nursing home and see, in your ancient partner's eyes, the excited anticipation of the young man reunited with his great love.

COURAGE CAN BE admired from any distance, but it can be discovered only through experience. Sometimes this has to be achieved in the midst of drudgery and hardship. Sometimes it is found through intense physical achievement that brings supreme joy as intention and action unite. Often, though, courage takes on meaning through an experience of profound suffering when what had seemed eternal or essential dissolves or disappears, and your faith in life, in yourself, or in God, hits the line. You lose a beloved person, a job, a relationship, your health, a sense of continuity with your own life. You flounder, shout, wail, panic, become depressed, blame, roar or retreat. *And then days, weeks or years later you move from that outraged place. You move onwards, inwards.* Not neatly, not conclusively. But somehow you face it – whatever 'it' is. You face the truth of that suffering within yourself. You face the truth of it, *and* the truth that it will not be adequately met with facile solutions or other people's platitudes, but only with your own version of resilience and compassion.

'Existence,' warns the analyst Irvin D. Yalom, 'cannot be postponed.' In not postponing existence, in not postponing *life* – while also acknowledging how helpless you feel and how great your need is – courage stirs and comes awake.

That doesn't happen neatly or conclusively either. A young man from our neighbourhood was in a car crash. He is totally paralysed. He needs a machine to breathe for him, and other people to attend to his most basic needs. He will never again be able to feel the earth beneath his feet or reach out to touch someone playfully or with desire. For two years he repeated every day that he wished he were dead. Then, between one day and the next, or maybe between one minute and the next, something shifted within him. Life asserted itself. Love asserted itself. *And he was able to meet that.*

Without knowing why, he finds himself the possessor of more courage than he knew he had, although he isn't calling it courage. He would shrug at the mention of the word if his body allowed it. Instead he simply says that, for whatever reason, life matters.

Each day he must practise versions of the courage he has already discovered. But in two more years, or five, or fifteen, he will need to discover courage all over again: when he sees his friends marrying, knowing that he will never marry; when he wakes up from a dream that he has been running and knows that he will never run; when the residual privacy he has is thoughtlessly invaded; when middle age and then perhaps old age bring him the possibility of fresh regrets, as well as deepening insight and wisdom.

James Hall is a Jungian analyst and well-known writer. In 1991, at the age of fifty-seven, he had a stroke that paralysed him so severely he had to be taught how to swallow. He communicates via a computer keyboard, and spends his time mainly within the walls of his Dallas home. Yet he was able to say to journalist Dee Wedemeyer, 'Life is, if anything, more interesting than before I was disabled. I don't worry now about such things as reputation and earning a living. With essentially nothing to lose, I am more open about what I think.'

After the stroke, Hall converted to Catholicism. Asked if he believes that God could heal him, he replied, '"God", as I conceive him/her, could heal me but would not. In a deep sense, there is nothing to "heal" me from. Obviously [I] could use physical healing to restore my previous level of function, but I am psychologically healthier than I have ever been.'

With Hall lives his wife, Suzanne. She has loved him since she was an adolescent. We can only guess at the courage it takes for her to mourn the husband who has now gone forever, while caring continually for a husband who is still a man but must in many ways be cared for like a baby. A baby, however, grows up and becomes independent. Carers of the permanently disabled have no such perspective.

Where does such courage arise from? How does it take hold? How is it lived, day in, day out? How do you prevent courage from curdling into resentment, rage, hostility, abandonment, despair?

Some people may be temperamentally more courageous than others, more open to life, accepting, resilient and flexible. But even those of us who might lay claim to none of those things can discover how courage is learned.

Reflecting on the two agonisingly painful years that have passed since the death of her thirteen-year-old son, William, after a hit-and-run accident at the side of a country road, Carol Mara said to me: 'I have learned courage I think from that moment that we knew he could die. I knew this was going to take much more than I felt I might have ever had, but I somehow knew that I would find it in myself to face what was going to happen.

'In the aftermath of William's death, I found myself doing things that I would never have imagined doing before, particularly say six months or so down the track when I felt that his death was not of consequence to the legal authorities. They didn't really want to know the whole truth. I felt, "I have to do something about this because no one else will." That's when I found the courage. I had to have enormous courage to put this on display to the world, to say, "*This* is what happened. Is this right? Shouldn't our system be acknowledging the loss of a life in a different way?" It took an awful lot of courage.'

Was it love or anger that drove her to act?

'I found the courage more out of love than anger, although I think that in doing that I was also able to deal with my anger in a constructive way in that I was actually doing something. But I could not let William's death – or William – be of so little consequence in this whole scheme of things. That led me to keep on going.

'If I hadn't found the courage to do what I did, I don't think I would have survived as well as I have. I would have felt that I had let William down and that I had not been true to myself about what was happening. There was a choice. I can remember fairly well when I had to decide, "Am I going to let this go?" I wanted it to be finished and done with but I thought, "I have to do something about this." If it had been stubbornness only, I'd have just been doing what was normal to my personality. But this was out of character for me. It was something new.'

That 'something new' Carol speaks of enlarges not only your perception of yourself, but also of the world around you, of life itself. Courage demands and gives an almost imperceptible degree of detachment, a willingness to look at the bigger picture; a willingness to acknowledge that you are making choices about your own life, even when you feel that fate or plain bad luck has dealt you a terrible blow, or many blows.

It is also likely that someone who is able to rise to the tremendous, unending challenge of surviving a premature death, or a complete loss of mobility, or who is caring for such a person, has been building up their intimate knowledge of courage, bit by bit, through a lifetime of subtle, undramatic, but basically trusting choices.

No matter how treacherous your personal circumstances may be, courage asks you to continue to experience and to express how precious life is. 'It is a great event to be born a human being!' teaches the Buddhist scripture, the Dhammapada. There is no greater challenge in life than to live as though you are aware of that.

I talk to Eloise. She is forty now and works with physically disabled children. She is open-faced, warm, funny, immensely appealing. Yet she spent most of her twenties in a heroin-induced haze. She made the money to support her habit through prostitution. 'It was no problem selling my body,' she told me, 'because I thought my soul had long gone.'

At twenty-eight, Eloise came close to death. She was beaten up by a client and taken to hospital, where one of the nurses turned out to be someone she knew from her school days. Janine took on the care of Eloise, took her home, fed her, built up her physical strength and insisted that she went to meditation and yoga classes.

Somehow, Eloise was able to comprehend that she had come to a crossroads. 'It was literally life and death. I had reached the pits. There was only one thing I hadn't tried – and that was to live decently. I could only sit for about two minutes at a time in meditation and I could hardly manage the simplest posture in yoga. I didn't care. Some part of me reached out and knew that this was the way I would save myself. That part of me held on even when the rest of me was going crazy and pouring scorn on it or saying to me I could never manage to get straight. I just stuck with it like an ancient mariner holding onto his bit of a raft and over time the raft got bigger and it turned into a whole life.'

But what about courage?

'First it was just stubbornness. It wasn't courage. I could see how stubborn Janine was! She was my inspiration although there were times when I hated her and thought she was just getting off on her "Rescuing the Fallen" trip. But that wasn't true. She is actually amazingly kind. She rescued me for my sake, not hers. Also, her rescuing could only go so far. My stubbornness had to kick in – and then, after a while, I had a bit more sense that I could choose at least to do what seemed to help other people feel better and act well, even if I couldn't make much personal sense from it, right away. I had to take a risk that it was worth doing. Then another. Then another. I often felt that was all I was doing. Taking more risks. When I was on smack and could have died any day, it didn't feel like a risk at all! Coming awake felt like much more of a risk, but there was a tiny flame of determination in me and I wanted that to grow. I'd been quite a brave kid, actually. I'd always stood up for my brothers and sisters when that was necessary, but I don't think I'd ever really grasped what it would mean to stand up for myself. There was no reality in it. That changed. Gradually I realised I, Eloise, want to live. Then I was willing really to do anything that was needed to achieve that.'

COURAGE IS LOVE'S miraculous face. It achieves its miracles through transformation. It allows the impossible to become possible; the unendurable to be endured; trust to be renewed; and the unexpected to become the inevitability that opens you to unprecedented insights about who you are, about what life is.

When courage stirs, it delivers the strengths you need but didn't know you had. This is not a straightforward matter. Those strengths come from quite a different place within you from your ego strength, or your conscious strengths that derive from and are expressed through thought, analysis and problem-solving, as precious as those faculties of the rational mind are.

When you are really desperate, when your basic trust in life is lost, something far deeper is required to match that need. From my own experiences of intense emotional pain, and the sense of absolute hopelessness and timelessness that can come with it, I know that a kind of dying needs to take place, a death of the old defences that would usually keep us from crying out, and from reaching inward.

Yet it would seem that only when you are desperate enough to descend into your depths and to cry out from that place in utter truth, as even Christ did, that *this is too much*, that *this is more than I can bear*, that you can finally release your own version of courage.

THE EVENTS THAT are causing you grief don't change when you begin to face them, but the present moment does change, and so does your guiding sense of how you can relate to life. This doesn't mean that you instantly face your future more hopefully or gaily. That may never happen. Perhaps the best that can be said is that you face life itself more truthfully and knowingly. 'What doesn't kill me, makes me stronger,' said the German philosopher Friedrich Nietzsche.

It is noteworthy and saddening to discover that Nietzsche ended his life without any of the faculties that had seemed to create and exemplify his 'greatness'. Deprived of movement, speech and probably comprehension, his physical shell lay comatose on a sofa in a version of living death. Yet when this 'body' of Nietzsche was visited by the young philosopher and scientist Rudolf Steiner, Steiner's exceptional perspicacity allowed him to see the surviving, perhaps eternal inner world of Nietzsche, which Steiner described as 'The soul of Nietzsche, as if hovering above his head, already boundless in its spiritual light . . . [as well as] the Nietzsche who bore within his body ideas drawn from widely extended spiritual regions – *ideas still sparkling in their beauty* even though they had lost on the way their primal illuminating powers [my italics].'

COURAGE CAN BE patient, a silent tenant in your heart that doesn't stir until it's needed. But that is only one face of courage. It is also energetic, daring, playful, imaginative, creative. No work of art is created without it. No feat of invention or exploration. No sporting success. No justly negotiated settlement. That's one of the reasons we dream about it, admire it, idealise those people who seem to personify it, and wish we could have more of it ourselves.

Acting courageously accelerates and engages the emotions as well as the body and mind. More interestingly, the love that drives courage and is fed by it need not be, in the smallest way, personal. Standing up for someone you don't know, or for a cause that does not directly affect you, is of no less value than protecting those you already know. It may even be of greater value.

Courage not only brings backbone, it demands it. 'During the time of the darkest night, act as if the morning has already come,' the Talmud teaches us. This demands that you stand up for what you know to be right and true even when doing so may isolate you and bring you grief. It also means never blaming someone who is suffering; never turning your attention away from that suffering to ask 'Why did that happen to you?', when you could be asking 'How can I help?'

To express love impersonally through acts of courage that also express trust and justice is the only meaningful way you have to acknowledge that you know your place within the human family. It is also the only way to acknowledge and to experience that you are more like than unlike every other family member, however special, different or painfully alone you may sometimes feel.

Taking on and making something of this membership in the human family is a challenge as old as human history. In Psalm 82 of the Hebrew Bible, we can read: 'Give justice to the weak and the orphan; maintain the right of the lowly and the destitute. Rescue the weak and the needy; deliver them from the hand of the wicked.

'They have neither knowledge nor understanding, they walk around in darkness; all the foundations of the earth are shaken.

'I say, "*You are gods, children of the Most High, all of you* [my italics] . . ."'

Without the courage to see and experience how all of life is profoundly and wondrously interconnected, there can be no meaningful expression of justice. Those of us who have wondered how it is possible to be vigorous in the pursuit of social justice in the outer world, while behaving like a pig at home, may recognise that, without heart, love, courage, such pursuit is hollow: merely a vehicle for personal rebellion, pride or ego.

Without courage, says Matthew Fox, former Dominican priest and author of *Original Blessing*, there is no spirituality. 'Courage is two French words for a large heart and without a large heart you're not a spiritual person.'

It's a tough statement. Maybe I can soften it a little by suggesting that in developing courage you also develop a version of spirituality, of grace, of compassion and of connective thinking, even if naming 'God' or acknowledging the mystery, the interconnections and the wonder of the universe is not for you. And in developing your spirituality, it is possible to develop courage; not least, the courage to *engage* with life, and to stand out against the monolithic institutions of rational thought and organised religion that scoff at what is numinous or mysterious, and wish it could be tamed.

I feel supported when Buddhist teacher Jack Kornfield reminds me that to open deeply to life 'We need tremendous courage and strength, a kind of warrior spirit. *But the place for this warrior strength is in the heart* [my italics]. We need energy, commitment, and courage not to run from our life nor to cover it over with any philosophy – material or spiritual. We need a warrior's heart that lets us face our lives directly, our pains and limitations, our joys and possibilities.'

This balanced stance of 'warrior's strength' would include our being able also to look at ourselves when we are in trouble and to ask of and for ourselves: 'How can I help? What do I need now? Am I creating space and time in my life to deal with this? Am I caring for myself tenderly and kindly? Am I

getting the help that I need? Am I bringing self-love to this
crisis rather than self-abnegation, self-pity or denial?'

The experience that *we can help ourselves* in a deep crisis, not
least by paying close attention to what is happening, and trusting that meaning can be recovered and compassion learned,
takes courage – and builds resilience. 'Meaning' need not translate as 'reasons why'. Some of life's most profound mysteries
will never be solved, no matter how we yearn and push for
something that resembles a solution closely enough to restore
a childlike trust that there is an order in the universe, which
the rational mind can follow.

'The eye goes blind/When it only wants to see why,' wrote
the Sufi poet Jalal-ud-Din Rumi, seven centuries ago. Often,
searching for reasons why something painful has happened
takes us far away from the experience itself and what it may
eventually teach. 'What am I feeling? Is this familiar? How do
I want to act? What effect is this having on others? Where is
this taking me?' Searching for reasons why keeps us looking
outwards instead of inwards. It separates heart from head. It
keeps us isolated within the cocoon of our own individual
pain. But that isolation – as overwhelming and as convincing as
it may be – is not the truth of the human condition. Terrible
things happen. In almost every life, terrible things happen. The
truth is: *that's what we share.*

Sometimes these 'things' are acts of nature; sometimes they
are acts of human cruelty. That the latter are generally harder
to bear than the former makes perfect sense. There is a sense
of personal betrayal in acts of human cruelty that far out-
weighs the randomness and impersonality of natural disasters.

Human cruelty leaves the recipient confused, disarrayed, untrusting, isolated, changed forever. And maybe one is, for a time, changed for the worse, in the sense that one may be, for a time, bitter, angry, depressed, distressed, vengeful, envious, despairing. From such depths, there is no easy emerging, and there can be no easy judging. Yet it is, paradoxically, not through looking outwards for reasons why that you find any peace worth having. It is through going inwards to meet the truth of your feelings, the truth of your attitudes. In that place, you make a vital discovery: that where suffering lives so, too, do love and compassion.

Zen master Hakuin seems to comment on just this when he writes:

> Not knowing how near Truth is,
> People seek it far away – what a pity!
> They are like he who, in the midst of water,
> Cries in thirst so imploringly.

WHEN I WAS feeling most helpless, during years of the legal battle that I feared would last longer than I could, part of what caused me such distress was my own incredulity that these events were happening, and that they apparently could not be stopped because I wanted them to stop, or because they made no sense, or because they were profoundly distressing and financially ruinous.

All those 'sensible' reasons were no more weighty than my hopes or wishes. But it was astonishingly difficult for me to grasp that. My incredulity settled like a carapace around my being. Like every experience of grief, it slowed me down, emotionally, physically and mentally. And when events continued to fail to match my hopes and prayers, disappointment, confusion and powerlessness added immeasurably to my distress.

Unable to flee that anguish, I had to learn vital, life-changing lessons.

'My child, despise not the chastening of the Lord; neither be weary of his correction: For whom the Lord loveth, he correcteth; even as a mother the daughter in whom she delighteth.'

Those lines from Proverbs did not cheer me. On good days I would make jokes about living as an addendum to the Book of Job. There were other days when I couldn't joke at all. When I was also diagnosed with breast cancer what I felt was a desperately uncomfortable self-consciousness that somehow I was being 'asked' to endure so much, mixed with a wretched loss of hope. I felt shame, too: shame that I was in this mess and could not get out of it, and shame that I was taking it so hard.

Looking back at that time, which is still extremely difficult for me to do, I can see that it was only by increasing my experiences of reality, *by doing what needed to be done* – cleaning and tidying the house; shopping, gardening; making meals and conversation; putting out the washing in the sun to dry and taking it in again; writing a novel that kept me in work and good company; listening carefully to other people's stories; looking after and being loved by my children and friends, and loving them back; paying attention to my dreams and to what was happening inside myself, no matter how unpalatable – that I slowly, slowly learned that even the loss of hope was something I could survive.

Along with that, and out of that, I learned that I could hope again, although not in the old way. I had become much more wary and gradually, over years – because in this matter I was a very slow learner – I gave up thinking 'This must end because it should, because I need it to, because it makes no sense for it to continue, because it is hurting everyone involved.' Such thoughts came to seem unbearably hollow to me and I literally could not endure it when other people voiced any of those same sentiments. Oddly enough, I gained courage and regained resilience when I gave up wishing that life was other than it was; when I gave up wishing that events were other than they were; when I surrendered to the painful truth of what was.

Surrendering may seem to be an odd way to practise courage. But I learned a great deal from an almost involuntary shift in attitude that I might, at other times, have been tempted derisorily to label as giving up.

Jungian analyst Polly Young-Eisendrath defines suffering as 'The discontent, the negativity or dissatisfaction that we often feel, sometimes in relation to pain or loss but also in response to ordinary hassles in life, such as a traffic jam or a bounced check.' She usefully reminds us that: 'Buddhists talk about suffering as that which separates us from engaging in our immediate experience. It sets us apart and can keep us apart from others. Commentaries like "why me?" or "poor me" or "stupid me" are symptoms of suffering. These thoughts and feelings pull us into agitations and annoyance. [Or panic and despair.] Surprisingly, suffering is often more disturbing than the original pain itself.'

My own experience was that at almost exactly the moment when I could extend my experience of reality *also to take in what I most wanted to avoid*, I experienced a strange kind of peace. It wasn't optimism, and it was not an end to pain or to suffering. But it was real and true, and it sprang directly from that raw sense of inevitability and a rather chilling knowledge that sometimes events simply are not going to be pushed around by our wishes, no matter how passionate those wishes may be.

IT IS ONE of life's most playful quirks that even the most insightful among us find it extremely difficult to discern which events in our lives will ultimately turn out to be our greatest blessings. Sometimes wonderful things happen, and then fizzle into nothing. At other times, events occur that we would do anything to avoid, yet it is these that have the potential to challenge and deepen us, to hone us into the person we needed to become; to increase our knowledge of life, and our authentic pleasure in it.

This view that every life circumstance contains the seeds of greater knowledge, compassion and resilience is an old theme of Dr Elisabeth Kübler-Ross. Her fame comes from her work with the dying, but it is impossible to work with the dying without also learning a great deal about living.

'Over the years,' says Dr Kübler-Ross, 'I have learned that every life circumstance, even a crisis, can nourish your soul.

Recently, the farm and home that I have loved so much for so many years burned down in a horrible fire. Everything that I owned, without exception, was lost.'

Before that fire devastated her home, Dr Kübler-Ross had said, 'I have found that all the bad things that happen to you are really gifts from God and blessings to make you strong. Those people who have never gone through any windstorms are weak and uninteresting, have no guts, no *chutzpah* . . . The biggest gift God gave to us is free will. You can hang your neck on the next tree or you can stick it out and become stronger.' Kübler-Ross's God is not the Almighty Patriarch in the sky. It is whatever manifests itself through life: 'The soul of you and me and every living thing is a particle of God that descends into the world. That is life.'

Following that fire, Kübler-Ross left Virginia and moved to Arizona, viewing what some of us might regard as the ultimate tragedy as 'an opportunity for a new beginning'. At the age of seventy, and after decades of voluntary involvement with literally thousands of lives, she is able to say: 'Perhaps one of trouble's greatest "side-effects" is that it teaches us that life is rarely the way we want it to be; rather, life is simply the way it is. And we are simply the way we are. What we need is the desire to look for the gifts in ordinary and extraordinary experiences.'

IN THINKING ABOUT courage, it is almost too easy to fly to the big events, to wonder how you would cope with what you dread most, even if you know that it is the small daily acts of courage that build the kind of life most of us could feel grateful to be living. Thinking about courage, you may crash into your fears: 'Will I measure up to this? Am I ready for it? Do I risk feeling less competent in my own life than I do already? How do I move high ideals out of a book and into my life?'

Such a collision brings an irreplaceable opportunity. Reading and talking about courage is helpful. Meditating on it is even better: holding it in your mind like a precious object, looking deeply into it, finding what is friendly about the quality, what fills you with awe, what terrifies you, what brings you peace. You can do that for days, weeks or months without discovering all of the personal meaning courage has for you. But alongside whatever thoughts you might have or discover is the need to put courage into practice – daring to engage more consciously and compassionately not with your own life only, but with life.

Do I dare to call about the job that interests me?
Do I dare leave the job that I hate?
Am I willing to risk opening myself to love?
Would it be out of place if I spoke up at a meeting?
Can I confront my boss about his racism?
Will I talk to the doctor about the lump in my breast?
Should I risk telling my friend her behaviour offends
    me?
Am I willing to risk looking silly while I learn something
    new?
Am I prepared to acknowledge how I have hurt you?
Dare I give money away to those who need it?

Could I give less time to what absorbs me most, and more
    time to others?
What does life expect of me?

There is no need to wait to act until you have sufficient
courage. 'Fear of fate,' wrote Swiss analyst and theorist Carl
Jung, 'is a very understandable phenomenon, for it is incalculable, immense, full of unknown dangers. The perpetual
hesitation of the neurotic to launch out into life is readily
explained by his desire to stand aside *so as not to get involved in
the dangerous struggle for existence* [my italics]. But anyone who
refuses to experience life must stifle his desire to live – in other
words, he must commit partial suicide.'

The struggle for existence *is* dangerous. Life itself is dangerous. We don't need the ugly synthetic dangers of drugs
and video violence to teach us that. We need only to experience what is real and true, like childbirth; like learning to
walk, to run, to swim, to cross a busy road, to climb trees, to
take our place in the schoolyard, to speak up for what we
believe in and dare to value. All of that can be treacherous,
dangerous, incredibly scary – and yet it is also what launches
us 'out into life'.

You don't leave yourself to find courage. You don't go to
any place outside yourself at all. Whatever courage you find
within yourself *as you are bringing truth and trust to your situation*
is already sufficient. But this can be discovered only through
experience, not through contemplation. When our fears keep
us timid or shamed, telling us that courage is for special people
only and not for you and me, it is exhilarating to defy that

miserable message, laugh at it, crush it with the fluid brilliance
of your indifference.

It is good to think about how soft courage can be; a sense
of things moving, of grace under pressure. These lines from the
Tao Teh Ching beautifully exemplify that:

> Nothing in the world is softer and weaker than water;
> But, for attacking the hard and strong, there is nothing like it!
> For nothing can takes its place.
> That the weak overcomes the strong, and the soft
> overcomes the hard,
> This is something known by all, but practised by none.

Finding that strength, and perhaps the will also, to be
courageous on our own behalf, as well as on behalf of others,
is crucial to self-love. More than that, it is crucial to an
understanding of what love is. In the giving and receiving of
love, no one is separate, no one needs to be left out. We are
not talking about finite qualities here: that if I take too much,
you won't have enough. That if I give you too much, there
won't be enough left for me. Love, courage – and all the
other transpersonal qualities that make our lives at once infinitely connected and infinitely unique – are available in an
abundance that is beyond the limits of our minds even to
imagine. We are so used to scarcity thinking. These qualities
defy that.

We have reduced ourselves to a way of thinking that reveals
a kind of mean, hoarding mentality, keeping what we value
most for those we love most; keeping some of what we value

hidden, protected for a future that might never come. We do this so 'naturally' and unconsciously that we rarely question it, no matter how theoretically committed we may be to the ideals of sharing, generosity, openness or democracy.

How stubbornly we resist learning that what is most precious in a life is not what we own. Not what we can buy. Not what we cling to, believing it will make us safe, happy or immortal.

'There is nothing to give up,' taught the spiritual teacher Nisargadatta Maharaj, 'for nothing is your own. It is like deep sleep. You do not give up your bed when you fall asleep. You just forget it.'

Finding strength only for others is as unbalanced as expending your energies only on yourself. Love is a universal quality. We need not spare others our love, and we need not exempt ourselves from it, either, in some false, distorted form of modesty.

Courage is as freely available to all of us and to any one of us as the sounds of waves crashing, of wind in high trees, of birds singing, of human laughter.

Those sounds, too, are always there, but sometimes we don't hear them. Wanting to hear them, readying ourselves to hear them, we need to turn our attention towards them. Courage can be like that. We need to turn our attention towards it, pay it more attention than we do our fears, even when those fears are clamorous, clingy, familiar and demanding.

Sometimes courage is learned that simply. By paying attention to what is happening, right now, in the present, and not avoiding it. Buddhists believe that this is our sole route out of suffering: to pay attention, to learn what matters and what does not, and to live life appropriately.

Simple? Yes. Easy? No. Just that first demand – to pay attention – goes against almost everything we learn in the West about surrendering ourselves utterly to distraction. Yet, says the Tibetan teacher Dilgo Khyenste Rinpoche, there are rewards for paying attention. (He means rewards in this life!) 'The more and more you listen,' he teaches, 'the more and more you hear; the more and more you hear, the deeper and deeper your understanding becomes.'

TO STEP MORE fully into courage's embrace, it may help to discover that you don't need to give up fear. Fear may be an old familiar in your life, and fear itself can be courage's best teacher. Sometimes it is only courage that allows us to acknowledge that we are afraid.

Indeed, in the presence of courage it becomes possible to take fear out of its hiding place, look deeply into it, ask it what it wants, how it thinks it is saving you, how you could learn what it wants to teach you without feeling driven by anxiety to attack, blame or self-justify, or to flee from your own life into the dubious safety of someone else's authority.

Seeking to avoid fear, we risk fetishising it. We long for a trouble-free Eden, for ourselves, and even more for our children. But they will learn courage *after* they leave Eden, not before, and they will learn it through their engagement with living, not through avoidance.

If they are lucky they will learn resilience as well as courage, and they will learn tenacity, that wonderfully fierce

quality that won't allow us to give up on anything that matters. And perhaps they will also need to discover for themselves
the differences between courage and 'being brave', and know
when 'being brave' – or defending themselves from recognising their own fears – is keeping them from courage.

Frankie Armstrong is a well-known British singer and song-
writer, and a brilliant teacher of singing. I owe my own return
to singing to her so I feel she is partly responsible for the hundreds of glorious hours I have had singing since I discovered
that 'spirit' or intention is far more crucial than an already
developed talent or skill.

Frankie is severely visually disabled and over a period of
twenty years has had very short periods of poor sight inter-
woven with much longer periods of virtually no sight. In her
inspiring autobiography, *As Far as the Eye Can Sing*, she
describes going to a self-development workshop at the beginning of that frightening time when she knew the
loss of her sight was going to be very serious indeed. To
appreciate this story you need to know that Frankie is enor-
mously vital, with enough energy and optimism to fill any
auditorium. At this workshop, she was paired off with a
woman she says she didn't particularly like. Earthy, sensual
Frankie had decided that the woman was a little 'heady' and
somewhat lacking in warmth. However, Frankie had no choice
but to work with her. She describes how that went.

'During that half of the time when it was my turn to talk
and hers to listen, intervening to follow up any statements I
made that seemed to affect me strongly, she said, "What happens if you say, 'I'm afraid of going blind'?"

'I said it and broke down in great waves of sobbing. She allowed this and suggested periodically that I repeat the statement. She was excellent. That morning *I wept out fears that I had never allowed myself to feel.*'

FACING WHAT ONE longs to avoid always demands courage. Yet as philosopher Ken Wilber points out: 'When you are no longer resisting present experience, you no longer have a motive to separate yourself from it. The world and the self return as one single experience, not two different ones.'

Even the most intellectually sophisticated people suffer from remnants of magical thinking that tell them that they can avoid an unpleasant reality if it is not fully admitted to their minds. If I don't notice that my husband rarely comes home for dinner any more . . . If I ignore the fact that there is a strange lump in my groin . . . If I overlook the reorganisation at work that will cut the management team by two-thirds . . . If I tell myself often enough that my elderly parents can continue to live independently . . . If I throw myself into work, even though my partner recently died . . . These are common ways to attempt to hold reality at bay but, unfortunately, they are also markedly ineffective. Reality has a way of lodging itself somewhere in our being. When we ignore it, pushing it into the realm of the unconscious, then sometimes it must make itself known to us even more dramatically, perhaps through physical pain, depression or anxiety, a breakdown in physical or mental health, or an accumulating emotional distress as the effort of denial takes an increasing toll.

Nini Herman's autobiographical book, *My Kleinian Home*, an account of what Herman calls her 'journey through four psychotherapies', offers a moving, insightful example of how difficult it can be to remain in touch with what is happening in your own life and being, *but how essential this is.*

Herman writes: 'I somehow managed to resist the temptation to withdraw to some island fantasy in my former, self-defeating ways . . . However painful it was to stay in touch to this extent, for the first time in my life, with a hard core of reality, the reward for risking it was not very far behind. For no sooner could I keep vigil with my basic fears of coming totally unstuck, than support came from all sides: from my colleagues and from J [her husband], from the children and from different friends I hardly even knew I had. I now discovered that the world, when it is approached with trust, can offer us a true response, even if it takes some time to decode the offering. For it is different in kind from our infantile demands which are for instant, total care, or for swift re-entry to the womb by the very shortest route.'

'LIVING AND DYING spring from the same root', Lauris Edmond reminds us, in a typically powerful line from her poem 'Hymn to the Body'. Writing of old women she says:

> Yet they know too, as I do, that living
> and dying spring from the same root, and there is
> still the shuttered bedroom, dark mirror in which

the impaired body may yet see itself quiver with
that frisking of nerves that points the heart's
direction, stirs an odd, unthinking delight.

Ah the wise body, so to declare itself for love,
and the inextinguishable hope of love, so to stand up
and shout its sweet defiance into the silence.

Fear and courage grow, I believe, from the same root, and
live on together also, back to back, side by side, feeding on just
that level of paradox that allows an old, impaired body its
'frisking of nerves' and its 'odd, unthinking delight'.

I could not have discovered anything that's worth knowing
about courage without fear. The days when I am not afraid
teach me very little about courage. Yet had fear entered my life
entirely unaccompanied by love, I cannot imagine how I
would have survived.

When my own need for consolation and support – for
courage – was at its greatest, I turned inward for help through
prayer many, many times. Reflecting on that now, I can see that
it is when I have felt most helpless that my pleas have been most
intense. One immediately thinks of a child, crying to the greater
power of the parent for help. Yet it is not the child only – the
child in all of us – who feels that suffering and cries out for
relief. Even in those moments of apparent helplessness, we make
a critical choice: to acknowledge that we need help and can ask
for it, or to fall into the grief and despair of the moment,
collapsing into our own smallness at just the time when that
smallness can apparently no longer contain our pain.

Asking for help is no easy matter. It takes courage to reach out, to remain open at times of great anguish. Open to kindness, to love.

Some of us may, through whatever openness remains to us, reach out to God; others to family, friends or even strangers. What or who we reach out to seems to me much less important than learning, through that reaching out – and through making ourselves available to be reached towards – that in the most painful, wretched circumstances we can touch and be touched in ways that speak volumes for our common humanity.

Talking to me about the support that she and her husband, Peter, received after the death of their son William, Carol Mara said: 'What happened to us is what every parent most dreads: that one of their children will be killed. The people that have sustained us most are those people who have recognised that in themselves: that we are living out their nightmare. They are the ones who could be the most truthful. They could appreciate what we were going through to some degree. In contrast, some people we might have expected to contact us on the anniversary of William's death didn't. We were feeling the loss again so intensely. I expected that to happen but it was very hard. We both felt that failure to contact us very deeply.'

Learning at first-hand how vital human contact is during times of greatest anguish, Carol and Peter have been able to make themselves available to support other parents suffering similar losses. More unexpectedly, Carol talks about remaining mindful of some of the qualities that made William's life happy and full, and how she is bringing those qualities into her own life. 'I often think about his qualities and try to incorporate some of them into my own life more than I did before. William was an adventurer and he liked exploring. He liked new places and new things. He was always willing to take a risk. Sometimes I say to myself, "I'm unable to do this," and then I say, "Yes, I will take that risk." Often this is in very small ways, but I try out new things more than I would have done before – even if it's just going on a really dreadful ride at Dreamworld. Also his friends were very important to him and he was very loyal to them, so I not only try to keep up that contact with his friends but to value more my own friendships with people and make sure I attend to them a bit more than I did before. You don't realise how much there is out there [in the way of support].'

ALL OF US are called on to find the courage to endure the loss through death of those we love; the loss of opportunities; the loss of youthful vigour and health; the need eventually to face the loss of our own life. Some of us must face all those things *and* discover what it means to live courageously throughout an entire lifetime, day in, day out, as we face the effects of divisive, inhumane prejudice.

In 1995 I had the remarkable experience of travelling through the southern States of America with a group of nineteen singers from all over Australia. Our goal was to hear gospel music sung in Black churches, and to sing as a newly assembled choir wherever that was wanted. We travelled to New Orleans, Louisiana; Birmingham, Alabama; and Memphis, Tennessee.

Everywhere we went doors were opened for us, food was cooked for us, arms were extended to embrace us, blessings were showered on us, in part because of the immense hospitality that is characteristic of southern Black culture, and partly because of the respect and affection many choir directors in the region have for our leader, singer and composer Tony Backhouse.

It was, in countless ways, a rare and profoundly moving time. We travelled 'White', and prayed and sang 'Black', starkly experiencing what leading civil rights expert Stanford Cloud has called, 'communities of [racial] isolation'.

The music we heard in those churches – many of them tiny, unadorned neighbourhood churches in poor suburbs – was arousing, dramatic, beautiful, and deeply healing. And when we sang the unaccompanied gospel that Tony Backhouse had taught us, and that we had rehearsed in hotel living rooms and parking lots, the reception was totally inspiring as the congregations clapped, called, prayed aloud, or stood and sang with us. We were singing their music, expressing their beliefs, and in our sung prayers they called to meet us: 'All right! Sing it! Sing it! Oh yes, Lord!'

That journey was, for each of us lucky enough to be making it, far more than a novel holiday. For me, it was a means to dive deep into a music that I love and to learn how to give myself to each song. Giving myself to music that itself comes out of immense suffering, yet is joyous, forgiving, hopeful, I learned a great deal. And spending time singing, praying, talking, laughing and eating with people who refuse to behave badly just because they are treated badly is undeniably liberating.

A day or so before we were to leave Memphis to make the long journey back to Australia, I met a remarkable woman, Sister Mae. Although I had met many, many remarkable people, my conversation with Sister Mae stood out. We sat and talked for a long time. I told her how good it had been to hear a woman reflecting on her wish to see an end to racism, saying out loud in church, during that day's musical programme, 'There ain't but one heaven and one hell. There ain't no two heavens and two hells. And if we can't get together down here, don't worry about climbing no golden stairs!'

Sister Mae had been laughing but now, as I spoke, her face grew serious. She looked directly at me. 'We are the most despised race on earth,' she said. 'The most despised, everywhere on earth, the Black race.' Her hands moved in her lap, drew together, came apart. 'And I don't know why.'

There was a dreadful moment of silence. I felt grief for her race and shame for my own. I searched my mind hopelessly for a response. Sister Mae leaned closer still towards me. Her hand went to her face. Laughter lines reassembled around her eyes. 'But you know what they say – someone calls you a cow, don't mean you got no four legs!'

'SUFFERING THAT IS not understood,' wrote Jung, 'is hard to bear.' And it is true that the apparent randomness and meaninglessness of so much suffering that floods our television screens – and the inner screens of our minds – is difficult even to witness. Again and again, I hear stories that persuade me that only by retrieving personal and social meaning out of pain, only by remaining at least fragmentally open to the healing forces of love and compassion, even in the face of extreme grief and confusion, can we avoid drowning in cynicism or collapsing in horror and fear.

Kanya Stewart is a New Zealand artist, writer and teacher of yoga, and a devoted follower of the contemporary Indian teacher Sri Sathya Sai Baba. Here she describes his help to her after her nephew Jason committed suicide, at the age of nineteen. It is difficult to imagine a more tragic death. Yet courage emerges in this story, too.

Kanya writes: 'Swami [Sai Baba] has been with me, my closest companion and comforter the whole way through. The moment I heard the news and in the hours and days of shock afterwards. I chanted His name and lifted Jason up into the light of His love.

'I flew immediately to Christchurch to be with my sister and her family. In many ways the whole experience could have been a nightmare, but Swami's loving support was evident every step of the way. There was so much love, so much love . . .'

Continuing her story, Kanya points to the possibility of growth and insight into our common human condition that tragedy allows. Like Kanya, I have come to believe that this, along with the discovery of the 'love, light and compassion that resides in our own hearts', is the sole purpose of suffering – if indeed it is valid to speak of purpose. But it takes tremendous courage and faith, and often a good deal of time, too, to get through to a point at which such insight is possible.

Yet, as Kanya says: '*We can survive the most horrendous of experiences. More than that, we are given the opportunity to grow strong and serve others. This is the greatest gift, an alchemy of sorts. Out of the pain and suffering that is an integral part of living in this physical realm we can discover the extraordinary love, light and compassion that resides in our own hearts. It's almost as though our capacity to open to that which is unimaginably painful and difficult is the key to unlocking the doors to realms of the most beautiful and sublime. This experience of tragedy has opened my heart fully to the suffering of others.*

'If I had a choice, I would have Jason back with us. Given that this is not possible, I give thanks for the opportunity to experience such unconditional love and deep sharing. At such a time, the boundaries that separate people dissolve and we have the chance to experience the oneness that transcends "me" and "mine".'

I AM SPEAKING to Lynne Segal, a woman I have had a warm professional association with for some years. We share interests, and now her three little children are at my son's school.

She is talking to me about her daughter Georgia who is in the same kindergarten class as her twin sister, Shannon. Georgia is unable to speak. She is normally intelligent, but severely dyspraxic. There is no passage outwards for the words that form in her brain. She might never be able to speak. I know some of this and have always been interested in this little girl, but I don't know much.

'Can she learn to sign?' I ask, brightly probably.

'No,' says Lynne. 'She only has the use of one hand.'

I am aghast, but not so aghast that I fail to notice that I am not hearing in Lynne's voice a single note of self-pity. I hear love.

MANY PEOPLE HAVE spoken to me of the dread they feel that, when faced with severe physical or emotional pain, or a life and death challenge, they will not be able to meet it in the way that they would want. Listening to them, I repeatedly hear phrases such as 'How do I know I will rise to the occasion?', or 'I might reach out and find that there's no one there', or 'It would be so dreadful if I wasn't up to it', or 'I don't know if I will be able to bear it', or 'I just don't think I'm going to be able to cope.'

Those phrases express something absolutely real: an uncertainty of trust that haunts us all, even those who do have some sense of a larger, unseen, loving force working within the universe and available to support them.

Canon Jim Glennon is an Anglican priest. Talking to broadcaster Caroline Jones, he spoke for many people who feel that they have been turned inside out by life and simply cannot continue to be the person that they once were. A terrible accident, the loss of a valued job or relationship, a major physical or mental health crisis: there are various forms that these changes take, yet the outcome is often extremely similar.

Out of his own hard-won experience Jim Glennon could say: 'Genuine breakdown makes you into a person that you did not know existed before, and that is a frightening and confusing experience. And it was confusing and threatening to me. After all, you just don't know why you are as you are.'

The pits into which he had fallen turned Jim towards God. This is an extremely familiar story, and one that can quite understandably further isolate or irritate people who do not feel that this option is open to them. What stands out here, however, is that this man was already a priest and had been a priest for some time. But it was not through ordinary life that he came to listen to himself or to God. It was through his *extra*ordinary anguish.

Elaborating on this, Jim said: 'I'm not someone with a hot line with God. I am really a rather prosaic person underneath but, in my weakness, God spoke to me and said, "Is there anything you can learn out of all this?" That was the one question I'd not asked myself, and He went on and said, "You are to learn to be more dependent on Me," and that was the turning point in my life.'

Whether at a time of crisis someone turns to alcohol, drugs, work or sex, to God, a counsellor or a friend – or inward to the resources of their own self, hopefully or despairingly – is an extremely personal matter that is nevertheless profoundly influenced by social, cultural and historical circumstances.

Jung believed that in facing a crisis in the present as honestly and consciously as we can, we also create an opportunity to bring the 'light' of increasing consciousness to what we have avoided knowing, or have been unable to know, from the past. In so doing, we can perceive the present moment in an increasingly broad and deep context, *and* see that hidden or oblique past with greater directness, complexity and truth.

Jung's own writings, and perhaps more especially post-Jungian writings, have probably never been more popular or influential. Yet Jung himself has been disparaged for years by many intellectuals who regard his interest in mysticism and the collective unconscious with suspicion. Nevertheless, it is impossible to avoid noticing that, in speaking of 'turning to God', or of 'seeing life differently', or of 'experiencing the meaning of life in a new way', the *emotional content* of what is variously expressed by a range of people, speaking 'through' their individual and diverse belief systems, remains remarkably similar.

Alluding to this in 'The Art of Living', Jung said: 'One should not be deterred by the rather silly objection that nobody knows whether these old universal ideas – God, immortality, freedom of the will, and so on – are "true" or not. Truth is the wrong criterion here. One can only ask whether they are helpful or not, whether man is better off and feels his life more complete, more meaningful and more satisfying with or without them.'

Jim Glennon had been an insecure child, and in adulthood had gained little help from his theological training or his years working as a priest. What emerged from his breakdown, however, was an experience of self-shaking profundity that had little to do with theology or dogma and everything to do with a massive intensification of his relationship with his God, and his own sense about why he is alive. 'What it meant for me, was that instead of asking God to help me with my problems, I felt God was saying to me that my problems were to help me with God. I was to depend on God more. It was like turning around 180 degrees.'

IT IS USELESS and facile to suggest that there is any simple way available to imbue yourself with trust – trust in yourself, in life or in any version of the divinity – before crisis hits. Trust can only be built up for its own sake, not as a kind of spiritual insurance policy or emotional prophylactic.

And, anyway, I have both observed and experienced that we simply do not know ahead of time what we will feel when faced with a truly life-shaking crisis, how we will react, what strengths we will find to call on, or even what ancient issues may reassert themselves, demanding extra of us even when we feel there is no more that we can take.

VIKTOR FRANKL WAS a psychiatrist and the author of an extraordinary book, *Man's Search for Meaning*, which he wrote out of his experiences of being an inmate in the Nazi concentration camp at Auschwitz. He, too, takes us deep into the challenge of facing life, *of valuing life*, whatever our individual or even collective suffering. He wrote: 'Whenever one is confronted with an inescapable situation, whenever one has to face a fate that cannot be changed, for example, an incurable disease, such as an inoperable cancer, just then is one given a last chance to actualize the highest value [which Frankl identifies as love], to fulfil the deepest meaning, *the meaning of suffering*. For what matters above all is the attitude we take towards suffering, the attitude in which we take suffering upon ourselves.'

In the decades since Frankl wrote those words, our attitude towards suffering has grown increasingly defensive. Almost invariably we experience suffering as something near to an insult: 'Why should I be having to put up with this?' The

immutable fact that suffering and death are an inevitable part of
all existence, that it is virtually only through some version of
suffering that we learn to distinguish between what is important and what is unimportant, and that it is through suffering
we glimpse the nature of our common soul, are insights that are
strangely difficult to pass on. One can read the words – and it is
possible to read similar words in many, many contexts. One can
hear them. One can even see them being lived out. Yet apparently it is necessary that the meaning of the words – more
importantly, the meaning of *suffering* – is salvaged anew by each
person, in their own way, at their own time.

Such meaning cannot be found through avoidance of suffering – though, God knows, most of us would try every avoidance
possible – but in darkness, in desperation, in cracking open to
the most humbling and overwhelming grief. All of which
demands from us the rawest, least diluted forms of courage.

In Psalm 22, the psalmist, David, expressed his rage and
loneliness and grief in this way: 'My God, my God, why hast
thou forsaken me? Why art thou so far from helping me, and
from the words of my roaring?

'O my God, I cry in the daytime, but thou hearest not; and
in the night season, and am not silent . . . I am poured out like
water, and all my bones are out of joint: my heart is like wax; it
is melted in the midst of my bowels. My strength is dried up
like a potsherd; and my tongue cleaveth to my jaws; and thou
hast brought me into the dust of death . . .

'But be not thou far from me, O Lord: O my strength, haste
thee to help me. Deliver my soul from the sword; my darling
from the power of the dog . . .'

One can only imagine the horror, the fear, the agony of loss of trust that David must have experienced in order to allow such a volcano to arise within him. He is not describing pain he has observed from some nice orderly distance; he is expressing pain – utter anguish – that *he is himself barely able to endure.*

Any one of us can also reach that dimension of anguish, when we, too, are feeling 'poured out like water', emptied of all our inner resources, when our 'tongue cleaveth' to our jaws, when neither our own words nor anyone else's are worth speaking any more, when our 'bones are out of joint' and our heart 'is like wax', and when we hardly recognise the body we have lived in all our life, and certainly do not feel at home in it. At such times, we *are* David and, reaching across 2500 years of human history, David *is* us. It is possible to say that in such moments we are most ourselves and least ourselves. We are most alone *and* most inevitably embedded in the oneness of the human condition.

But the human condition is not experienced through suffering only. It is also what brings us the greatest possible direct joy.

In the next psalm, the twenty-third, David describes a quite different internal state. 'The Lord is my Shepherd,' he cries out in a thrill of recognition, trust, love and relief. Far now, emotionally, from 'the dust of death', he is able to say with fabulous relief: 'I shall not want. He maketh me to lie down in green pastures: he leadeth me beside the still waters. He restoreth my soul: he leadeth me in the paths of righteousness for his name's sake.'

David has not, however, forgotten how it was in the unending darkness of despair for he goes on: 'Yea, though I walk
through the valley of the shadow of death, I will fear no evil:
for thou art with me; thy rod and thy staff they comfort me.

'Thou preparest a table before me in the presence of mine
enemies: thou anointest my head with oil; my cup runneth over.'

And now comes David's great cry of hope that he has
endured all that he will be asked to endure. Again, we can so
easily see ourselves when he says, touching wood, his fingers
crossed, 'Surely goodness and mercy shall follow me all the
days of my life: and *I will dwell in the house of the Lord for ever*
[my italics].'

THERE IS A great deal in everyday life that pulls us away from
being courageous. We do not live in courageous or even
heroic times. In a culture that overtly and persistently thrives
on divisiveness and competition, that lauds winners then cuts
them down, and that condemns losers while also relying on
their complicity, it is all too easy to see ourselves as victims and
to blame others for the difficulties that are part of every human
life. Within such a culture it takes a deliberate commitment to
the cultivation of self-love *and* care for others to remain
responsible for each and every banana skin we drop – and to
look around us to check that no one else is skidding.

We live in a culture that adores talk. Despite that, it remains
a rare and moving experience to hear someone actually take
responsibility honestly for something they have done, to hear

someone say: 'I did that. I am sorry. How could I do things differently?', or 'I am sorry that happened. I deeply regret it. How can I now help?' Such simple honesty requires courage. And it builds trust.

Instead we are far more likely to hear others *or ourselves* say versions of 'I only did it because . . .', or 'She made me', or 'I never did it at all.'

Paying close attention to what is true, and learning to distinguish it from what one might wish were true, develops trust. Such trust – offering it, being worthy of it – is a crucially important aspect of loving, of taking other people seriously, and of not using them simply as stepping stones on whatever your current individual route might be. But this is not the glamorous side of courage. There are no medals, no parades, no promotions for taking responsibility for your own life. Nor for taking care that what you say is true rather than expedient.

The interior rewards, however, are great; not just great, but tremendous because they keep you in faithful, knowledgeable contact with yourself. And from that place, you are available to have faithful, open-hearted contact with others.

'If one can conceive of a fully integrated person,' wrote dear Dr Winnicott, the famous paediatrician and psychoanalyst, 'then this person takes responsibility for all feelings and ideas that belong to being alive . . . it is a failure of integration when we need to find the things we disapprove of outside ourselves.'

IN A SOCIETY where there can be few winners and many losers, it is more usual to be passive, resigned or cynical than courageous. Often a persistent voice inside ourselves tells us that even making a gesture towards courage is too hard. Better to stick with the known, the safe, the easy, the predictable. Yet the balance to that view is discovered through experience: that there is a great deal within us that *supports* our practice of courage.

There is a lovely story told about St John of the Cross, who was imprisoned and tortured for his attempts to revitalise his religious community. He realised that he was slowly dying in prison. He wanted to escape, but in doing so he risked being captured and tortured to death. Yet if he stayed immobilised, he would die anyway. Choosing the greater risk – to escape – which carried with it at least some chance of life, he engaged his heart: his heart that wanted to go on beating and living at least as fervently as his mind must have been warning him against the dangers of escape.

Gloriously, his escape succeeded. In joy and triumph he wrote this poem of appreciation for the source of his courage:

There in the lucky dark,
none to observe me, darkness far and wide;
no sign for me to mark,
no other light, no guide
except for my heart – the fire, the fire inside!

At a more recognisable, everyday level, whenever I returned to the writing of this book I had to face my fears that it is crazy to take on subjects such as these. Who am I to do it? How dare I? Almost every day I had to remind myself that I am not daring to write this book because I am already courageous. I am writing it because I *need* courage. And I have learned that what we pay attention to reverberates in our lives.

TALKING ABOUT THE life and death of her son Jonathan, writer Anne Deveson gave me a wonderful example of precisely how powerful words can be, or even – as in this case – a single word.

'My son had died and we were to bury him the next day. We do not belong to any formal religion, we rarely go to church, but I wanted a priest to conduct the service because I felt the need for ritual.

'I asked a man I had met through work, and I asked him because he seemed thoughtful and kind. When he came he spent quite some time finding out about Jonathan, what he was like, why we loved him, what did we remember about him, what might other people remember about him. He asked about his illness – which was schizophrenia – he asked about the difficult times and the good ones. He gave me a sense of someone *caring* about Jonathan, this young man who had taken his own life because he could endure it no more. And when you are to bury your son, you desperately want people around you who will care, not just for you, but care about what has happened, care about this life that has ended.

'Just before the priest left, he suggested that we all join hands in a short prayer – Jonathan's brother and sister, the priest and I. One word shone through all his other words. He prayed for us to have courage. It came to me like a surprise, something I hadn't anticipated, a strength that radiated through the whole of me, bringing all my disintegrated, shattered and weeping pieces together, making me whole. It helped me through the following day. It was a word I used aloud when we moved off to the graveside together, and it's a word that has stayed with me.'

A SERIES OF pictures pass through my mind: women and men caught in an intense drama without time to choose between fear or fearlessness. A child needs rescuing from an attacking dog. A gunman must be disarmed before he resumes his random shooting. A friend must be found on the side of a mountain before sundown. A house burns; people scream to be saved. One man attacks another in a parking lot, ready to kill. A truck must be lifted off the body of an elderly woman, lying beneath giant tyres. A farmer and his dog return again and again to the banks of a flooding river to bring terrified stock to safety.

To cast aside your own instinct for self-preservation in order to save others' lives is always a brave thing, and in life-threatening circumstances it is heroic. It requires the capacity to forget yourself and your self-protective instincts to respond to the precise needs of the moment. It is often the rare experience of being utterly awake in the present with no possibility of thinking of future or past. In such a moment, what's needed are the qualities we associate with the heroes of mythology and legend: self-sacrifice, intense concentration, superhuman strength, and unwavering tenacity.

However long it takes, though, the crisis passes. The task comes to an end, for it is a task – one that takes you to an intensity of existence hovering somewhere between the realms of the human and the divine. The hero returns to earth. And it is on earth that the time for reflecting must begin. For how should anyone make sense of such an experience except by metaphorically 'going to ground', turning inward, looking at how their most personal internal landscape has been changed by an external event?

PERHAPS THE HEROIC moment is repeated. Acute crisis workers, such as fire fighters, rescue team workers, ambulance drivers and some police, expose themselves to such tasks repeatedly, sometimes over an entire working lifetime. Maybe for them the extraordinary becomes earth: the place where they most comfortably land.

For the rest of us, however, when our pulse has ceased to race, and the cries for help can be heard only in memory, something needs to be made of what we have been through. The exceptional experience must be hauled in, like a flailing fish at the end of a long line, so that it can be stowed away and eventually integrated, because it is not possible to survive any extreme experience and not know yourself differently, and like yourself more, or less.

IT IS NOT useful to think about courage without also acknowledging how awesome that human capacity for heroism can be. Taking risks to save a life, or for a cause larger than your own self yet one with which you feel truthfully aligned, builds that quality that is rarely spoken of now but that used to be called 'character'. I would define character as the confidence that you can trust yourself in and out of a crisis, and that others can trust you, too.

In a neatly interdependent way, character builds resolve: a sense of purpose that sees you through the self-doubt that inevitably precedes a challenge. It takes you through until you are completely absorbed by whatever needs to be done, and you and the task are one.

Thinking about that – saving a life, causes larger than yourself – there's a sense of physicality, of vulnerable human bodies being out there 'on the line', the line being that imperceptible border between life and death because, at its most extreme, human bravery does demand the risking of 'life or limb', though not for your own sake only.

Yet, for all the magnificence of human endeavour that we can associate with bravery and valour, heroism cannot be entirely cleansed of a grim history. Heroism is a hungry myth. It has devoured the lives of countless numbers of men, mostly young, over three millennia. During wartime the myth becomes especially voracious, consuming men by the tens of thousands in a single day and, increasingly, women and children unlucky enough to be in the way. Eighty million people have died as a direct result of war in this century alone. And how do we know it is only eighty million? Perhaps it is eighty million and thirty-nine, each one of them entitled to more life, each one of them grieved for, mourned over and their loss of life regretted.

The widespread adoption of the hero myth, which occurred five hundred years before the birth of Buddha and a thousand

years before the birth of Christ, coincided with what writer
Andrew Harvey has described as 'the shattering of the harmony of the old goddess archetypes'. Is it too neat an equation
to suggest that as the hero rose, the goddess fell?

The rise of the hero myth, with its emphasis on a particular version of masculinity and on individual achievement,
brought to an end a period in human history when even the
dominant cultures lived in harmony with nature and respected
her forces, an attitude that came to be preserved over the next
two millennia only by the least aggressive cultures, including
those of Australia's Aborigines, in which – and I think this is
absolutely noteworthy – instinct and intuition continued to be
cultivated, and were valued beyond 'reason'.

As reverence for nature dwindled within those primary societies – and of course I am thinking of the Greeks and Romans
particularly – men's attachment to the intellect soared, partly in
response to what we would now see as the often savage demands
of the ego. And there was, as Andrew Harvey expresses it, a
'separation of the Creator from the creation, an increasing sense
of divorce between heaven and earth and the triumph of a
divisive, categorizing, dissociative kind of knowing.'

Poetry makes sense of this, too. The Hindu mystical poet
Rabindranath Tagore writes of seeing light, but no fire. It's a
fine image of dissociative knowing: losing track of the source
of things, and also the consequences.

'I see a light,' he says, 'but no fire. Is this what my life is to
be like? Better to head for the grave.'

Through its intricate associations with war and imperialism –
the taking of land and life – the role of the hero has traditionally

demanded, and still demands, a high degree of dissociation: a belief that the life of an enemy or a colonised 'native' has less value than your own. A belief that you can actually or metaphorically kill or subjugate and not also be injured by these acts. A belief that you can poison the earth, and not stunt your own and your children's growth.

When my own children were very young, they used to recite a most beautiful little verse at school as a grace before their meals, a verse that reminded them each day of where their lunchtime bread came from:

Before the bread, the wheat.
Before the wheat, the grain.
Before the grain, the sun and rain,
And beauty of God's love.

Most of us have forgotten where our bread comes from. Most of us have forgotten where we ourselves come from, as well as where we are heading. We live dissociatively throughout our lives, blind even to the most primitive understanding of the rule that all actions have a reaction – for better or for worse. Dissociative thinking keeps us stunned, believing the lie of our own powerlessness.

Pouring poisons down our kitchen sinks, we are acting
    dissociatively.
Making poisonous movies for our children, we are acting
    dissociatively.

Forgetting to sing, or dance, or honour our bodies, we are
acting dissociatively.

Denying the actions that cause others grief, we are acting
dissociatively.

Allowing ourselves to be lulled into old myths of
nationalism, we are acting dissociatively.

Forgetting the lessons of history, mythology and spirituality,
we are acting dissociatively.

There is courage, and honesty, in coming back to the source
of things, and in thinking about consequences. That's what it
takes to wake up.

VERSIONS OF THE hero myth survive in the line-up of our
inner archetypal figures – the Warrior, the Seeker, the
Destroyer, the Creator, the Ruler – and are endlessly recycled
in movies, although there often what we see is a hero exerting
power over others. We rarely see him reflecting on his experiences and learning how to live. We rarely see him liberating
himself by enduring his own deep-seated fears. And we almost
never see that our hero is a woman.

But this need not be a case of either/or. It would be tragic
to abandon all the thrills of being a hero in our own lives, or
of developing physical courage and the mental stance that goes
with it. There is something dazzling about the sheer eventful-
ness of human bravery. In part because most of my risks have
been intellectual or emotional rather than physical, I can be
touched by versions of physical endeavour that go nowhere

near the hero's line between life and death: Robyn Davidson crossing Australian and then Indian deserts on a camel's back; strong, purposeful Jane digging out entrapped roots of a long-gone tree to make way for fresh planting; my sister Geraldine creating tranquil, settled gardens from the rubble of a building site; the ease with which a kind male stranger changes the flat tyre on my stranded station wagon; women known to me only through films and books who must carry an entire family's water each day from well to home, balanced on their heads.

There is tenaciousness and 'character' in all of that. But in mythic heroism, whether ancient or modern, there is too often the agony of premature death: of another human being; of an insect, animal or bird; of an irreplaceable corner of our planet.

'WHEN SOMEONE HAS something to do, let him do it with all his might,' urges the Dhammapada. This is not an invitation to ferociousness. It is a way of reminding us to pay attention to what we are doing. Paying attention, we have less need to be mythic heroes. Paying attention, we can afford to take our own lives seriously enough to be truthful about everything that we do. Yet, still paying attention, we can feel safe enough to leave ourselves entirely behind, to pay total, embracing attention to something far outside ourselves. Paying attention, we need to make fewer and fewer distinctions between inside and outside, between you and me, between us and them, because we feel trusting, safe and loving enough to do that. Paying attention, we learn reverence for all forms of life because eventually we can't help but see that everything we think, say or do (or even dare to hope) is interconnected and has its reverberations. Paying attention, we learn that those reverberations trail behind us and create the universe in which we live.

Day in, day out, for any one of us living a life of work, friends, care of children or aged parents, getting older, getting sick, losing loved ones, seeking God, laughing, crying, making love, making dinner, having a partner, not having a partner, feeling appreciated, feeling misunderstood, sleeping, waking, tidying up, getting upset, getting over it, learning something new, worrying, rejoicing, putting the garbage out, preparing to die, *doing our best*: in all of that long haul that takes us from our birth to our death, it is not heroism but courage that we need.

There are physical elements here, too. Nothing we can ever do is separate from the body. But what can arise within us, when we make room, is that ineffable version of courage – courage of spirit, emotional courage – which can exist as forcefully in a physically paralysed human being as it can in the most elite athlete quivering on the starting block.

Courage is what it takes to be fully human. It's what pushes us to survive the daily navigations between the known and the not-known; to deal with the inevitable; to create useful distinctions between what we can change and what we cannot. It is what will allow us to go into our own particular versions of hell. It is what will give us the strength and the grace to re-emerge, and still find life worth living.

Fidelity

To be faithful to another —

whether a person, principle or divinity —

means being faithful to oneself,

transparent to oneself.

PIERO FERRUCCI

$\mathcal{I}$ t was impossible to avoid. Each time I mentioned that I was writing about fidelity, people began to talk about sex. I wanted to widen the context: to talk about fidelity to oneself and one's friends, to one's destiny, beliefs, values, vocation. Perhaps about fidelity to one's faith, to God.

'Yes, yes,' people would say, 'but what about sex?'

IT IS TRUE that in contemporary society the sole conscious vow of fidelity that most people make is to their sexual partner when they specifically promise that they will make love with no one else. But as desirable as sexual fidelity may be, and I have come very late to believe that it is indeed desirable, what value can such a version of fidelity have if it sits alongside behaviours that are untruthful, unkind or unloving?

People can be – and often are – 'virtuously' sexually monogamous, while being untrue to the vows of love. Can we call those people 'faithful', therefore, when they are angry and abusive to their partner, belittling or sarcastic, or withholding of words, affection, money or safety? If so, then we would need to ask, faithful to what and to whom?

WE WILL GET on to sex, but not without thinking about love. And not before thinking about the self, that difficult-to-define sum of all you are, because the capacity to be faithful in any remotely meaningful way arises not from containment, but from a sense of freedom; not from wishful thinking or other people's rules, but from the unceasing continuity inside, which is the self.

The self is the source of our freedom. It is the place from which we make all our choices. It is the place from which we create the truth that is our own life.

It is to the self, first, that we owe fidelity. Not in order to take us into narcissism, but to lead us out of it. Shakespeare described this perfectly when he wrote his famous lines:

This above all: to thine own self be true,
And it must follow, as the night the day,
Thou canst not then be false to any man.

TO BEGIN TO experience how you can 'to thine own self be true', it is necessary to leave behind the familiarity and dubious comforts of narcissism. The narcissistic person has little sense of self, little capacity to be true and little authentic freedom. To fill that emptiness of self (which can feel treacherously sad), narcissists gobble other people. When they no longer need someone, they spit that person out. Often that person then ceases to exist for them.

When they themselves are no longer needed, they shout, whine, fall into victim mode, blame someone else or become dangerously angry. This is – broadly – because being their own emotional caretaker, and responsible for everything they do, is not part of the narcissist's agenda. Things are *done to* narcissists – good things and bad things – and the people doing those things are judged 'good' or 'bad' accordingly. If narcissists themselves are abandoned or hurt, the person who has committed that treachery will not be quickly forgotten. That person will loom large and may, with time, loom increasingly large because narcissists harbour hurts and nurse grudges, often at the expense of more positive experiences.

WE WERE ALL narcissistic early in our lives, and had to be for our own survival. As infants, we took what we needed from our mother and roared and howled when our needs were not met. We didn't stop to consider our mother's needs. For us, those needs had no existence. Only our own needs had any reality and we ruthlessly split mother into 'good' and 'bad', determined entirely on whether she had satisfied us or not.

Most of us outgrow this stage. We move through childhood, sit, stand, walk, and our emotional horizons also broaden. It gradually and sometimes painfully dawns on us that our needs must fit in with other people's. Sometimes we have to wait, and at other times even waiting doesn't bring the results we want. If we are lucky, we discover that while we are waiting we can meet many of our own needs ourselves, even when we wish this wasn't necessary. Bit by bit, experience by experience, we learn that it's possible not only to take care of ourselves, but also to have interest and energy left over for other people, too. We don't get angry or defensive when someone asks something of us. Most of the time, we like it.

It's that awareness of other people that pulls us out of the cocoon of our narcissism. We may not want to leave that confined space, but we have much more psychic room to move once we do. And, looking around, waking up, we come gradually to understand that some of the painful or unpleasant things that happen in our world are caused by us, and not by others' failings. That's a crucial element in emotional maturation and the development of self: knowing that there is no one to blame.

THERE ARE, HOWEVER, many people who grow out of biological childhood into adulthood and even into old age without outgrowing this early pattern: needing, howling, oblivious to the reality of other people's needs, smiling and charming when their needs are met, snarling when they are not. Such people may act cruelly, ingenuously, ingeniously. They may be the most seductive people you will ever meet. They may cling ferociously, tyrannically to their relationships. But they are rarely likely to be faithful: not to others, not to themselves.

WE LIVE IN a narcissistic society. That makes the practice of fidelity – knowing how to be true to our own selves, and knowing we are capable of being true to others – exceptionally difficult. Narcissism and fidelity do not fit well together. We are subtly and not so subtly encouraged by movies, marketing, advertising and pop culture, which also permeate government and political rhetoric, to regard each other not as precious 'selves', deserving of respect and trust, but as objects for consumption. Greed is far sexier than gratitude;

competitiveness is much 'hotter' than co-operation. Power and money are what *matter*.

Mostly we live in a heightened state of insatiability, wanting what we haven't got, forgetting and discarding what we already have. Brittle, fragile relationships are normal, with each person watching their own back, rather than the face of the person they most want to love and be loved by.

I meet a young woman at a train station. She is clearly distressed. Talk spills out of her. She is on her way to stay with her mother for a week and is upset and anxious about leaving her boyfriend. 'It's not that I'm afraid he will go off with some other woman or anything,' she says, looking afraid that he will do just that, afraid that, in the space of a single week, whatever holds them together will dissolve or be disrupted.

In this atmosphere, trust is not easily developed, and 'love' curdles through neediness and anxiety. Neither partner is free.

There is relatively little in contemporary Western life that pulls us out of the self-interestedness of childhood. A public culture that trivialises what is important, sensationalises what is unimportant, and promotes gross sentimentality over genuine feeling is narcissistic. So are the political cultures that uninhibitedly encourage consumerism, divisiveness and exploitation of people and natural resources. So are the social cultures that promote individualism and addiction.

Your addiction may be to high-status work or the agitation and the distractions from your inner world that accompany it, but that also keeps you tightly trapped. Any addiction, whether socially approved or not, is narcissistic. It keeps the focus on you and your needs. Not enough is left for other people. Not enough is left for yourself.

The cult of self-development, or even a spiritual path that doesn't wake you up to do something about the painful realities of this world, can be just as narcissistic, just as entrapping. Stephen R. Covey, author of the hugely successful best-seller *The Seven Habits of Highly Effective People*, points out that 'Much of the self-esteem literature has created a kind of narcissism of taking care of the self, loving the self, and nurturing the self and has neglected the next step: service.' Challengingly he asks, 'You may be good, but what are you good for?'

The more widespread and normalised narcissism becomes, the more we all lose out. Narcissism endangers our planet; it endangers the survival of the human race. Human beings are social animals. We have the capacity to live and work, play and fight, rejoice and weep, within groups much bigger than our immediate family. It absolutely supports our psychological health to have a whole range of people to care about and take an interest in. We all need at least a village's-worth of friends, acquaintances, challengers and allies.

Yet increasingly people find themselves isolated and bereft, yearning for a greater sense of belonging, hungry for a group and all the benefits it brings in reminding us that caring for each other may well be the only truly worthwhile thing we will ever need to learn.

CARING ABOUT PEOPLE lovingly and well demands fidelity. 'He that is faithful in that which is least is faithful also in much,' said St Luke.

To bring fidelity to life – taking on what it means to choose to be consistent, persistent, trustworthy, committed, truthful, loving, and delicate in your discernment between what matters and what does not – you need to be capable of vigilance, of staying awake to the subtlety of what happens between you and other people. This means caring about details as well as the big picture. It means learning that what may be a small thing to you may carry much greater meaning for someone else. Your own view may not change as you discover this, but it is usually possible to express your respect for a different view and to take this as an opportunity to deepen your knowledge of that person. Because fidelity also asks that you care about other people and yourself equally and simultaneously.

This is not so easy. It involves being 'transparent' to your own self-deceptions; taking responsibility for what your needs are; facing what is unpalatable about your intentions or behaviour. It involves developing the strength and clarity of mind to distinguish between intention and action, knowing that what you desire and how you act may sometimes need to be two quite different things.

It means acknowledging that the way you feel about someone may sometimes ask something difficult of you. It may mean, in thinking about yourself and those you love, that you must look inward sometimes, as well as outwards. It means taking stock often, and pausing.

NARCISSISM RARELY PAUSES. Narcissism tells you to *get it while you can* (people, sex, drugs, *experiences*); that *if it feels good* that's reason enough to do it; that wanting something means that *you should have it*. Narcissism tells you to *forget anything that's a hassle*.

Narcissism tells you *other people's needs are a drag*. They have no right to make demands; you have no need to meet them.

Narcissism tells you to *follow your emotions*. Doing something because it needs doing is not the point. Your feeling state is your only valid point of reference.

Narcissism feeds on the saccharine end of the inner-child myth. It's big on tantrums, sulking, refusals to explain. It is deaf to the knowledge that the greatest act of infidelity you can commit is when you fail to grow into the full splendour of your adult self; when you fail to grasp that your childhood is over now, and that your life in the present is yours to make.

Narcissism whispers something different. Narcissism tells you how appropriate it is that your inner child rules your emotional household: that there are no boundaries, no bedtimes, and no needs that matter but yours. Narcissism confuses freedom with acting out.

Narcissism assures you that your inner child is never going to grow up, and is certainly never going to leave the sheltered home of your own concerns.

NARCISSISM ALSO TELLS you that unpleasant truths are not true. Narcissists are unable to tolerate and learn from a view about themselves that differs from their own.

Offered such a truth, they will attack, deny, withdraw, sulk. They will shout and blame, 'But you always . . .', and 'I never . . .'

Somewhere, far inside themselves, narcissists know truths about themselves that are far worse than any unpalatable truths someone else could come up with. This is why they react to a pinprick as though it were a dagger.

LYING ON ROUGH grass, leaning out over the edge of a smooth lake in the days when the world was still young, gazing deep into the water to find his own reflection, Narcissus – before he fell in love with his own dazzling, reflected self – was searching for something. It is not too hard to imagine that what he wanted to find was love, or at least some reassurance.

We all want that. It is bleak and dangerous for any of us to live without affection.

He was just a boy, our young Greek. He was new to the world, inexperienced, easily impressed. That he looked outwards instead of inwards to find what he was searching for makes his fate all the more poignant.

WHO YOU ARE, teaches Sri Sathya Sai Baba, is made up of three persons. 'There is the one you think you are, the one others think you are, and the one you really are. Work towards making all three the same,' he urges. 'Then there will be peace and bliss.'

In the language of contemporary psychotherapy, bringing 'the one you think you are' close to 'the one others think you are' involves using awareness to bring the 'self' and the 'persona' (or false outer self) into unity. It means risking being truthful inside and out, trusting that who you are is fine, and that you do not need to hide behind a constructed self in order to please other people or satisfy their expectations of you, or to keep yourself diminished or inflated in your own eyes.

How you do this is simple – and extremely demanding! You watch what you express through your behaviour and attitudes. You don't watch in order to judge yourself or punish yourself. You watch in order to find out what's going on and *to change whatever behaviour needs to be changed.*

That's the only way to become conscious or awake. It is immensely and permanently challenging, but the benefits are enormous. It will allow you to have increasing choice in all your actions and reactions. And knowing that you have such choices will set you free.

THE THIRD PART of this trinity – the guiding force Sai Baba refers to as 'who you really are' – is your spirit, soul or Self, which includes ego and transcends it.

EGO EXPRESSES OUR rational, conscious side (although in protecting our ego we often behave completely irrationally). Self includes that side but also takes in what is poetic, intuitive, instinctive, creative, symbolic and sympathetic – those qualities that allow us to make meaningful connections with other people and with ideas that engage the heart as well as the mind. It is this side of ourselves that brings us into contact with nature, and into an understanding that we ourselves are part of nature.

Our creative, intuitive side meets our rational mind, circuitously and indirectly, in the languages of dreams, fantasies, music, painting, poetry, physics, and in the space beyond language that we reach through reverie or meditation, or sometimes when we forget all about ourselves and laugh.

In writing about this complex, elusive concept of self in *Intimacy and Solitude*, I used Jungian analyst Marie-Louise von Franz's strong phrase 'solid ground inside oneself' to describe that inner reality that a knowledge of self brings. I still love that phrase and find it useful. It offers an inspiring sense of balance, and of spaciousness.

You are unlikely to have access to that solid ground inside yourself all the time. Anxiety, depression and fear – most of all, fear – can take you away from it so that you may feel as though you are at the end of your rope, at the edge of your own life, running out of steam, dangerously close to the precipice. (How telling that all these phrases use the language of physical landscapes.)

But even from the most fleeting initial experiences of the self – of how simultaneously personal and impersonal the self is – it is possible to learn to shift from ego-perspective to the vastly more loving perspective offered by the self. Caring about *who other people are* (listening to them, watching their hands, their faces, remembering their stories) helps to bring about that shift. Caring about nature also helps: noticing the life that is teeming all around you. So does caring about yourself. Not caring for your suffering and woundedness only, but caring for your creativity, your energy, vigour, joy, your capacity to exult, sing, cook good meals, write bad poetry, have sex, wallow in the bath, dance, laugh with your mouth wide open, dig in someone's garden, walk with long strides, and lie still on clean sheets doing absolutely nothing.

EGO URGES YOU to take *careful* care of yourself. Ego worries that you might be tricked, taken advantage of, manipulated. Ego warns you that there are dangers everywhere. Ego wants you to know that, in the real world, dog eats dog. Ego knows that you can never have enough. Ego says if you don't take this chance, there may never be another. Ego says there's no one more important than you are. Ego fears you don't matter. Ego whispers that you could be sidelined, disgraced, victimised. Ego needs you to be right. Ego is in a rush. Ego blames others. Ego says, 'Look out.'

From the place of the self, the view is different.

Self knows that you are already unique. Self wants you to give freely of yourself. Self wants you to be free. Self is spacious. Self sees how like other human beings you are. Self can bear failure and learn from it. Self knows that dogs do not eat other dogs. Self needs time to dream. Self speaks eloquently through the language of dreams, poetry and symbols. Self trusts that we do not always know what's best for us. Self expects the unexpected. Self has no beginning and no end.

Self supports your knowledge that you are constantly making choices and that the deepest reaches of your life are created by those choices.

FIDELITY ASKS OF us that we have a sense of who we are beyond the easy descriptions of work, age, sexuality or marital status; that, through living observantly, we discover what our values are. And that we find ways to live out those values *while always recognising through our decisions and actions* that our values are meaningless when they don't take into account that others' interests are as important as our own.

SOMETIMES, THOUGH, IT may be just the right thing to be self-interested, even when that may have the potential to hurt another person or go against what they want. When you genuinely care about others' feelings, this can seem like quite a hurdle. Your most familiar sense of self can feel jeopardised. But to be loyal, loving, and true to others, it is absolutely necessary to know what supports your own self and what does not, and to be willing to act appropriately.

I came across a situation that illustrates this when I met Juliette, an interior designer who is in her mid-forties. A decision to put herself first had occurred when she ended a five-year working partnership because she was no longer willing to tolerate her business partner's extreme pessimism.

Telling me about it, she said: 'Actually, Jackie isn't just pessimistic, sometimes she's downright paranoid. It's a hell of a shame because she's also incredibly bright and we were doing well financially and so on, but I was coming in at the beginning of every week knowing most of my energy would go into propping her up. We had talked about it millions of times, gone to counsellors, done the whole "changing our behaviours" trip, yet nothing changed. Or it didn't change enough. Her attitude was and is bloody stuck. Inside every cloud is another cloud. Or shards of glass. Last March I realised I had two choices: to stay and put up with it knowing she won't change, or go. By May I was out of there. I miss Jack like mad sometimes, but I would never go back.'

FIDELITY NEED NOT ever imply being 'stuck', rigid, dogmatic or glued to a single point of view. It's much more likely to be the insecurities of a fragile ego that put you back repeatedly onto the same boring, unexamined old track. From the perspective of self (taking into account both the bigger picture and your own needs; taking into account the freshness of *this* moment), you become conscious that you are making choices constantly. Making them with your eyes open, rather than closed, is always empowering and sometimes wonderfully exciting.

In acting on her own behalf, Juliette was not automatically 'unfaithful' to Jackie herself or to the partnership they had shared. Juliette was acting in a way that reflected her own truth. It was harming her to stay in the partnership and feel increasingly drained and depressed and, whatever she did, it was not changing or relieving Jackie's pessimism either. Skill was called for, however, for Juliette to remain just as true to what had passed between them when they had shared common goals as to their diverging agenda in the present.

Juliette had chosen her action, and was solely responsible for it. Neither she nor Jackie would have been helped had she decided to tell Jackie it was all her fault that the partnership couldn't work; that Jackie was a paranoid bitch and that no sensible person would ever want to work with her.

Such inflated accusations – which deny all that has been good, and grossly exaggerate what has been bad – are commonly used to create sufficient space between people to make a separation possible. What they also do, however, is whip up so much hurt and confusion that the truth of the situation is lost, and so, too, are the chances for retrieving out of the separation a friendship or mutual esteem.

Listening to Jackie express her hurt, Juliette was able to find in herself the grace to tolerate that distress. She neither blamed Jackie for her feelings, nor pretended that she had nothing to do with how upset Jackie was.

This doesn't mean that she took onto her own shoulders how terrible Jackie's life would now be. She simply (or not so simply) stayed with what was true: that she had to go, and that Jackie was upset.

FOR MANY PEOPLE, putting themselves first as Juliette did can seem daunting, or even impossible. Those women – and it is almost always women – have learned to get their needs met through meeting other people's needs. Such unselfishness does not always express fidelity to yourself, however. It can be distancing, confusing and exhausting.

If your soul longs to give over all your waking hours to the service of other people, then it will be a glorious and not a debilitating experience to follow your soul in that way. You will find the strength you need through the day and sleep soundly through the night. But if at the end of your day you feel depleted, resentful, martyred or wasted, then some of what you are giving to others needs to be retrieved and given to yourself. This is not bad, or selfish. It is loving and compassionate and fair.

Self-awareness can tell you what changes need to be made, and exercising your will – your awareness of choice, in attitude at least – brings about those changes. Martyrdom is a habit.

Usually it is an extremely deleterious habit in that it drains the
liveliness out of life and causes your body to slump, your shoulders to droop and your spirits to fall. .

I am writing about this lightly. Yet I feel the intense pain of
it. There is insecurity about your right to be alive in here.
When such feelings dominate, it is hard to be faithful to yourself. I have martyrish tendencies myself. Sometimes they have
been more than tendencies: they have been the brutal compulsions running my life. Keep running, keep helping, keep
going. Viewing martyrdom as habit, as an attitude of mind that
really will slip away when another more enlivening attitude
takes its place, keeps the proportions right.

'Why do we focus so intensely on our problems?' asks
Jungian analyst James Hillman, and then suggests, 'Somehow
we desire our problems; we are in love with them much as we
want to get rid of them.'

I'm not sure about that. I think it is more that we get used
to those problems. They are like the awkward limp we hardly
notice because we have had it all our life; or the routine patter
we fall into with friends from the past. It becomes difficult for
us to recognise ourselves without those patterns. And this can
be true even when it is something that we really do want to
shift or change.

This tendency to act and react in familiar, patterned ways
becomes even more marked when we are anxious, afraid or
distressed. Then *it's familiar territory almost always that we fall back
on.* The neurosis may be uncomfortable, but it's where we fit.

After all, as with any other role that has us at its mercy, we
have learned to be a martyr at some time for some good

reason. Perhaps slipping into martyrdom happened bit by bit, while we were looking in some other direction, away from ourselves, forgetful of our capacity to choose freely. Perhaps it did initially give us something valuable. Maybe it was a way of connecting with other people that was rewarding. Maybe it offered a sense of purpose, or provided a structure that we needed. Or it could be that it was the way we learned to be like our own mother, and to show respect for all that she painstakingly did.

But as vital as caring for others is, it should never cost us our own happiness. It should never shrink our soul life. Taking care of others best happens when it flows out of the love we nurture and feel for ourselves; out of the love we feel for life itself, as well as out of the feelings of love, duty or responsibility for those people whose lives can sometimes seem dangerously more important than our own.

YOU MAY NOT be stuck in a painful version of fidelity to the 'martyr' part of your personality. Maybe the role that holds you in thrall is 'the headmistress', 'the eternal optimist', 'the captain of the leaky vessel', or 'the clown'.

It is usually tiring to be stuck in a single role; impoverishing always to be the listener and never the talker; always the responsible one and never the risk-taker; always the fool and never the banker; always the initiator in sex and never the one who is seduced; always the navigator and never the driver; always the one who is right, and never the one who is finding out.

From the perspective of the self, there are many attitudes and roles you can play with, give names to, try out and learn from. It is not inauthentic, or unfaithful to one's self, to experiment with changes in attitude or behaviour *if it feels as if it is entirely your own choice to do so.*

When we are young, particularly, we try out all kinds of roles, finding out what fits, what feels authentic or foreign, silly or charming, painful or rewarding. As we age, and come to know more and more securely 'who we are', it is still possible to extend our emotional and behavioural repertoire. Sometimes new roles are forced on us, anyway. We must leave our homeland. We become a widow when we had only ever expected to be a wife. We were once busy mothers, and now preside over a silent house. We are paralysed, and may never again run or walk. We lose our place in the workforce and must recreate a meaningful rhythm and routine out of our own resources. Our sight goes and we must learn to negotiate the outer world by touch and sound.

None of this means that we cease to be ourselves. On the contrary, it can sharpen our taste for life wonderfully, increasing our fidelity to what really matters, and our indifference to what doesn't.

The crucial thing seems to be to find a way to live right in the heart of your own life – not on the sidelines and not as a stranger. Where your own life doesn't fit or suit, it matters more than anything else in the world that you find a way to make whatever changes are realistic, loving and possible. This takes patience, courage and a belief in yourself, but acting on your own behalf in this way rapidly develops those qualities also.

Far too commonly we allow great chunks of our lives to break loose while we mourn what we have not done, regret

what we have done, fail to make the changes we need to, or
envy other people their lives instead of truly settling into
our own.

Sally Gillespie, my inspiration on these matters, is alarm-
ingly stern when any of her friends dares veer away from their
own reality to enter the realm of the If-onlys. 'When you pay
more attention to someone else's life than to your own, or if
you surrender to the kind of envy that tells you that someone
else's life is preferable to your own, then you are, in a really
deep and crucial way, abandoning yourself,' she warns. And it's
true that, while few of us grow beyond our childhoods without some regrets, and while most of us have at least a few
regrets that can loom large on shaky nights, if we do turn
away from our own lives to gawp enviously or regretfully at
others' lives, we lose a precious, fleeting opportunity to live
fully in our own.

LIVING YOUR OWN life faithfully and freely, and not as an
afternote to Princess Diana's life or as a pale version of Princess
Stephanie's, helps you to maintain a steadiness and intimacy
within yourself that provides the basis for all your outward
dealings. The two princesses may not, in fact, be sources of distraction for you! But few of us could say with hands on heart
that we do not spend more time paying attention to the pulp
fictions that pass as news than we do to our own true stories
and the true stories that will save us. It is much less demanding to read about the princesses than it is to pay attention to
your own dreams, to write regularly in your journal, to meditate and pray, to reflect on and learn from your instinctual life,

or to catch up with your own shadow. And even if princesses are decidedly not your style, it is much less confronting to flirt with the advice of Sogyal Rinpoche, Matthew Fox or Clarissa Pinkola Estes than it is to sit in the peace of your own room, asking your questions and listening to a 'small, quiet voice' that gives you your own answers.

Yet that, too, is an expression of fidelity.

Jungian analyst James Hollis says that, 'While maintaining fidelity to outer relationships, we must become *more fully the person we were meant to be*. Indeed, the more differentiated we become as individuals [by which he means, the more you become yourself], the more enriched will be our relationships.'

HOLLIS'S CONFIDENCE THAT we enhance all our interactions with other people by feeling more at home in our own lives, and being more fully ourselves, is heartening. In my experience, it is also true. But what are we to make of his notion of 'the person we were meant to be'? The phrase is a loaded one and sits, waiting, at the heart of this question of fidelity. *Faithful to what? Faithful to whom?*

'The person we were meant to be' seems to imply a deterministic view of human development that contradicts all I have been suggesting about freedom, will and choice. The idea of destiny is not simple, however. It raises the prospect that there is an essential meaning to each life and that the task of each life is to find and live out that meaning. Or find it *through* living it out. This may be an idea more familiar to those influenced by Eastern thinking than Western, yet psychoanalyst Viktor Frankl captured just this idea when he wrote, 'Everyone's task is as unique as is his specific opportunity to implement it.'

With rare exceptions, we grope towards the discovery of our destiny through the experiences of a lifetime; through active reflection on the choices we have made and the chances that have come our way; through reflection on what brought us to the bull's-eye first time round, as well as on the ghastly mistakes that taught us it was time to move on.

Destiny should not be confused with fate. Fate's what happens; no choice there at all. Whether fate is what is 'meant to happen' or is hazardous, I have no idea. What I do know is that railing against fate makes your voice hoarse and your fists bloodied but changes nothing.

Destiny is more expansive and mysterious. It finds its expression in everything we do that feels in our bones as though it 'had to happen'. Such moments may arrive seemingly haphazardly but are actually reached through choice, through repeated expressions of will.

A man meets the same woman a dozen times in a dozen different places. Meantime, he dates several other women. They are wonderful women, but everything feels a little flat. Maybe he's flat himself, he speculates. Maybe it's all too late. Maybe he has missed his chance for that particular version of happiness. He doesn't settle, though, for less. Then, for the thirteenth time, he meets the same woman. She walks into a party on the arm of another man. He doesn't see that other man. He looks at this woman as though seeing her for the first time. He sees someone new. He feels new himself. Throughout his being he is smiling. The woman is also smiling. Three weeks later they are living together. Six months later they are married. They honeymoon in Venice. It can happen.

Each choice we make replaces other choices. Thought and will are incredibly important here, yet destiny cannot be discovered through thought alone. Destiny is often discovered instinctively or by 'chance'. An image comes to my mind of someone moving through the dark, hands outstretched, looking for signs to establish where she is going and whether she is safe. Her eyes cannot see through the darkness; through her ears she can hear no sound; yet she must continue forward. No other direction is possible. *She is on her way.* Perhaps in those raw moments, fate and destiny draw together. Something happens that shifts her to a different place.

I reach for a book. It seems to have been written just for me. You sit on a bus. Behind you, two strangers talk instructively about something that is urgently concerning you. You meet a man at a business conference, far from home. He tells you that you remind him of his son. Only later do you find out that his son was a boy you met at camp when you were fifteen, and have never forgotten. I find myself thinking about my friend Susanne in Munich. A fax arrives. She has been dreaming about me, and has this to tell me . . .

That's synchronicity at work. It's always at work. Mostly we don't notice it. A couple of years ago I interviewed the American writer and Jungian analyst Jean Shinoda Bolen. She told me that she pays those moments of synchronicity at least as much attention as her dreams. They are telegrams from her unconscious: messages that invite her to an increased level of awareness.

They are more than coincidences. They are gusts of fate tugging at our sleeves. 'Pay attention,' they are saying. How we respond to them, whether we pay attention or swat them aside, reflects and illuminates our destiny: the sum of all that we can be, the expression of our uniqueness.

'THERE ARE HUNDREDS of ways to kneel and kiss the ground,' the Sufi poet Rumi reminds us. How glorious it is when we choose to do something that expresses love, gratitude or compassion, and *choose to do it in our own way*, knowing that through each small act we are expressing and intensifying our fidelity to who we are and simultaneously needing to cling to 'who we are' less and less.

THE TASKS AND challenges of any life will involve many 'firings' in the Kiln of Learning, some of them unwelcome; some showing us how to be awake to the gifts that are also part of every existence: the blessing of the sun rising, of birds calling, of grass and plants growing, of human voices singing and laughing, of someone moving towards us with words of love.

At my son's Rudolf Steiner (Waldorf) school the children learn to use their hands as well as their minds, and are supported in the awakening of their instinctual and spiritual lives, as well as the life of the intellect, so that they will be prepared for whatever their particular destiny asks of them.

This education, which arises from Steiner's exceptional understanding of our spiritual nature as well as of science, is intended to help the children discover what their unique talents and needs are *and* how to remain open and relatively uncompetitive in order to be free to respect others' talents and needs.

I grew up in the 1950s and 1960s, a time when ideas about destiny were decidedly not part of the explicit curriculum. Nevertheless, a similar idea about fidelity to one's vocation or calling was instilled in me because we were taught at my Roman Catholic convent school that if we had a vocation for the religious life but refused God's calling, we could never be happy in what we ourselves chose. (Those were the ages of dogmatic religious certainty, of course.) I remember hours of fevered prayer, asking to be spared the honour of a religious vocation, fearing a dire outcome if I attempted to pitch my selfish little will against what I then perceived to be the mighty will of God!

Twenty years later, I was a successful publisher, working as managing director of The Women's Press. The job was a voracious beast, as most worthwhile jobs are, but I felt immensely lucky to be doing work that brought together, as it did, feminist politics and high-quality publishing, then my two great passions. Yet for all that good fortune, destiny intervened. I became restless, less certain. There were aspects of the work that I managed increasingly less well. I felt gaps growing at an alarming pace between myself and other staff members. That was confusing and distressing. It created a jagged disjuncture between our rhetoric and our practice.

Conversations, and especially several striking dreams, pointed the way to leaving publishing to embark on a new path of full-time writing and psychotherapy. I didn't want to leave a profession and job I had loved, yet gradually it seemed essential and then inevitable that I loosen my ties to the known and move on.

Fifteen years later, I remain conscious of how hard that decision was to make. Nor has it been easy to live out. Both writing and psychotherapy are areas of work where you can never feel sufficient. A gap constantly yawns between what you can offer and what your subject matter or client deserves. Yet increasingly I sense how that all-important change did have the stamp of destiny on it for me. It has become virtually impossible to imagine that I could have been faithful to *myself*, could have been free to be myself, had I not made those choices.

Practically, I can see that making those particular choices has allowed me to continue to bring my private passions and professional work into a unity, and has given me time to be available to my children in ways that would have been impossible had I remained a full-time publisher.

But there is more to it than that. Making those choices, or accepting them, has meant that I am able to live my work as much as any other aspect of my life. That doesn't mean that I always like what I am doing. It certainly should not suggest that I find it easy or transporting! It only means that I cannot imagine what else could have taught me more about my own strivings, and put me more closely into contact with the myriad ways in which others attempt to make something of their lives.

IN CHOOSING WORK that aligns self with body, thought and feelings, there is of course a breathtaking expression of privilege. But even for those of us who have such choices, the urgings of the soul are often difficult to hear.

Prestige, status, money, security, familiarity, power: these all speak to us more loudly and compellingly than the far more mysterious and subtle messages of the soul. Yet those messages can be heard: by watching what you really care about; by knowing when your body as well as your mind feels alive; by being conscious of what engages you; and by being mindful of what sets you free.

THAT ESSENTIAL FREEDOM to take responsibility for what we are doing, for what we choose, for the emotional tone we create around us, ideally extends from the smallest details of our lives to the most profound.

Can we be faithful to ourselves and not speak up in protest when someone is humiliated or hurt?

Can we be true to what we believe is right and stand by while others are treated unfairly in the workplace?

Can we afford to shrug with resigned indifference when someone attacks another person in the name of racism or sexism?

Can we stand by when the actions of our governments trample over what we believe are basic human rights?

These are questions that are as relevant to the practice of
fidelity as they are to courage. For surely each time we forget
what our values are, or refuse to take responsibility for the feelings or attitudes that could express them, we betray our human
family, as well as ourselves.

I am aware, writing this, that it is not everyone's desire to
concern themselves with the big decisions of politics and government, with civic or social concerns. And it is all too easy
for the people who *are* concerned with such matters, to
become excessively careless about what is happening under
their noses at home.

At the very least, though, a faithfully held lifeline to your
self, your soul, and to all the other souls with whom you
share this divinely wondrous planet, gives you reason to rebel
against passive living, powerless living, a way of living that
tells you that what's happening out there is too feral, too far
gone, too impossible to understand or affect. Living faithfully
– or let's just say, living open-heartedly – demands, I believe,
that you cultivate a *willingness to act when that is called for.* You
may have been symbolically or even actually lying low for
twenty years, but when the moment comes for someone to
get up, stand up and speak out, *it is you who can do it.*

'WHOEVER HAS NOT known himself knows nothing,' the Gnostic Gospel, the Book of Thomas the Contender, announces, 'but he who has known himself has already understood the depth of all things.'

It takes courage, and a wild, crazy fidelity to the sheer impossibility of being fully human, even to stand on the edge of understanding 'the depth of all things'. It means being willing to play life *un*safely. To *be* the fool as well as the banker. It means not putting on a light every time darkness falls. Not running away from sorrow. Not suffocating anger. Not sugarcoating depression. Not turning away from your own envy, jealousy, hatred, scorn, pretending those emotions don't matter, or that they belong to someone else. Not ignoring death.

It means unravelling your constant failures, but doing this with spirited curiosity and without succumbing either to inflation ('Everything that happens is somehow my fault') or self-pity ('I am too much of a worm to affect anyone else with my thoughts or my behaviour so I might as well behave just as I wish').

THIS IS THE kind of attention I mean. I notice that each time I am talking to Jemma on the phone her voice sounds faint and increasingly less energetic. I become reluctant to call her. There is something about her self-pity that drives me nuts. I try to cut her short. Her pleading feels like an attempt to hold me. I can remember a time when it was fun to call her, when we could laugh together and talk intensely about a whole bundle of topics that interest us both. Now I tell myself that I have too little time to spend any of it on duty calls, and that

Jemma's lack of emotional stamina is a barrier to any mean-ingful contact between us in the present. She annoys me. Why should I put myself forward to be annoyed? Surely that makes no sense? Talking about this with a mutual friend, I am able to bring my friend totally on side. 'Poor old Jemma,' we agree. What we don't say, but think, is: 'It's a shame that she has become such a bore. But what a good thing it is that we are still so bright and full of energy!'

WHAT I AM achieving here is a great line in self-justification. Not only have I managed to extricate myself from the responsibilities of an old friendship without an obvious scar, I have also managed a neat little turn of self-inflation *en route*. The loss I may feel for the absence of the old Jemma, my good friend, is buried beneath my unasked and unanswered questions.

Those questions would push me to explore why self-pity arouses such strong feelings of anathema in me; why friends need to be amusing for me to justify time for them; why I need to construct a self-serving drama to withdraw from this friend-ship if it has already run its course.

Pondering those questions, I may find that I am allowing a little more compassion to arise for myself as well as for Jemma. That may make me less defensively contemptuous of what I have been calling her self-pity.

I may discover that I am a little anxious myself that, if I am not in top form, people may be less inclined to call me. It occurs to me, too, that the unilateral ending of a relationship that has been important to me is strikingly uncourageous.

However uncomfortable it may be, I need to find a way to let Jemma know what I am feeling, and to give her the chance to express what her reality is.

To be true to our friendship, I need to listen to her deeply, allow her to talk without any self-righteous interruptions or justifications from me. However tempted I am to interrupt and say my piece, I need to stand back, shut up, not argue with her or impose my reality. Doing this, I may discover that it is grief or depression in her voice, not self-pity. Or perhaps she has lost confidence in my interest in her. Or it could be that my withdrawal painfully (even unconsciously) reminds her of the shattering time when her mother went back to university as a mature-age student and seemed to have almost no time for her children – although that, of course, is not how Jemma's mother would see it . . .

THIS TINY, BANAL scenario, which could easily be painful enough to fill your emotional horizon for many days, is a simple example of how demanding it is in reality to 're-own' the feelings you may have projected onto someone else.

Yet unless we are prepared to explore where we are in any difficult situation – which is much harder than sitting in self-righteous judgement on another person – it is virtually impossible to clear the way to think about that situation less judgementally, and ourselves, and whoever else is involved, more truthfully.

BUT WHAT, YOU may be asking, about the person who mis-reads *me*? What about the situations where I am unfairly blamed or misunderstood? How should I react when my reality is overlooked or trampled on? How does fidelity fit in then?

Does fidelity demand that I should stand back to let that happen? That I should lean forward and offer whichever cheek hasn't yet been slapped? Or should I stand up for myself, be truthful, bold, heroic?

ANYA, A YOUNG teacher, phones me to say that she has been several times to see a well-known psychoanalyst. She is furious because her version of who she is seems to be getting lost in the most absurd kind of exchanges. Far from helping her, these exchanges are moving her away from whatever solid ground already existed inside herself to much more treacherous ground where she must be unfaithful to her own truth if she is to continue in this process of analysis.

Four or five meetings into the therapy Anya tells the analyst she is unhappy and is thinking of leaving. 'You were extremely nervous when you first came,' he tells her. 'Perhaps you should think about why you were so nervous.'

'That's not correct. I wasn't nervous,' Anya tells him. And she tells me that because he had been highly recommended she really wasn't nervous at that first meeting. Her 'nervous-ness' – if it exists at all – has arisen as she has observed that he finds it difficult to remember her details; that he confuses her story with someone else's, another patient's she assumes; that he yawns and looks bored.

'The silence also makes you nervous,' he informs her.

'I wasn't nervous.' Anya tries again.

The analyst is silent.

WHEN SOMEONE OFFERS a view of you that differs from your own, that view may be loving, interesting, irritating or predictable. A week, or even an hour later, it really won't matter much.

However, when someone unlovingly *insists* that you are in some fundamental way different from the person you recognise as yourself, they do you a disservice. At such times the greatest balance is to be able to call on your own truth, and to have some truth to call on.

Of course, you cannot always see yourself as others see you. There will be times when any new information comes as a shock. What matters though is that there is room to say, 'I don't see it that way. This is how I see it,' *without being told that you are wrong.*

WE WORRY SO much about sexual infidelity, about who is sleeping with whom, and whether it matters. But it is my rather sad observation that sexual infidelity infects far fewer intimate relationships than those commonplace wounding verbal attacks unloosed like poisoned arrows out of the attacker's own fear, insecurity or inability to contain their own unacceptable feelings.

Time and time again I have witnessed people who are supposedly bound together in love saying things to each other that express no version of love that I can recognise, but only rage, self-loathing, insecurity and contempt.

Some years ago I lived near a painter then in her late thirties, a woman named Mariko, who suffered greatly from her capacity for wounding self-criticism, which flourished no matter how successful she became in the eyes of the world. Throughout those years she was honest with her partner, Jim, about the painful insecurity she felt – she had been adopted as a two-year-old child into a family that was in the process of disintegrating – yet whenever he allowed himself to become gripped by envy or confusion or self-pity, Jim would accuse Mariko of undermining him. 'You think you are the only one who can succeed around here, don't you,' he would scream at her. 'You want me to fail. I know you do! If you weren't so full of yourself you would make more time for me.'

When Mariko tried to express what she actually felt – that she wanted success and security for him at least as much as for herself – Jim could only become even more rabid and accusatory. In the wash of his own narcissistic self-pity, and in the grip of what the Jungians would call his shadow (ideas about himself that he had repressed or disowned), he allowed himself no moment's space to listen to her and learn something true about the inner world of the woman he professed to love. More seriously, he allowed himself no moment's space to consider what meaning this particular accusation had *for him*.

From the perspective of self, or even simply because the same sequence of events had happened often, it would have taken Jim just moments to pause and wonder if his judgement of Mariko could possibly be incorrect. And then just another moment to ask himself: 'What am *I* feeling here? Why am *I* reacting in this way? Why am *I* getting so stirred up on this same topic again and again and again?'

In doing this, he would not be taking attention away from Mariko because *his attention was not with her, anyway.* Throughout these painful encounters, and despite all his yelling at her, his attention remained on himself or, more precisely, on old wounds from his past. He was spewing this out to Mariko, transforming her in his mind into the source of his pain, when in fact the source of that pain was within himself.

Only by shifting his attention, clearing his way through the thickets of his own emotions, could Jim have returned to himself. Then, gradually and perhaps with some help, he could have learned to see Mariko as a separate person, learned to listen to her stories as separate from his stories, and expressed to her the love and appreciation that perhaps he longed to show.

That precious opportunity for Jim to bring light to his own darkness, to discover something important about his own envy and, more fundamentally, his own lack of inner safety, arose repeatedly, and was repeatedly lost. So, too, eventually, was that relationship and the chances it offered for giving and getting love.

WE ASK SO much of our sexual relationships. We *sexualise* so much of what we need to get in many different ways. We ask that our sexual relationships make up for everything ghastly or painful that has ever happened outside our own bedroom, and sometimes for what happens inside it as well. We ask that they be the place where we can 'be ourselves', even if we don't know who that is and don't want to find out. Often we expect to be able to dump all our fury and confusion onto our lover – as Jim did on Mariko – then expect that same lover to provide us with intense excitement, safety and care. Even by 'rational' standards that exclude any understanding of unconscious processes, this is truly bizarre. We ask that our lover save us from loneliness, even when we are boring or belligerent company. We ask for a continuous rerun of the unconditional love and intense regard we once received from our mothers, even though we ourselves are no longer babies, and our lover is as ravenous as we are.

Most tragically, even when we profess that it's not just sex we want but love, our behaviour shows how furiously we are battling for ascendancy and power.

Caroline Josephs is an old friend and Zen practitioner with whom I have had many talks over the years about just these kinds of questions. Caroline has long since concluded it is possible to have a truly loving sexual relationship only when the two people concerned are also open to a shared love for that ineffable force for good most call God, or the Infinite, which adds a crucial bolster to their own personal love and also lifts the hothouse atmosphere that can soon be as oppressive as it once was exciting. She says, 'I really believe that you can't have a sexual and a love relationship without each having a relationship with the Infinite – or with some spiritual path. *There has to be that third element.* Then it doesn't matter what age, what gender, what sexuality the people are. That's irrelevant. They relate to each other *through* that Infinite, *through* that other dimension.'

That is indeed my own experience: that when one person can love another through the unitive mystery that is God, and feel the presence of divine love shining through that person, it is impossible not to treat that person with kindness, goodwill, respect and absolute pleasure, and impossible not to feel the deepest possible gratitude that such a person is in your life. I have experienced that, in the presence of such love – that person loving you and God loving you through that person – petty complaints, irritations, comparisons and restlessness dissolve into meaninglessness. What flowers, instead, is the sweet eternal, open-hearted rose of love that neither drops its petals, loses its scent, nor ever dies.

BUT WHAT ABOUT people who do give every evidence of having a joyful, respectful relationship that expresses mutual esteem, but are not spiritual people? 'With them,' Caroline suggests, 'the spiritual commitment takes a different form. Maybe it's their love of nature, their shared commitment to the earth. But they must have this encompassing aspect of the light and the dark.'

Not everyone will agree with Caroline's view, but I think she is most usefully implying that the symbolic light and dark that is part of all our natures does not have to be literalised into extremes of behaviour switching from the ecstatic to the profane. Nor, out of fear of both light and darkness, does there need to be a huddling in the middle ground where not much except boredom, inertia and resignation is felt any more.

'When people are without that third element,' Caroline continues, 'there's a distortion of spirituality into power relationships which somehow reflect the questions: 'Who has the authority here? Who is God in this household? Who's on top?' This reflects that old paradigm of the structure in the church and in organised religious thinking. It's the old patriarchal construction of hierarchy and organised power. Women can be involved in that, as well.

'My downfall in past relationships has been not looking after my own integrity – as one person in relationship to another. That's got lost in this power struggle. Two small selves fight and clobber each other and feel afraid. Whereas in the other kind of relationship, where God or Infinity or Nature is also present, two small selves connect in the larger self.'

THE UTTERLY BASIC foundation of impersonal love, which comes from a trust in something larger than ourselves – which need not be called God – definitely supports a sense of who we are and how we can be with each other.

'A spiritual life of some kind is absolutely necessary for psychological "health",' writes Thomas Moore in *Care of the Soul*. 'At the same time,' he warns, 'excessive or ungrounded spirituality can also be dangerous, leading to all kinds of compulsive and even violent behaviour.'

British family therapist Robin Skynner, veteran of forty years of clinical practice, has also found that high levels of mental and spiritual health are linked. 'Each promotes the other,' he says. 'Healthier people do seem to feel a greater emotional sense of connection and belonging, and that sense of meaning and connection is a vital part of health.'

Expressing that 'sense of connection and belonging', and cultivating it through the love you give, infinitely enhances the love that you as an individual could ever offer. What's more, it brings you into the presence of your own soul.

This rich experience of love takes the sting of intense neediness out of personal love, and frees you from the anxious, narcissistic demand of yourself that you should watch out not to give too much, check on what you are 'owed', and guard against being cheated.

Sufi teacher Hazrat Inayat Khan reinforces how inappropriate it is to reduce love to a currency. He writes: 'When a person thinks "I am too good or too kind to you; I have been too devoted to you," that person forgets that *kindness, goodness, and devotion are larger than the horizon* [my italics]. No one can be too good, no one can be too kind, and no one can be too devoted. When there is a discussion between friends, and one says, "I have done so much for you, I have suffered so much for you, I have had so much pain on your account, I have had such a difficult life for your sake," then he is entering into business. He wants to keep a diary of what he has given in the form of love and kindness and goodness and sacrifice. A true friend makes every sacrifice he can and never thinks about it; he does not even allow his mind to ponder upon the subject . . . If a person has learnt the manner of friendship he need not learn anything more; he knows everything. He has learnt the greatest religion, for it is in this same way that one will make a way to God.'

WE EXERCISE FIDELITY, or fail to, constantly in relation to others. Not just to our sexual or love partner, but also in relation to friends, family; in the way we think about our work, our moral values; and in our thinking about the reasons why we are alive, and what meaning life itself has.

Yet such an integral view of fidelity is not what we pay most attention to. *Will you, Janet, promise at all times to take the time to know yourself, to be true to your deepest values and, in so doing, to be open to all other human beings . . . and to the infinite manifestations of beauty and wonder within nature itself . . .? Will you, John, promise at all times . . .*

We save those promises, or a slim version of them, for sexual fidelity only. This is in part because of the ancient worries men had as to whether they were indeed father to the babe. But they stay around also because our enculturated associations of fidelity (and infidelity) with sex are incredibly strong. So strong that most initial acts of rebellion, whether by a teenager wanting to flee the stale breath of parents or a spouse eager to escape the tedium or lack of truth within a marriage, involve thoughts of sex, if not the translation of those thoughts into action.

It's easy to see why. The idea of sex as a vehicle for liberation or defiance is as deeply entrenched in our individual souls and cultural psyche as any more romantic or idealised view that links sex with love, comfort, nurture or even transcendence. We absolutely associate freedom with the idea of being able to do what we like sexually; and the idea of constraint with not being able to do what we like sexually.

Sex – and the physiological and emotional drives that propel sexual activity – also has something in common with feats of physical courage. Each gives us a precious opportunity to be fully in the moment, to be awake to our own physicality.

More than anything, sex allows us to unleash our sensate nature. It gives us a chance to take in and offer back gifts from our five senses: smell, touch, sound, sight, taste. It pulls us into (and will expel us from) a mini-drama that has at least the potential of crescendo, fortissimo and diminuendo. It gives us permission to forget our anxieties about who we are and how old we are. Making love, we are not old. Or, if we are still young, we never will be old. Sex is our boldest defiance not only of age, but of death. 'Sex,' said that professional rogue and writer Henry Miller, 'is one of the nine reasons for reincarnation . . . The other eight are unimportant.'

SEPARATING, FALLING APART after sex, there is again a mirroring of the aftermath of courage. Eyes opening, blinking, body heat evaporating: we return to earth. T*his is who I am.* And, sometimes, *this is all I am.*

If we are lucky, we lie after sex in the arms of our lover, daily tensions dissipated, breathing in the other's closeness, comforted by the feel of bare skin against bare skin, by the smell of two entwined bodies, by unconscious memories of our infant self lying cradled in the arms of our own mother, and perhaps by stirrings of the deepest collective unconscious memories of our Divine Mother: 'Darkness within darkness. The gateway to all understanding.'

That sexuality, sensuality and spirituality can and do coexist, and can and do bring us closer to the mystery of the infinite,

to all other human beings and not just one, is brilliantly cele-
brated in each of the mystical traditions.

The Christian mystical tradition had a very restricted run
from the seventeenth century, when the rational, scientific
view took serious hold, until 300 years later when the Eastern
and Western traditions began to look much more closely at
each other, and join in intensely positive collaborations that
promise to take us to a new depth of understanding of humanity as well as the divine.

From pre-seventeenth-century Christianity, however, many
glories do survive. Julian of Norwich, a fourteenth-century
nun and mystic, was a celebrator of Meister Eckhart's creation-
centred spirituality, and a reveller in the feminine face of God.
Hers is just one of many voices again singing out to us across
the centuries, singing from all corners of the earth, to inspire
in us a taste of the sensuality and ecstasy of living in continual
consciousness of our relationship with the in-dwelling God:

As the body is clothed in cloth
and the muscles in the skin
and the bones in the muscles
and the heart in the chest,

so are we, body and soul,
clothed in the Goodness of God
and enclosed.

WE LOVE, FIRST, with our body, mind and emotions fully engaged. The infant's joy in life is blissfully promiscuous. Her smiles are for everyone who coos, admires, and delights in her. Along with her smiles comes the beating of her tiny clenched fists at her sides, exuberant kicking, great swathes of dribble falling from the tiny lake that is her opened mouth. But for all the rapturous, generous sharing of her smiles, the baby's great passion is for her mother, possessor of the breasts through which vital milk flows, and possessor, too, of an intensity of emotion that surrounds her, holds her, makes sleep possible and illuminates waking.

THOUGH WE YEARN to make love as adults, we often split ourselves into pieces. We split the objects of our admiration into pieces also. We fall in love with the way a head of hair swings; with a body that has spent many thousands of hours in a gym; with a smile that reminds us of our favourite uncle; with a bank balance that promises respite from our own endeavours; with a talent or drive that matches or substitutes for our own.

If we are lucky, the rest of the person falls into place. We wake up, little by little, to find out who the person really is. Perhaps her hair swings like Rachel Hunter's, but she is not Rachel Hunter; she is herself. The smile is like our uncle's, but the smiler is not our uncle; he is himself.

Often, though, we are unable to bear knowing who the whole person is. When we no longer like the segments we are getting, we begin to behave badly. Often we do this to the accompaniment of a self-justifying rhetoric that grinds the other person into even smaller pieces. We blame that person for not being who we imagined they would be. We skilfully belittle them, reducing them still further in our gaze.

Sometimes we become incredibly angry with the person for not being who we wanted them to be. We may smash them with our words, or with our fists.

Or maybe we use contempt to create distance. When we talk about the person, we may display to other people, as well as to ourselves, that in our perception of them the person is not a whole, living, breathing human being. We may say of that person, who breathes and sleeps and hopes much as we do: 'He was a waste of my time', or 'She was a lousy fuck', or 'It's obvious that he's a loser', or 'There was nothing to her.'

If we are in a relationship with only an abstraction or a bit of a person, it is easy to add on other bits. The issue of fidelity, or infidelity, becomes irrelevant. There would be some logic at least if these other part-relationships added on what we were 'missing'; however, while sometimes they do – a person who is a 'devoted' spouse and a 'hot' lover is the most obvious and banal example – in many cases they do not. Often people have the same part-relationship repeatedly or simultaneously.

Many men and perhaps increasingly women, too, will have multiple relationships that focus on one aspect only – often sex, although it could also be or include any other sensation-inducing connection, such as drugs, alcohol or even making money. (It also used to be making revolutions, but that particular means to a connective end lacks the fizz it once had.)

Depending on how satisfying that focus is, the relationship may last from less than twenty minutes to a lifetime. What doesn't get challenged, and is sometimes barely even touched, are the tricky, sticky negotiations, the leaps of faith, the dazzling feats of daring and the profound, lasting satisfactions that are involved when two people face each other honestly, attempting to see each other truly, and to be seen, as two whole people diving side by side into the ocean of love.

I AM NOT interested in judging the ease with which one part-relationship may slide into or out of another. There can still be pain involved; there can still be riotous joy, release, creativity and learning. And there can undoubtedly be fantastic sex even in a coupling where personal love is absent.

In Isabel Miller's novel *Side by Side*, set in 1960s America, Sharon has her first sexual experience with Candi: 'Blonde, great build, pure clean happy face.' Sharon has been in love all her life with Patricia but, for the moment, Patricia is far out of the picture. Going into work the morning after, Sharon's lesbian boss, Marnie, takes one look at Sharon and says, '"Feel better?"'

'"Yeah. It's funny. I don't even love her."'

Marnie has been around the block more than once. Miller has her say, '"There's something to be said for lust, too. It's as rare as love, actually."'

That two human beings who scarcely know each other can have exuberant, even ecstatic sex is a tribute, surely, to those vitalising, primitive biological functions that we too readily ignore when we are upright.

But when even the greatest sex is over, what next?

In the context of love, two people opening their bodies and hearts through sex affirms and strengthens the connection between them. 'Lovemaking is one of the deepest acts of prayer in which adults can engage,' says *Original Blessing* author Matthew Fox.

Such a statement means, I believe, that sex, like prayer or meditation, has the potential to allow you to lose yourself and find yourself simultaneously; to know that naked in your lover's presence you are nothing and everything; to experience that your sensations and your lover's sensations are indivisible; to find that reaching into and being reached into are twin aspects of a single gesture. All of that is also true of prayer and meditation. Turning your mind inward and outward, you lose and find yourself in the nature of mind, glimpsing that reaching towards and being reached to also takes place in a single gesture, and that all of life is sacred.

THERE IS NOTHING that we can do to or through our bodies that does not also affect the rest of who we are. Snip your little toe while you cut your toenails and feel yourself flinch. Eat tainted food and you will probably vomit violently until it leaves your body. Endure angry or aggressive sex; have sex because you are bored, lonely or vengeful; do what you really don't want to be doing – and the toxicity is harder to expel. Ask any woman or man who has been raped; any child who has been sexually abused; any person who feels trapped by their own obsessions. Perhaps you can dissociate from what you are doing, or from what is being done to you. This does not mean that it has not happened, or that it has no consequences.

Before we begin to grasp even at the most primitive levels the unity of all things, we live in a dream. In that dream it is perfectly possible to cut off your own right hand and believe that your left hand can make up for the loss. It is possible to be filled with a longing to be loved and cherished, yet have sex with someone who doesn't know your name. It is possible to have sex with one person while your attention is totally focused on someone else. It is possible to have sex with someone you have dressed up to look like someone else. It is possible to say to one person that you love them, but that they are not exciting enough so you must have sex with someone else. It is possible to be turned on sexually by someone you loathe, and turned off by someone you like. It is possible to walk dangerous streets in search of dangerous sex. It is possible to whip someone for money and piss on their face. It is possible to have an orgasm while hanging in a noose.

Doing any of these or a thousand other things – or not doing them – has a significance way beyond questions of personal or social morality. Prurience, personal distaste, religious abhorrence, moral retributions, threats of eternal damnation: none of these have in any significant way dented humankind's appetite for sexual practices that have nothing to do with love, or for activities that are dissociative and unknowing.

And why should they? The illusion of not-knowing that body, feelings and mind are one is not going to be shattered by threats from a pulpit. It is not shattered by grimly truthful warnings about disease or death. It is not shattered by the pain of broken marriages, the cries of desperate children or the pleas of outraged parents.

The dream of not-knowing comes to an end, I believe, only when the dreamer reclaims her body as essential to herself, *and begins to regard it with love*. This is never an insight that comes from outside herself, or from intellectual knowing only. Perhaps intellectually she has known this all along. Maybe this has even added to her splitting: to the separations and disjunctions within herself. Now, through something happening that is familiar, connecting with an insight that is less familiar, she *experiences* that what she is doing or having done to her body, profoundly affects *who she is*. She experiences that she is being unfaithful to herself, or that someone else is being unfaithful to her, and thinks to herself: 'It need not be like this. Things could be better. I could feel better. *This is not how I want to live.*'

Observing the effects of that insight, sifting it through the sieve of her short or long lifetime of experiences, she discovers something healing: 'I am *free* to treat myself with love. I am *free* to treat others with love. I am *free* to be treated with love.'

DOM BEDE GRIFFITHS, an English-born Catholic priest who spent most of his long life in India, strengthening his Christianity through his deepening knowledge of Buddhism and Hinduism, acknowledges the harm that Christianity has done to separate people in the West from a loving, faithful relationship to their own bodies.

'Human love is an expression of divine love,' he has said, 'or ought to be. We degrade it, we profane it, but really, the sexual energy is a power from God and it is meant to be an expression of this love of God.'

Religious proselytisers who rant against sex, and the sexual libertarians who claim the right to do anything at all to their own bodies, and sometimes to other people's as well, make strange bedfellows. But both groups demonstrate, in their different ways, that they believe sexuality exists as something separate from the rest of life: as a 'thing' to be elevated or despised.

Both are reluctant to see human beings as a unity. Separating any aspect of the human being from all other aspects, aggrandising the physical and sexual either through fear or avidity, throws a person severely out of balance. To the proselytisers, the body part of the equation and maybe the emotions, too, are something you must learn to control with your mind. The body is not 'the garment of your soul', but a messily disruptive reminder of your animal nature that should be tamed and subjected to a set of rules organised by people who know you better than you do.

To the sexual libertarians, your body is also something distinct, something you use for pleasure, certainly, but something that can also be used as a vehicle for distraction, sensation, control, aggression, power, money. You do things to it. Other people do things to it. You do things to other people. What could be more straightforward than that?

Neither view expresses an awareness that the human body – and everything that happens to that body in health and sickness, in bed and out of it – is deserving of understanding and of love.

Bede Griffiths again: 'We've neglected the body, the senses, sexuality, even the imagination, and concentrated on the mind and the will, to reach God by that. And that has created a neurosis. You see many people today concentrate on the spiritual, the supernatural, and they neglect the body, the senses and their sex, and they become neurotic. And that is why so many people leave the Church. [Or reject even the idea of Christianity.] Christianity doesn't answer their *human* need.

'Our task as Christians today is to recover that other dimension. Tantra [Buddhist and Hindu traditions of practice that transform the energy of passion and aggression into spiritual awakening] is important. It teaches you that the body itself is part of your human person which God has entered and is transforming. And your sex is part of your human *being*. Today we emphasise your sexuality is part of your human nature. You've got to deal with it. You can't leave it out. You shouldn't indulge it. And you must allow the Holy Spirit to work through it until it becomes a dynamic force opening you to God.

'So we have to learn how to open ourselves to the body, to open ourselves to the senses, to sexuality, to the imagination, *to the whole human reality.*'

IT IS IN this context, the context of a striving towards *the human reality*, that I listen to the stories people tell me about their relationships, their failures and successes, their fidelities and their infidelities. What I hear is this:

Love drove this scenario; fear drove that one.
This helped make me whole; that shattered or reduced me.

This I can feel easy and wholehearted about; that I would
    prefer to forget.
This brought me close to another person (and myself); that
    made me feel alone.
This was truthful; that was not.
This I can feel good about; that I do not.

IN FINDING OUT what could inspire us, what would feel
wholesome, trustworthy and healing, we need to listen to our
hearts. Our hearts can lead us out of anxiety and dissociated
sex, towards a sexual expression worthy of the self. We listen to
our hearts through our bodies, through understanding what
makes us feel alive and expansive and not only stimulated and
explosive. We can listen to our hearts by taking time to pay
close attention to our intuitions and feelings; and through
interested solitary reflection.

Doing that we may discover that we should take sex *more*
seriously, even knowing that, once we have taken it seriously
enough, it will take us into playfulness and laughter, as well as
into commitment and intensity.

'A sexual relationship is an act of communion between
body and spirit,' Vietnamese Zen master Thich Nhat Hanh
says. 'This is a very important encounter, not to be done in a
casual manner . . .

'When we are approached casually or carelessly, with an attitude that is less than tender, we feel insulted in our body and
soul. Someone who approaches us with respect, tenderness,
and utmost care is offering us deep communication, deep
communion. *It is only in that case that we will not feel hurt,*

misused, or abused, even a little. This cannot be attained unless there is true love and commitment. Casual sex cannot be described as love. Love is deep and beautiful and whole, integrating body and spirit . . .

'Sexual communion should be like a rite, a ritual performed in mindfulness with great respect, care, and love. Mere desire is not love. Without the communion of souls, the coming together of the two bodies can create division, widening the gap and causing much suffering.'

BUT SUPPOSE YOU are not in love? Suppose you are living in a relatively loveless partnership, or in no partnership at all? Should you then forego the pleasures of sex for its own sake, waiting – maybe for far too long – for sex to come wrapped in the garments of love?

I don't have a simple answer to that. All I have is a series of hunches, built up through years of my own mistakes and listening to others talk about what they regard as their mistakes and hearing, repeatedly, that loveless sex is rarely worth ruffling the sheets for. Even when the sex was lovely, I hear, loneliness followed, or worse: shame, awkwardness, false promises. For you need to know what it is you are wanting from sex. What that is differs for different people but most people are searching through sex for human contact, excitement, tenderness, touch, familiarity, adventure, playfulness, a feeling of being alive in their own bodies, a renewal of confidence that they are lovable and capable of giving love. Yet many people are having sex often and getting none of those things.

Bringing sex back into the place where it belongs – a part of yourself; one way of being human – you can discover that some of what you want from sex can be arrived at in other ways, with less risk, as much delight, and more freedom. More crucially, it is effortless to discover that there are other ways than sex to find those things, and to find them beautifully and satisfyingly, not as substitutes only.

Exploring the map of your own body and learning how
     to live within it vigorously as well as tenderly, helps.
Learning to care for other people and to develop
     interests that you have in common with them,
     helps.
Throwing yourself into all the physical realities of life,
     helps.
Working up a sweat, helps.
Making opportunities to eat well and laugh a lot, helps.
Developing a watchful and knowledgeable relationship with
     nature, and finding in that subtle reflections of your own
     nature, helps.
Cultivating beauty and sensuality in all your environments,
     helps.
Expressing yourself creatively – singing, dancing, writing,
     drawing, acting, chanting, working with clay or in the
     garden – helps.
Taking time to be with adults if you are mostly with
     children, or taking time to be with children if you are
     mostly with adults, helps.
Finding friends across all age groups, helps.

Creating your own means for transcendence – music,
   astronomy, mountain climbing, meditation, chanting or
   dancing – helps.
For some people, slowing down helps. For others, getting
   going helps.
Observing that no feeling state, however compelling, remains
   static, helps.

None of those activities replaces sex. But often sex doesn't
quite live up to sex either. What we miss, often, is what we
idealise, not what we have had or will ever have again.

ROSALIND IS FIFTY. She's the principal of a girls' school,
physically attractive and vibrant, but on her own admission
much less needy of men's admiration than she once was.

'I was really quite pretty but, like so many young women, I
needed someone else to affirm that. I ended up in so many
beds in part because that was the affirmation that counted
most for me. I wanted to be desired, and being desired meant
much more to me than the actual sexual act, even though I had
and have a robust sexual appetite.

'But what a price I paid for that desire! When I think of
the risks I took, the dangers I put myself in, the boredom
that I endured before and after and sometimes during!
After all, what are you left with after the pursuit, and the
conquest? Damp sheets, some embarrassment, sometimes a
few laughs, and very, very occasionally, the beginnings of a

real friendship that might have been better off begun out of bed anyway.'

Has Rosalind ever had sex that was better than that rather dismal version?

'Yes. I was in love through most of my late thirties and early forties. I really did love this man and am certain that he also loved me. For four of our eight years together we assumed that he would be able to leave his marriage once the kids were more or less grown up, and that we could then marry and would be together always. The commitment and trust between us were rock solid. His wife knew that he was in a relationship with me and she must have known that he loved me. I am sorry about the pain that caused her but I also truly believe that he and she were not ever that close, and that she was pretty content with her work, her children and a good circle of friends. There was certainly no sense that she was the hang-dog left waiting at home.

'He and I were utterly open with each other. We shared most of what we thought. We shared interests. We adored talking, talking, talking. And I loved sleeping with him: touching, petting, patting, snuggling up. All of that was as wonderful as the actual sex we had together.

'In our fifth year together, his wife died very suddenly of a stroke. It was disastrous. She was not quite fifty. It was actually unbelievable. She and Robert had had five children. The eldest three were at university but the younger two were still at school. Naturally he felt that he should give all his spare time to them. We never discussed moving in together. It seemed wrong, somehow. That was her territory. The children shouldn't be taken to a new home. All of that was understood between us. So for several more years we saw less and less of each other, then he had a kind of breakdown.

'We had stopped making love long before that, and closed up in other ways, too. It all went together. It does, doesn't it?

'We've still got a number of mutual friends, and sometimes I see him at a dinner party and we still talk and talk extremely fondly and gaze at each other and hug, but it's as though there's a wall of fog between us. On my side of the fog I have vivid memories of sharing everything with this man. Feeling absolutely no shame with him about any aspect of my being, and feeling totally accepting of him also.

'Maybe on his side of the fog he feels much the same. Yet we can't reach through it. He seems fragile still, like someone who's been through a very long and terrible illness and will never quite recover. He's working again, doing big deals in the city, out to lots of social functions, and so on. But it can't be the same.

'When I eventually went to bed with one or two other people it was a pale version of the real thing Robert and I shared. What I disliked most was that I felt so self-conscious. I was worried about all the usual boring things – my size, my desirability – and what a distraction I found that! I couldn't pay that intense depth of attention to my partner while I was worrying about myself. Yet it absolutely was not selfishness on my part. It was a separateness that could not be bridged through sex alone. That must be what makes the differ-ence. When you love someone, when you really, truly love someone, then for the time you come together, you *are* together. It's the best possible bulwark against loneliness. Sex is not the bulwark. Not for me anyway. Love is. That's immensely precious, don't you think?'

TO CULTIVATE FIDELITY does not mean constraining yourself, although it may certainly involve sometimes giving up what you want to do or feel 'driven' to do. It may also mean choosing to do what is very difficult. These are not expressions of constraint; they are expressions of freedom: freedom to be true to yourself, freedom to exercise your regard for other people.

Freedom *is* an expression of awareness that you can choose the attitudes that create your life. That's all.

It means not making the rules too simple, and not being ingenuous about an apparent lack of rules either. The question, for example, of whether Rosalind and Robert were, during their years together, 'unfaithful' either to themselves or to the vows Robert once made to his wife, seems to me not easily answered.

Conventionally, of course, the answer would be that, while Robert was married, having a sexual relationship outside that marriage was unfaithful. Yet would it necessarily have been more 'faithful' to have left his family, divorced his wife and married Rosalind?

Perhaps it may have been more truthful. It was Rosalind, after all, who had become Robert's wife in any real meaning of that word. But Robert was also a loving and devoted father, and there is fidelity in that, too.

Theirs was not a life that I would choose. Having lived out almost every possible permutation of this complex situation, I could now say that, for me, sex within a relationship that is compromised by lack of freedom to love and to be loved with a full heart, is too meagre. And that within a relationship where love and trust *can* be fully present, the attraction of sex outside that relationship simply disappears.

But still the picture isn't simple. I could now also argue that leaving a relationship that is debasing or dead is no less an act of fidelity than staying in a relationship that is half-alive and trying to resuscitate it. And that leaving a relationship considerately and truthfully, rather than hysterically, accusatorially or self-righteously, is no less an act of fidelity than giving up a behaviour that hurts your partner for the sake of your shared love and the life you could still have together.

WHEN YOU ARE given the opportunity to love someone in their entirety – when that person honours you with the opportunity to be as close to their body as you are to their mind and soul – and when you dare to allow that person to love you in *your* entirety, then having sex with someone else for the sake of slaking a transitory itch begins to seem absurd. Just as absurd, maybe, as *not* having casual sex might once have seemed.

Lust – which can translate as that transitory itch – can be the catalyst for all kinds of change and creativity. Matthew Fox speaks positively of it, but adds a useful caution. 'Lust by itself is, of course, not all of our sexuality. Meister Eckhart says, "If you want to treat your passions well, don't go into asceticism, don't mortify your senses and kill them. Rather, put on your passions a bridle of love."'

Fox continues: 'What's a bridle? A steering instrument for a stallion. There's a stallion of lust inside all of us. There's a stallion of anger inside all of us. Our passions are holy. We can't go any place important without them but we need to bridle them. We need to steer them. If you can't steer them, then they're going to ruin your life.'

AT ITS BEST, sexual love is an expression of strong, positive feeling, as well as a means for feelings to expand and explode through the body so that one is entirely present to what is happening, and thoughts, distractions and even memories are momentarily laid aside.

It is a time, too, when each of our five senses joins to form the perfect chorus that is the backdrop as well as the means to an experience of ecstasy. Few writers have captured this more exquisitely than the author of the Song of Solomon: 'The flowers appear on the earth; the time of the singing of birds is come, and the voice of the turtle is heard in our land . . . Arise, my love, my fair one, and come away . . . My beloved is mine and I am his: he feedeth among the lilies.'

WHERE TRUTHFUL, CONSCIOUS fidelity lives and breathes, there is also love. Love for oneself, for others, for life. That love is palpable. After six months or sixty years, it is there in their smiles when the two people meet. It is there in the interest one shows while the other talks. It is there in the pleasure they take in their friends. It is there in the delight of having time apart and coming back together. It is there, too, in their sorrows. It can still be there when they face the end.

Is it too pat, or too simplistic, to suggest that where infidelity is, there is fear? Fear of boredom, of intimacy, of commitment or truth? Fear of being alone. Of not getting what one wants? Fear of no longer being desired? Of growing old? Of being forgotten? Fear of the awesomeness of love?

Yet it is only love that can soften fear, dissolve its effects, and let something else emerge. A teaching from the Hindu scripture the Isa Upanishad reinforces this: 'Who sees all beings in his own Self, and his own Self in all beings, loses all fear.' Not only loses all fear, discovers love.

IN THE END, fidelity is nothing more than finding out who you are, and learning to be true to this, so that, as night follows day, 'thou canst not then be false to any man'.

It is not discovered through other people's rules and injunctions. They may be inspiring, cramping, or quite irrelevant. Fidelity is discovered patiently, sometimes almost stealthily, through paying attention to all aspects of life, including those that involve the body and are called sexual. 'The chief aim of the individual is to create out of himself the most significant product of which he is capable,' wrote analyst Frances Wickes.

Our knowledge of fidelity is often honed in the dark, literally as well as symbolically. It takes us deep into the most personal and private areas of our lives, yet how we live out our ideas and ideals of fidelity also has profound interpersonal and social consequences: 'For we are family one of another.'

Restraint

Be still and know that I am God.

PSALM 46:10

*B*efore drawing breath comes a whole tumble of questions. What is restraint? Why should it be a virtue? Haven't many of us spent a couple of decades attempting to *increase* our range of emotional expression? A couple of decades attempting to be true to whatever feelings arise. Shouldn't we be attempting to explode into life rather than imploding into death?

And surely it's a fact that only rather dreary people are restrained? Isn't there something cramped and pinched even about the word itself? How could it be psychologically healthy to repress oneself? The goal of the therapeutic endeavour is to liberate oneself from repression. To be free, free, free. What place could restraint have in psychological good health?

THAT SALLOW YOUNG man, sulking at a dinner party, clearly thinking himself too good for the rest of us, preferring his own company, not speaking to anyone, barely reacting when he is spoken to, nothing to say really, not worth speaking to either: the kindest thing one could say about him is that he is restrained.

What about that drab woman in your office, the one who never speaks up at meetings? It's impossible for her to get on the wrong side of anyone; she takes absolutely no risks. Who knows what she's thinking. Who cares. Talk about restraint! You could sit a dummy in her chair and it would be livelier company than she is.

And haven't you also been to bed with someone who turned out to be a total wet blanket? Passive. Inhibited. Reminding you of nothing more than weak, milky tea left to grow cold? *Restrained*. Yuck.

RESTRAINT IS THE virtue that may on first glance appear the runt of this fairly awesome litter. Few people wake up in the morning and reach inwards to locate their golden source of restraint, believing that it will support them through the day. Yet once you can untangle it from its web of negative connotations – most of which more fairly belong to *constraint* – you could find that this is the virtue on which all the others depend.

CONSTRAINT IS IN part a habit. When it takes hold, it shrinks a person's openness to life. If you have always wanted to learn to play drums, but don't; if you would relish the chance to give up your safe job to work as a gardener, but don't; if you long to travel to the next town or continent, but don't – then constraint temporarily has you under its heel.

Some people are more temperamentally inclined to be constrained (pleasing, modest, acquiescent, submissive, timid, downtrodden) than others. But when constraint is actually restricting your life, it should alert you to a fear of acting or reacting that's been built up through a myriad of difficult experiences that are still waiting to be brought out into the light, addressed and understood.

RESTRAINT IS NOT a habit. It is, every time it happens, a fresh act of will, an expression of your freedom to decide for yourself. An expression of your choice to act – or not. Your choice to be true to what you believe is important, or not. Your choice to be loving to yourself and thoughtful about the social good, or not.

I AM TALKING to a young woman who has been a dope smoker for years. She is trying hard not to smoke while she finishes a book that she has been intermittently writing for what she describes as 'long enough'. Going without the dope is painfully difficult for her, as anyone who has any kind of addiction to comforting substances will fully understand. Not at all sure of what she might say, I ask her: 'Can you feel that it's worthwhile? Can you trust that doing without will give you something more valuable in the longer run?'

Her face lights up. 'Yes, absolutely. But it's still very hard.'

'Does this feel as though it's loving of yourself?' I press on.

She thinks carefully. 'It does. But that's because I really want this book to get done. You smoke four million joints. Then you think, what's the harm in four million and one? But each one makes a difference. If I smoke, I don't even *see* the computer!'

Allowing ourselves to know that we can take the time to reflect and choose how we will act is difficult. Taking the time to choose how we will act is also difficult. Choosing not to act on every impulse, or in response to entrenched and maybe unconsidered emotional habits, is difficult. Who among us doesn't know that, to our cost? My own worst mistakes, my deepest regrets, arise from the moments when an unwise reaction spewed out of me – and could never be taken back.

The idea of pausing, 'taking your time', of not acting or reacting before you are ready, is far from fashionable. Some people, and especially some young people, are increasingly going into an extreme revolt against the frenetic demands of contemporary life and spend months or even years chilling out from the heat of this freneticism. But the majority of us live life running, reacting instantly to whatever is asked of us and, in turn, demanding from life immediate satisfaction.

In 1909, reviewing a biography of the first Queen Elizabeth, Virginia Woolf said of sovereigns: 'They may not stand aside, but must always act.' Today most of us behave like sovereigns. But where do these crazy compulsions come from? Who do they benefit? *Who owns us*? And if this way of life is not working for us, why do we believe that we have no right to stop it?

THESE DAYS, I work as a writer and psychotherapist. For years I worked as a publisher. I am also a mother. If I appear on radio or television, or am being interviewed by a journalist, questions can be thrown at me that may have nothing to do with what I have learned from any of those roles. Is this because I am reassuringly opinionated? Only in part, I think. It is also because, in a small way, I am a public person. Public persons have reactions to anything. To everything. At this time. At any time.

Perhaps, as an introvert, I would like to think about my reaction. If it is a question about something important, then I know that I will do that subject matter, and myself, a disservice by rushing in. But there is no time to pause. The time to react is now.

React now; regret later.

WHAT MARKS CONTEMPORARY life almost more than anything else is its speed. Speed has become a synthetic virtue. We can fly around the world in less than a day, talk to dozens of people simultaneously on linked telephones, connect with millions of people on the Internet. We have long ago forgotten what waiting for a letter meant. We think only of the immediacy of e-mail and the fax. 'Instant' is a word lavishly used by advertisers. They know it will assure and allure us. We abandon our old computer when a new one can work more quickly. Never mind that we ourselves cannot type or even think faster, however brilliant the machine. We trade up our cars, too, even when we know that speed limits on roads mean we could anyway not drive the new car any faster than we did the old.

No one wants to wait. Waiting wastes time. We confuse the value of our time with our own self-worth. We regard other people's time as capital. We talk about time as though it were the master and we were the slaves. This expresses an entrenched personal and social anxiety. We ask about each other's 'time' with the care we once asked about health. And the two are linked. Having little or no time is a danger to our health. It's common to complain of having no time at all. Fewer complain, bitterly and truthfully, of having far too much time, of being sidelined from the world of paid work where 'no time' is a badge of honour.

When people say they have no time what they mean is no time to pause, to collect themselves, to dream, to think something through, to consider if what is being asked of them or what they are asking of themselves is fair, just, humane or loving. Does it expand their life or contract it? Does it put them more in touch with who or what they really care about? Or does it take them further away?

WE RUN OUR lives according to bizarre external agendas. We boast if our children walk or talk a month ahead of their contemporaries, learn to read before they go to school, or can do two music examinations in a year instead of one. At my daughter's genuinely caring school, some girls are offered the opportunity to move through the first three years of high school in only two years. It is considered to be a privilege for these academically adroit girls to race through the normal curriculum and have time left over to crunch through other experiences that, presumably, girls who must move at the more conventional pace may not have.

But is it self-evidently a privilege to *hurry*? To hurtle into the future any more quickly than time itself carries us?

DESCRIBING HIS EARLY morning routine, sixty-year-old writer Robert Fulghum – who lives on a houseboat in Seattle – says: 'I arise about six o'clock every morning. Instead of turning on the light or the radio, my wife and I light candles or oil lamps. We like to begin our day with this softer, gentler light. We listen to music as we build a fire in the fireplace, especially in winter. After the fire has been built, the next hour of the new day is spent in talking to each other. These morning rituals bring us into the day in a gentle, nourishing manner, so unlike the hurried and panic-stricken way we began our days when we were much younger. Now we open our day with a consciousness of attitude. We're together, and we pay a lot of attention to each other.'

YOU MAY BE saying: 'It's all right for him. He's old or he's rich or he doesn't have to get to a job or care for the kids. He's got a partner he actually wants to talk to. For the rest of us, living in the real world, life can't be like that.'

But I wonder. Fulghum speaks of 'a consciousness of attitude'. Even with kids, jobs, noise, competing interests, it's possible to bring a *consciousness of attitude* to the vital question of whether life has to be lived at an exhausting gallop or can sometimes just be lived.

'Understanding that we can put difficulties aside is incredibly helpful,' Buddhist teacher Jack Kornfield reminds us. 'We don't need to face our problems all at once, and we don't need to do so in every circumstance. As with all aspects of nature, there is a proper place for our hearts and minds to grow.'

When we rush we breathe shallowly. Everywhere I go I see tired, stressed women and men, and too often children also, unaware that as they rush towards the moment that has not yet come, heads forward, chests cramped, shoulders tight, they are taking tiny breaths in, letting tiny breaths out. Maybe they don't know that the Indian yogis believe that a person's life span is measured not in years, but in breaths. Those same yogis who themselves can live for years without food or water, or for months buried underground, have observed that creatures that breathe quickly, such as birds, dogs and rabbits, have a relatively short life span. Creatures that breathe slowly, such as snakes and tortoises, live much longer. The heart of a mouse beats one thousand times per minute. An elephant's heart beats about twenty-five times per minute; a whale's heart beats only sixteen.

Any activity that is going to express not just what you know, but who you yourself are, takes time. It not only takes time to effect, but it emerges from within, from time spent dreaming and drifting; from lying-on-your-back, staring-into-space time; from time spent sitting out on the back steps or in a café with a mug of tea; from time that is emptied of external concerns. In their race from one organised activity to another, or from the blackboards of school to the screens at home, many children have no chance to learn that this 'doing-nothing time' may be time that is not just well spent, but best spent. And many adults who once knew it live as though they have forgotten.

IN EVEN THE most demanding life, sometimes it is worth doing the most ordinary everyday activities slowly. Setting out cups for tea; brushing your hair; drying dishes; polishing the car; walking with awareness of your feet rising, falling, rising, falling: any activity grows in grace and beauty when you slow it down and become aware of the subtle flow of movement that makes up any single action.

Hurrying, you lose much of that grace and beauty.

Slowing down so that you know what you are doing, you are reminded of what you already have: clean water, clean cups, tea; an arm that is strong enough to lift a brush and move it through your hair; a car that can take you places; feet that can also take you places; earth to walk on. That is already so much, and yet it is so easily overlooked.

GOING OUT OF the house this morning, rushing to get my children to their two separate buses, I did not see what colour the sky was, never mind how exquisite and perfect the plants are that flower in a fall from big round pots on my concrete front steps. It is spring as I write this, and white geraniums, scarlet and orange nasturtiums, pink-and-red-striped busy lizzies, alyssum and white paper daisies grow from their shared earth with touching splendour. By their side stands 'Sidonie', Australia's first lavender. Her flowers form on the end of strong, tall, elegant stalks, and are so blue they are almost purple. Pausing, I have time to think not only of how beautiful they are, but to think of Colette, too, the French writer whose mother's name was also Sidonie.

These are flowers that will bloom even for the most neglectful gardener. But first they must be planted.

ALL THE VIRTUES come to life through your capacity to make a choice. It is restraint, though, that offers you that precious moment – the merest split second sometimes – in which you know that you are doing the choosing, *that you are free to do the choosing.*

YOUR LIFE IS created from the consequences of millions of choices. No one has made them for you. No one can make them for you. They are entirely your own work. By the time you reach mid-life, some of those choices will be enscribed on your face, telling a story that is available at a single glance. Even if you can afford or favour cosmetic surgery there is nothing that can be surgically changed about the look in a person's eyes: the gaze that speaks of compassion or mistrust, selfishness or selflessness, interest or inertia, greed or contentment.

The vital capacity to decide whether you will be generous, kind, good-humoured – or not – is what distinguishes human beings from all other living creatures. It is what makes our acts of cruelty so much more devastating and perverse than the acts of one animal attacking another. Animals attack for food or to protect their territory or their young. Human beings also attack for pleasure, or out of a misplaced belief that they can placate their own misery at someone else's expense.

WHOEVER WE ARE, however we live, we need time and internal space to reflect. How else can we learn from our successes as well as from our mistakes? How else can we know what effect events have had on us, or discover how we think we ourselves have affected other people?

Reflection is the core activity of consciousness. It is impossible to broaden and deepen our awareness of ourselves, and of life itself, without it. Reflection needs more than time. We need to undertake it from the perspective of the heart as well as the mind. Without heart, it is all too easy to pervert it into yet something else with which we can beat ourselves, yet something else where we can fail. On the other hand, without mind, it is all too easy to become soggy and self-serving, and to learn little that is of much value.

I am aware how confronting it is for many people to begin the process of learning to reflect on their own lives. This is not an intellectual difficulty. It more usually arises out of a lack of self-trust that assumes that whatever they will find, it will be grisly and disheartening.

Traditional Christian teachings on original sin have a lot to answer for. The notion that we are innately sinful, and that without great effort we will slip back into our 'naturally' sinful condition, is utterly repugnant to me.

Our spiritual nature is love. ('God said, Let us make humans in our image, after our likeness.' What other likeness could there be but love?) Consciousness – waking ourselves up; committing ourselves to know more truthfully who we are through observing how we behave as well as what we think – can bring us back to love, especially when we use it to recover and reclaim for ourselves the unitive qualities of patience, reverence for nature, intuition, sensual knowledge, and reflection.

REFLECTION IS LEARNED in silence and it reveals silence to us. Silence is not emptiness; it is the container within which fullness is found.

One of the most agonising effects of mental illness can be the loss of silence. If your mind is more than usually filled with chattering or clamorous voices that you can never silence, this is a torment of a most excruciating kind.

From the Tao Teh Ching we learn:

The highest form of goodness is like water.
Water knows how to benefit all things without
striving with them . . .
In choosing your dwelling, know how to keep
to the ground.
In cultivating your mind, know how to dive in
the hidden deeps.

Moving from clamorousness and mental and verbal activity into silence can take place in small stages. It can happen by becoming conscious of the places where you are anyway silent, such as in the bath; lying in bed at night waiting for sleep; on the way to work, hanging from the strap in the middle of a swaying bus; in your car; pulling weeds; or walking to and from the local shops.

It is possible to extend that silence gradually until it seems familiar enough that you can welcome its constant presence into your awareness without any other accompanying activity. It is possible to welcome silence and feel welcomed into it for its own sake only, and for yours.

As you discover that silence is not emptiness, you can also discover that restraint is far from inert. The way to discover this is not through abstract thought, but through experience, personal investigation and practice.

'We will establish peace not only by doing but also, and more importantly, by being,' Jesuit writer and teacher William Johnston points out. In that he reflects the teaching of Taoism: of non-action (*wu-wei*) leading to non-violence; of allowing nature to act – which means that even without our actions and interventions, everything anyway changes.

ALL THE MYSTICAL traditions honour practices that are centred in silence, practices that 'leave behind the senses and the operations of the intellect', as the author of the sixth-century text *Mystica Theologia* expressed it. This is not to discount the senses or the intellect: on the contrary. It has never been more necessary that we should bring knowledge to love and love to knowledge. Fatuous declamations of 'love', without thought of how love and justice are to be expressed for the social good, are narcissistic and futile. But intellectual knowledge, without the gifts of love, is equally sterile. In the best possible expressions of human endeavour, Eros and Logos align, dance, flirt, move towards each other and, if you let them, marry.

There is more, though. Beyond the senses and the intellect is silence.

The early-seventeenth-century German mystic Jakob Böhme takes us directly into the mystery of our relationship with the infinite when he says: 'Cease from all thy thinking and willing, then shalt thou hear the unspeakable words of

God . . . *When thou art quiet and silent, then art thou as God was before nature and creature*; thou art that which God then was; thou art that of which he made thy nature and creature.'

THE RELIGIOUS SOCIETY of Friends, founded in the seventeenth century and more familiarly known as Quakers, pays particular attention to the practice of meeting 'the Light within' in silence, centring Meeting for Worship in a silence that is broken only if someone attending meeting feels moved by the Holy Spirit to briefly share what they find stirring in their heart as much as in their mind. That Quakers have, despite their small numbers, played a continual and unflinching role in a wide variety of social justice matters is not unaligned to that central practice of entering the silence in the belief that each one of us, *and no one of us any more than another*, has within us 'that of God', a divine light that seeks to illuminate and transform all of our lives.

Not simply believing, but putting into practice that belief in the universality of divinity within, makes sense of the Quaker refusal to kill under any circumstances; to take part in any war, no matter how purportedly 'just'; to validate separations between people on the basis of race, class, sexuality or gender; to believe that revelation began or ended with any particular group of scriptures; to pay attention to honorifics that exalt one person over another; or to turn away from the most needy, on the grounds that their plight is distinct from our own. But while most of this activity is socially, outwardly directed, it arises from and enters into that inward silence, in a constant cycle of weaving and mending, seeking and finding, mending and weaving.

Writing at the end of the nineteenth century, Quaker Caroline Stephen said: 'The one corner-stone of belief upon which the Society of Friends is built is the conviction that God does indeed communicate with each one of the spirits he has made, in a direct and living inbreathing of some measure of the breath of his own life; that he never leaves himself without a witness in the heart as well as in the surroundings of man; and that in order clearly to hear the divine voice thus speaking to us we need to be still; to be alone with him in the secret place of his presence; that all flesh should keep silence before him.'

DANIEL GOLEMAN WRITES for the *New York Times* and is author of the fascinating, useful book *Emotional Intelligence*. He cites self-awareness – which he defines as 'recognizing a feeling *as it happens*' – as being 'the keystone of emotional intelligence'.

The capacity to reflect on one's actions – and to understand what drives them – is, in my experience, just as important. Nevertheless, Goleman's view underpins my own fascination with the possibility that freedom can arise from restraint.

Self-observation arises directly from your capacity for restraint. Goleman describes it in greater detail: 'At its best, self-observation allows . . . an equanimous awareness of passionate or turbulent feelings. At a minimum, it manifests itself simply as a slight stepping-back from experience, a parallel stream of consciousness that is "meta": hovering above or beside the main flow, aware of what is happening rather than being immersed and lost in it. It is the difference between, for example, being murderously enraged at someone and having the self-reflexive thought "This is anger I'm feeling" even as you are enraged.'

That 'slight stepping-back' Goleman is pointing to is what you experience each time you pause, watch your thoughts and know that you and your thoughts are not one, or when you watch your feelings and know that you and your feelings are not one. However convincing those thoughts and however passionate those feelings, there is still something other: a central, potentially unifying 'I' that is the self. The self that is observing the thoughts and therefore cannot also be the thoughts; the self that is observing the feelings and therefore cannot also be the feelings.

RESTRAINT BEGINS WITH a moment of intention.

I am ill. A friend comes to work in my garden. She knows that among my many concerns is an anxiety that I have not been able to weed and clear a particular patch that is overgrown and threatening the life of some timid plants. My friend is a devoted gardener. I feel safe in her hands.

A couple of days later I am up again. I go out to the garden. It looks wonderful. I am thanking her in my mind. Then I notice that she has cut back a native plant that took two years to get to be the rather spindly delight it was when I last saw it.

In that moment, I have a choice. I can choose to speak to my friend honestly. I can tell her that she has cut back a plant that I would have left alone. That is, after all, the truth. Alternatively, I can choose to thank her again for the work that she did in my garden. She has done it in her own way, not mine. In that, I see our differences one from the other.

If I did speak to her honestly, she would inevitably be hurt, in almost exactly the way I myself would be hurt had I done my best, then been told that my best was wrong. In that, I see that she and I are much more similar than we are different.

I *choose* not to speak about that plant, but only about her kindness and the pleasure it has brought me. Choosing, I am practising restraint.

Six months later, the plant explodes into flower far more lavishly than it has ever done. But that's not the point. Even if the plant had died, that moment of restraint would still have saved something more precious than the most exceptional flowering plant. It saved my friend's heart from unnecessary hurt; it gave me the chance to express and gather love.

I HAVE HAD to live through many storms and their aftermaths to learn that love is as powerfully expressed through the moments we hold back from taking action *for the sake of someone else*, as in the moments we step forward to make our claims.

This is yet another example of the value of sacrificing short-term satisfaction for the sake of long-term happiness. Or maybe not sacrificing anything, but just holding someone else's needs in the circle of your life.

There is a splendid illustration of this in Jane Smiley's novella *The Age of Grief*, where a husband holds himself back from confronting his darling wife about her adulterous relationship. Of course, it could be argued that he is merely a wimp, or is afraid to risk his wife leaving him for her lover.

Both those assumptions could be true. Certainly it would seem that as long as the affair is not out in the open, they can carry on as though all is well in their marriage and even in their joint dental practice. But Smiley's skill does not allow the reader the comfort of such simple conclusions. Instead, she shows that it is only because David is capable of love that he can hold back *for Dana's sake*.

At the end of the novella Dana reappears after a night's absence. David asks her: ' "Well, are you leaving or staying?"

' "Staying."

' "Are you sure?"

'She nodded.

'I said, "Let's not talk about it for a while, okay?"

'She nodded. And we looked at each other. It was two-thirty.

'The big girls would be home in forty minutes.

'Shall I say that I welcomed my wife back with great sadness, more sadness than I had felt at any other time? It seems to me that marriage is a small container, after all, barely large enough to hold some children. Two inner lives, two lifelong meditations of whatever complexity, burst out of it and out of it, cracking it, deforming it. Or maybe it is not a thing at all, nothing, something not present. I don't know, but I can't help thinking about it.'

I AM NOT valuing here the refusal of one person to discuss with another person what matters to them. That's not restraint. That's a defective effort to control, which usually arises from and expresses fear.

Restraint holds you back from saying anything that may give you momentary relief or even pleasure, but that causes hurt, confusion or retaliatory anger. It expresses love at best, or at least an awareness of choice and some insight that others' lives have a value equal to your own.

Restraint also allows you to face what is difficult, but true.

Andrew, a close friend, calls me from New York. He is in his mid-thirties and has been half in love for years with a woman who also loves him, but is a committed wife and mother. 'Which virtue are you working on now?' he asks.

'Restraint,' I tell him.

There's a tiny pause. Then he says, not quite laughing, 'There's too much of that in my life. Too much fidelity. Too much restraint.'

I ask, 'How would you wish it could be different?'

'That I had more choices. That restraint was more balanced with abundance. That I was giving less to my work, which really doesn't make me happy, and had more left over to find out what would make me happy.'

He pauses again and then says, 'An old lover rang me the other day. She said, "Are things going as they should?" I replied, "Things are going as they are. That's how it is."'

What Andrew is saying exemplifies, I think, not only how restraint can be challenging or plain difficult, but also the value of being able to face what is true. That doesn't mean that knowing the truth or living truthfully provides the instant satisfactions or relief we crave. On the contrary. But it does mean that we are far less likely to be cultivating harmful, unconscious disjunctions between our outer and inner worlds. This alone will make us feel safer and 'more in charge'.

I can hear, listening to his voice, what restraint is costing Andrew, but he knows, and I know, that the costs would be worse if he and his friend acted. Out of consideration for everyone involved, including themselves, they are choosing not to act. That doesn't make things easy; it only keeps them real.

The great Indian leader and peace activist Gandhi came to think so highly of truth that he subtitled his autobiography 'The Story of My Experiments with Truth', and said, 'My uniform experience has convinced me that there is no other God than Truth.'

However, as family therapist Robin Skynner has pointed out, before you can experience the value of truth, or tell the truth, you have to know what the truth is. Unsurprisingly (given that distinguishing truth from not-the-truth depends a good deal on your capacity for reflection), the more psychologically healthy someone is, the more possible this is. Skynner says this is because such people, whom he calls 'the healthies', 'have a more realistic view of what's going on around them, and what they're like themselves. In addition, they'll really "believe" in honesty . . . So healthies will interpret a myth like "Honesty is the best policy" not as an injunction but as a simple fact that's obvious from their experience, and do so in such a way as to encourage telling the truth in a wider, more open way about a more complete range of topics.'

Less psychologically healthy people have a rather different relationship to truth. They will often see the 'truth' as something they can barter with, or bend to suit their own whims. With little capacity to reflect, they may quickly come to believe their own rhetoric, even when it is patently at odds with the facts before them. Of them Skynner says: 'It's more difficult for them to tell the truth in any objective sense, because for a start *they're tending to project all their faults on other people, and to blame everyone but themselves for anything that goes wrong* [my italics].Unlike the more healthy, they don't even know what the truth is. In addition, because they see the outside world as basically hostile, they'll feel morally justified in "doctoring" the truth in order to defend their own interests against all these unfriendly forces.'

RESTRAINT CANNOT BE practised without some degree of maturity. When young children are growing as they should, they are naturally impulsive and exuberant. Swiss analyst and writer Alice Miller suggests that 'Warm and genuine feelings are unable to grow without the vital soil of exuberance.' Being asked to wait a minute can seem to those children like an agony. Taking a back seat is an impossibility.

Learning gradually, gradually to know that they can wait, learning to move their protective impulses away from themselves towards someone else at least sometimes, is part of what civilises each child. When the processes that teach children such civility are undertaken in a leisurely and affectionate way, and they go well, they fit children to live with others in a civil society where each person must constantly accommodate themselves to others' needs.

Restraining children is not the same as teaching them restraint. Restraining children is something that is done *to* them, with more or less love, and more or less goodwill.

Constraint can certainly be taught through the imposition of will. Restraint, however, is an expression of free choice and can only be taught through modelling: through the children experiencing how they themselves benefit from their parents, friends, teachers sometimes *not* reacting, or reacting in ways that do not put themselves first. As they learn how they benefit from this, *and learn how to reflect on it*, they are likely to want to find out for themselves, too, how restraint expresses choice, a learned willingness not always to act or react; a learned willingness to pause, or to give up something for one's own sake, others' sake, and eventually for the sake of those not-so-abstract ideals, peace and social justice.

These are extremely difficult lessons to learn, especially for people whose nature is fast moving, assertive or tempestuous. A lack of restraint can utterly determine the tone of someone's interactions with other people, even when those are relatively impersonal. 'Completely desist from defending your point of view. When you have no point to defend, you do not allow the birth of an argument,' suggests endocrinologist and writer Deepak Chopra.

I think carefully about what he is saying.

I remember innumerable times when my point of view has at least momentarily been infinitely more important to me than the people with whom I am arguing. Yet did I ever change their minds through the force of my most passionate arguments? Did they ever change mine? I remember allowing

myself to become distressed, outraged, agitated, even contemptuous far more often than I was ever enlightened, and
infinitely more often than I brought, in that frame of mind,
light to others.

Jane is a beekeeper. She talks to me about what she has
learned about restraint from going into her hives. The bees
have a highly organised, complex, fascinating social system. She
enters their world as an invader, but is more or less welcomed
according to the speed and thoughtfulness with which she
acts, and the state of mind she carries with her. 'If I go into the
hive feeling agitated, then I agitate the bees. I may even be
working slowly and carefully, but that in itself may not be
enough. They pick up my mood, my vibrations immediately
and if that *mood* is hurried or distressed, it takes me a long time
to settle them. It's the same with people. If I take up an issue
with someone when I am agitated, then soon they are
buzzing. They become unsettled. I become further unsettled.
It takes a long time to find harmony.'

THERE ARE INNUMERABLE moments in every life when
restraint is quite inappropriate. If your baby has fallen in the
goldfish pond, this is not the moment to practise restraint.
When your friend tells you a wonderful joke, there is no
virtue in holding back your laughter. If the impulse arises in
you to kiss your lover who has placed her lips remarkably
near your own, then restraining from doing so could border
on the ridiculous.

The instincts that push you to rescue your water-exploring baby, to laugh at a great joke, to kiss your lover, to eat when you are hungry, to sleep when you are tired, are in themselves beyond the value judgements of 'bad' or 'good'. The discriminations of 'good' and 'bad' become appropriate when you relate those drives to the particularities of time, place, circumstance. It is good to eat when you are hungry; less good to eat all day. It is appropriately gratifying to kiss your own lover. It is not appropriate to force a kiss on someone who does not want this.

Sigmund Freud's insights into the nature of the unconscious mind led him to the view that what we can perceive and 'control' through the rational, conscious mind is pretty limited. Much of what we do, how we act, even how we feel, is out of the sphere of our conscious awareness. This partly explains how we can keep falling into the same behavioural cesspit, even when we truly believe we want to make a change.

Freud argued that our behaviour as adults is set in train by psychosexual events in early childhood and continues to be determined by unconscious motivations (which reveal themselves through our slips, such as turning up late or 'forgetting' to go to a meeting that had seemed to offer the chance of a lifetime), irrational forces (flying off the handle at your boss because she unconsciously reminds you of your nasty aunty), and biological and instinctual drives.

Those drives – which can seem so 'natural' that we may be barely conscious of them and have never thought of examining them – broadly speaking push us towards the taking of pleasure and the avoidance of pain.

That sounds wonderfully healthy. Problems arise, however, when cogs spin, land in the wrong place, and people become totally confused about what will bring them pleasure, and how to avoid pain.

As an extreme and obscene example, think of military dictators putting literally millions of people to death in a futile attempt to avoid their own pain (and finding thousands of followers to carry out this vile work in order to avoid *their* own pain). In the Freudian model, they are curbed neither by their ego, which ought to let them know that it isn't rational to sacrifice human lives for the sake of ideology, nor by their superego, which ought to keep them in touch with the traditional values of all societies, which say that killing fellow humans is not a good thing.

Instead what occurs is a monstrous alignment between a perverse version of the superego that says that there are ever-more perfect ways to kill, and a version of the death instinct that says that as long as you are killing successfully you will avoid pain and postpone the dread of your own death.

That this makes no 'sense' to anyone except the perpetrators is highly significant. At these dangerously low levels of human psychological functioning, there is little or no capacity to pause and consider whether your actions are affecting others positively, and often there is little or no capacity to care.

RESTRAINT OFFERS A space between intention and action and the opportunity to protect others from actions or reactions that should exist only in your imagination. The more conscious you are of that space, and the freer you are to occupy it, the more easily you can choose whether and how to act.

TO REFUSE TO be responsible for all of one's actions is to refuse to be fully human. We are familiar with the terrible cry 'I was only carrying out orders.' Just as terrible is 'I only did it because he made me', or 'I only did it because I am already a victim myself.'

Buddhism helps us to understand that what fuels such statements – and the actions those statements attempt to defend – is profound ignorance. It is no coincidence that Buddhism offers humankind no external saviour. The historical Buddha taught through the example of his own life how we can save ourselves from unhappiness, *not how he can save us*. The Dalai Lama reinforces this when he teaches: 'We are our own masters. No one can protect us.'

People who refuse to grasp the truth of what they are doing are ignorant – in our Western sense of that word. The Buddhist view of ignorance (or delusion) comes much closer to the real tragedy of such experience. All human beings are trying to find happiness and trying to avoid suffering, Budhhism teaches. That is what unites us. *But it is impossible to create our own happiness by causing suffering for someone else.* To imagine that it is possible – perhaps by looking at the financial gains some exploiters make, or the perverse glee of the sadist, or the transitory power of a bully – is to become deluded by short-term pseudo-benefits that do not carry within them even the smallest seed of long-term happiness.

IN THE GREAT Hindu text the Bhagavad Gita, the god Krishna
also reflects on the pain of being in the grip of ignorance. The
warrior prince Arjuna asks, 'What power is it, Krishna, that
drives man to act sinfully, even unwillingly, as if powerlessly?'

Krishna tells Arjuna and us, 'It is greedy desire [unconscious
drives] and wrath, born of passion, the great evil, the sum of
destruction: this is the enemy of the soul.

'All is clouded by desire: as fire by smoke, as a mirror by
dust, as an unborn babe by its covering . . .

'Desire has found a place in man's senses and mind and reason. Through these it blinds the soul, after having overclouded
wisdom.'

Then Krishna gives us hope. He understands that we will be
pushed sometimes by our confusion about what will save us or
make us happy to do harmful or crazy things. However, we can
realign ourselves with goodness – love, God, the self – by using
our mind (*consciousness*, which is far greater than the rational
mind).

The text continues: 'They say that the power of the senses
is great. *But greater than the senses is the mind. Greater than the
mind is Buddhi, reason; and greater than reason is He – the Spirit in
man and in all* [my italics].

'Know Him therefore who is above reason; and let his peace
give thee peace. Be a warrior and kill desire, the powerful
enemy of the soul.'

MANY PEOPLE GO through their entire lives as slaves to their
drives or impulses. They genuinely believe that their feelings
are more powerful than they are, or that something mysterious

within themselves causes them to do what makes them unhappy and prevents them from doing what could make them happy.

Yet the rule of thumb on human behaviour is so simple. Doing what harms others will hurt you also. Doing what relieves others or offers them happiness will at least bring you peace.

Applying this formula to life is self-evidently not so simple! We live in a greedy, arrogant, angry society. Those emotions and attitudes are not just outside us. They live within us. It is only with consistent awareness, consistent reflection, and a consistent regard for the truth that we can reduce their power and let other qualities flourish.

IT IS OUT of the most mundane of activities, as well as the sublime, that the opportunities arise for us to come awake, to move from the 'not-knowing' state of unconsciousness into the 'knowing' state of consciousness. Understanding this, we learn that in every mistake we make, there is some meaning to be grasped.

Denying our mistakes, acting as though they have not happened or were caused by someone other than ourselves, we lose a precious chance to retrieve that meaning. Yet it is really only through the reflections that we manage to make *before we act*, as well as *after the event*, that we come to know the depth and reality of our own life, and move from the sweet but necessarily fleeting innocence of childhood to the consciousness of choice that defines true adulthood.

A WOMAN IS at the supermarket. She spends twenty minutes in the parking lot driving round and round waiting for a place. During that time the baby wakes up. The baby's crying. The toddler is saying, 'When we get there? When we get there?' The first time he asks, his voice deep and serious, it sounds touching, even a little impressive. When he asks for the tenth or fifteenth time, and the woman has just missed another space, it sounds grating.

The woman gets out of the car, straps the baby onto her back, holds the toddler's hand, makes her way towards the supermarket. As she approaches the door, an angry young girl bursts through it. 'Drop dead, cunt,' the girl says to the woman.

The woman knows that the outburst has nothing to do with her. She struggles to find pity for the girl. It's hard.

As they walk around the aisles, the baby starts grizzling. Occasionally people glance at the woman. She knows that they are thinking they can't hear Céline Dion properly over the supermarket music system if some woman can't keep her baby quiet.

The toddler needs to pee. The woman crouches down, very carefully so that she won't tip the baby on her back too far forward and puts her mouth in the same region as her toddler's ear.

'You have a nappy on, sweetie. You could wee in that,' she says.

'I want to wee! I want to wee!' calls the toddler.

The mother can remember a time quite clearly when she thought getting tired in the office meant getting tired, and when problems in the office meant problems.

She makes her way towards the public toilets. They are closed. There is no one to ask why they are closed. What difference would it make, anyway? The toddler is crying now and has forgotten how to talk. The baby is also crying. There are only a few things in her trolley and many things on her list.

The woman abandons the trolley. She picks up the toddler and carries him on the front of her body. He rocks backwards and forwards against her. That makes him hard to hold. The baby bobs along on her back. As she is leaving the supermarket, the woman sees someone she knows. The man is well dressed, poised, smiling. He waves. The woman would like to wave, but doesn't have a free hand. She nods instead, and hurries out.

She makes her way around abandoned trolleys, past a group of adolescents who look at her as though she is made of shit, and weaves her way carefully past reversing cars. Still carrying her two children, she feels like a three-headed beast. When she reaches her own car, intending to open the doors and persuade her toddler to crouch on the ground and pee there in perfect privacy, he looks up at her. He smiles.

'Don't want to wee. Don't want to wee,' he says.

The woman puts the toddler on the ground. She takes his hand. They go back towards the supermarket. They have to walk very slowly because his legs are short. The baby is grizzling again. They get into the supermarket without any hassles. They take a trolley. She stands the toddler in it. There are half a dozen items in the trolley, then ten, then a dozen. The list is shrinking. The baby's asleep.

Suddenly the toddler says, 'Need to wee, Mummy. NOW. Need to wee.'

The woman is very tired. She would like to lie down and go to sleep and not wake up until Céline Dion is ready to retire. Instead, she abandons the trolley, reaches down, picks up her toddler, runs as fast as she can with him out to her car, shouts at him, tells him he has to wee outside or nowhere, puts the baby to her breast to shut it up, pulls the weeping toddler back into the car with one hand while holding the baby on her breast with the other, throws her head back on the headrest of the car, and wonders why she was ever born.

Moments later, the toddler climbs onto whatever is left of her lap. They are tightly wedged, damp, disarrayed, but the baby is sucking noisily and happily, the toddler is twisting his hair, sucking his thumb and leaning into the curve of her body, and the woman is – at last – sitting down. It could be much worse.

RESTRAINT IS SOMETHING we have the chance to practise every day. Some days we might call it forbearance. Often, as with the woman in the supermarket, the meaning of restraint is revealed only when we are at the absolute edge of our limits. Then, wonderfully, it extends our limits.

Only the exercise of love through the practice of restraint would allow that mother to keep as relatively calm as she did, to remain as flexible to the needs of her children as she did, to give herself over to the service of their legitimate needs as she did – and not scream or rant or abandon them.

When, on some other day, one extra ghastly thing happens and she does 'lose it', what she is losing is her capacity for restraint. But because she loves her children, that capacity will return, even if she loses it repeatedly. And to say that *it* will return is not quite right either, because none of these qualities ever leave us. W*e move away from them*. We can return to them.

This mother might notice – because she is capable of reflection – that she moves away from restraint most rapidly when she also feels out of touch with herself. When she feels that she has been emptied. When she feels that her partner is not pulling his weight. Or that her own mother is less interested in the children than she might be.

Because restraint is a powerful means to express love and sometimes – as with this mother – loving selflessness, it flourishes most easily where love also exists. In general, the mother who can be patient way beyond the point at which a saint would have questioned his calling is doing so either because she is blessed with an exceptionally equable temperament or – more probably – because she does have the love and support in her life that she also needs.

IT IS WITHIN the crucible of relationships, and especially family relationships, that we can learn most about restraint, and learn most about how restraint expresses love, and also vital versions of respect.

Susannah is an impulsive, sociable woman in her early forties who paints fabric and also runs a small florist shop. She has a sixteen-year-old daughter, Marla, who has been insisting that she won't stay at school. Marla's father, Ross, is a psychiatrist who has not lived with the family since Marla was an infant; however, she remains his only daughter. He is adamant that Marla should be forced to stay at school. Any school. He knows that she will regret it forever if they allow her to have her own way.

Marla wants to take up work as an apprentice hairdresser. Susannah rarely visits her own hairdresser. Hairdressing is not the world she imagined for her clever daughter. She hears her own prejudices and fears articulated bombastically by Ross. She recoils from his certainty that he knows Marla's needs better than Marla does.

Susannah remembers her own confusing adolescence. She knows that in the midst of such confusion it is virtually impossible to see anything except in terms of black and white.

The more Marla and Ross rage at each other, the more Ross also sounds like an adolescent. He has become obsessed with the matter. He calls Susannah to speak about it several times a day. So does Marla.

One evening, Susannah and Marla go to the movies together. On their way home, Marla turns to her mother and says Susannah has failed her in not protecting her from Ross's rage. She then begins to cry and say that her life is hopeless because she has always been the pawn between them and could never please both of them at the same time.

This heart-breaking tirade continues through most of the night. Susannah observes how Ross's certainty that Marla's future will be in ruins if she leaves school early is echoed in Marla's certainty that her past has been ruined because of her parents' separation.

Susannah feels shattered. With enormous difficulty, she listens to everything that Marla has to say. At three in the morning she says she has to go to bed. Marla accuses her of never listening to her. Half an hour later, Marla crawls into Susannah's bed and sleeps alongside her, as she often did as a younger child.

In the morning, Susannah feels like a total wreck. She is absolutely sure that she has failed Marla. She gets up reluctantly, showers, goes to the kitchen.

There she finds a completely cheerful Marla, eating a huge breakfast. Marla begins to talk about the movie they saw together, laughing as she reruns several scenes past Susannah.

Susannah wonders which of them is crazy. She goes on listening, and eating breakfast. As Marla leaves, she announces to Susannah that she has made a decision to stay at school, but just until the end of the year.

Susannah longs to ask Marla how she came to this decision. It is, after all, a total turnaround from her adamant position of the previous day. For a few seconds she also longs to tell Marla how wretched she feels about the cruel things her daughter said to her and after a night of lost sleep.

Instead, she kisses Marla, tells her she loves and trusts her, and goes about her day.

HUMAN BEINGS ACT, react, interact, largely out of habit. This is not itself a bad thing. It is absolutely inevitable. For all that I have said about the benefits of developing the virtue – or the art? – of restraint, it is also a version of bliss not to have to be in a state of self-consciousness most of the time.

Why one bundle of emotional and cognitive habits makes itself at home within any particular individual is a fascinating mystery. There are many psychological, and probably socio-logical, theories on offer. I suspect most of them are in the region of the bull's-eye, rather than right on it. Temperament; family patterns; community and social values mediated through church, school and the public culture; physical and mental health; the way others perceive you in terms of race, gender, class, lovability; the way you perceive 'life' and learn to attribute meaning: all of these factors and probably many others, too, play their part.

But what does seem more predictable is that, at times of stress or heightened anxiety, most human beings have a reac-tion or at least a tendency towards a particular kind of reaction that, over time, they can begin to see is somewhat predictable.

I am not sure that this applies to moments of extreme crisis. I suspect it doesn't. In one extreme crisis a person may behave capably or even heroically; in another, where different anxieties altogether are aroused, that same person may be incapable even of physical movement.

In less extreme but perhaps not less taxing situations, there is generally more predictability. In my own case, for example, when I am stressed or anxious (and I find it difficult to dis-tinguish usefully between those two states because for me they usually co-exist, as do anxiety and depression), my thinking becomes catastrophic. Only the worst can happen; only the worst will ever happen. This is not unusual, but for each individual who suffers from it, such bleak universality is poor consolation.

Those experiences of intense anxiety not only cause me to think illogically, they make themselves known to me somatically through tension in my upper body, neuralgia that shoots pain up my skull from my teeth (so I can no longer 'get my teeth into' what's troubling me), tightly binding headaches, and a feeling of being shut in that I can experience as almost unbearably claustrophobic. It's interesting (from this distance, writing about it) to notice how those physical symptoms cluster in the region of my head, and seem to assault it. This is worth noticing because, although I am struggling with feelings, I am usually attempting to think my way out of them. Yet my thinking function seems, at such times, to be under unending attack from these upheavals in my psyche. And so it is.

For you, the physical symptoms of emotional distress could be quite different. Pains in the stomach, constipation, diarrhoea, acute back pain, restlessness, repugnance or cravings for certain foods, sleeplessness, the need constantly to sleep: these can all be symptoms of emotional pain expressing itself through the body and asking for and needing attention from the organising, unifying 'I' that can perhaps, if what's happening is not too overwhelming, help alleviate the symptoms and reach some understanding about the cause.

The seeds of one's individual, dominant reaction to stress, depression and anxiety are planted in childhood when the soil of one's being is fertile and utterly ready for growth. Glorious seeds are planted then, in everyone. But in what will later emerge as a reaction to life being too hard or seeming to ask too much, something happens that has a particular significance to that human being, and a responsive pattern gets laid down. This 'something' may be a whole series of 'somethings', or it may be a something that is of little consequence to the people who were also around at that time, or is unobserved by them. That is why, when someone is struggling to make painful unconscious material conscious, it is disrespectful and freshly wounding to say, 'Oh that! You got over that in half an hour!', or 'We all managed to get the cows milked before school. What are you moaning about?', or 'It wasn't like that. It was like this', or 'You're making too much of it.'

For yet more reasons, the *effects* of psychological pain do not come in neat proportions to the activating events. Addicted as most of us are to simplistic, cause-and-effect thinking, this is difficult to understand. If one person can come out of a child-hood spent in Auschwitz and nevertheless be a *mensch*, why does someone who only spent a year in traction at the age of nine have to make such a big deal of it?

On those disproportions, Viktor Frankl, who did spend three years in Auschwitz, has this to say: 'Suffering completely fills the human soul and conscious mind, no matter whether the suffering is great or little. Therefore the "size" of human suffering is absolutely relative.'

PEOPLE WHO ARE anxious or stressed may or may not have physical symptoms of pain, but their minds will certainly be crowded with compelling, painful thoughts. I have come slowly to see that what my processes of catastrophic thinking are doing are undermining my belief that I can cope. In other words, along with thinking, 'This is ghastly, this will never end, this can only get worse', are the fearful thoughts: 'This is ghastly *and I can't do anything to change it*. This will never end, *and I can't do anything to stop it*. This is the finish of my capacity to cope, to write, to work. *I can't do this any more.'*

My anxious and depressing thoughts tell a particular story. They tell the story of what the Jungians would call the archetype of the Orphan who knows that she is alone in the world, who knows that there is no one there who can help her, save her, or even understand her, *and who fears that she cannot go on saving herself.*

Your narrative in times of darkness and stress may tell a different story: that you will never get what you want; that you can only get what you want in secret; that if people knew what you are really like they would abandon you; that you will never get more than you give; that you will never be the favourite one; that you cannot please your father or your superego; that you will always be crushed; that you can't dare to let down your defences; that your prizes, honours, money and status are a sham.

Your depressing beliefs may not be conscious. Often they are acted out and can be perceived only through working on your dreams; through careful reflection on what your *actions rather than your thoughts* can reveal to you; or through careful observation not only of your own reactions, but also of what attracts you and repels you in others' lives.

In my own more externalised but no less 'true' life – the life
I live in relation to the outer world – I largely express the
Warrior archetype, not the Orphan. Taking on the writing of
this book is typically a warrior activity: fighting off the sly, persistent demons of my own self-doubt, and the giant dragons of
my own unworthiness, I risk my writing life and reputation to
reach the 'prize' of greater understanding.

Without the Warrior, I could have done almost nothing that
has been important for me in the outer world (with all the
reverberations that any outer action has on the inner world):
living independently from the age of sixteen; leaving my home
country at twenty; ending an early, ill-fated marriage; co-
founding The Women's Press; being able to persist despite the
attacks on women's writing and feminism that shadowed our
early days; moving on from the Press to extend my own writing; writing books that reflect and arouse strong feelings; finding the strength to stand up for what I have thought was right,
in my own defence and in defence of my children.

The Warrior has stood me in good stead, and is there to be
discovered in your own psyche and expressed through your
own life, if this hasn't already happened. But what the Warrior
cannot do, and should not do, is crowd out the Orphan.

The Orphanage is the place my feelings rush me to when
I am at my most inwardly beleaguered. That such a time is
when I could be most helped by the strengths of the Warrior
is an irony that doesn't escape me. This is not, however,
what happens.

What makes matters worse is that while the Warrior – like
every other archetype – does have a negative aspect as well as

a positive, and the Orphan does have a positive aspect as well as a negative, I, for my 'bundle of reasons', have unconsciously learned to attach my positive experiences to the Warrior archetype and my negative to the Orphan.

That I was 'orphaned' as a child is only part of the story. My mother died after a two-year illness when I was eight. My father was physically present during my childhood but was, in my experience of him, emotionally distant. But long before this time, long before any time that is available to me to remember, I was sliding between the archetypes of Warrior and Orphan. I have written in my first novel, *Running Backwards Over Sand*, about the child Zoë's grief when her mother dies, and her devastating sense of failure that she cannot save her. Those feelings were also my feelings. Zoë loves her mother passionately, chivalrously: she is every bit the ardent young lover, the idealistic young knight. There was little sense in Zoë, or in my own child self, that someone else should or could save the mother, or even the child herself. Zoë did not know how to be a child who looks to adults to save her. This was at once her strength and her downfall. Instead, with that agonising mix of grandiosity and helplessness that seems to be at the heart of so much that is baffling about the human condition, Zoë psychologically (and unconsciously) took it upon herself to save her mother and, *only through that mission*, to save herself. This was her challenge, and her failure had to be endured simultaneously with her loss.

In any life, there needs to be no literal, outer orphaning for the Orphan's beliefs to establish that *there is no one to save me* and, at the worst times, that *I cannot go on saving myself*. Such beliefs may be briefly or occasionally part of many people's experience, but they may not be the beliefs that erupt almost automatically whenever the going is especially tough.

IN HIS INSPIRING discussion of how the ideas of German psychologist Max Wertheimer respond to that critical question 'How do we shift from one mind-set to another?', Psychosynthesis therapist and author Piero Ferrucci writes: 'In order to have new ideas, we have to open ourselves to life as it is, not as habit would have it. *We need to surrender to reality* [my italics].'

Back we come again to the heart of the matter, for this is yet another way of talking about facing the truth. Daring to see reality as it is, and somehow allowing our feral, fearful inner archetypes also to catch a glimpse of a different reality from the one they/we steadfastly and faithfully believe to be the truth, is, of course, a crucial task of consciousness. The particular 'ways of seeing' that any one of us has, no matter how mistaken or eventually neurotic, began *as a means to care for ourselves*, as a means to hold us together when our ego-consciousness was fragile and raw. Surrendering that way of thinking can seem as dangerous as facing those initial terrors. Even to bring one's mind around to the concept that most of one's thinking is made up of and produces subjective illusions can seem dangerous, terrifying, absurd. Where, then, is reality?

Ferrucci quotes the nineteenth-century British biologist Thomas Huxley: '"Science seems to me to teach, in the highest and strongest manner, the great truth which is embodied in the Christian concept of the entire surrender to the will of God. Sit down before fact like a little child, and be prepared to give up every pre-conceived notion, follow humbly wherever to whatever abysses Nature leads you or you shall learn nothing.'"

Accepting our own fallibility and looking at our own mistakes, not to discredit ourselves but to learn from them; listening to other people's views of experiences we have shared, with curiosity as to what we may learn from them; watching for the patterns in our reactions and actions to find what they reveal; sifting out the differences between our dearest hopes or convictions, and the facts before us; developing the intention to remain as securely as possible in the present moment, rather than racing back to the past or forward into the future: all of this supports us in our attempts to find and face our truth.

This isn't easy. None of it can be done without reflection. None of it can be done without restraint. But only by refusing to settle for anything less than the truth can we heal ourselves and 'open ourselves to life as it is'. And only by giving up our 'pre-conceived notions' – however valued or hard won – can we adjust our subjective illusions to the objective reality, bring our outer and inner worlds into a unity, and bring the unhappy battle often taking place within our own minds to an end.

SOME YEARS AGO I observed a series of counselling sessions where the counsellor was working with a husband and wife who had been married for ten years or so. The husband, Bram, desperately needed to leave. The wife, Jenny, was equally desperate that he should not go.

Bram had explained at length how claustrophobic, unhappy, even suicidal he felt within the marriage. He was certainly prepared to go on being an active parent; however, he believed that if he had to go on as an active husband also, he would be colluding in his own living death.

Jenny's incredulity in the face of these exceptionally strong statements remained total. 'But you love me!' she kept saying. 'We've always done everything together. We both believe in marriage, that marriage is forever. You couldn't get along without me. You have always needed me. Haven't you always needed me?'

The pathos of her situation was obvious. And her physical gestures exemplified that, as she tugged at her clothes, straightened them over and over again, left the room repeatedly for glasses of water, ripped up tissues, bundled them into balls, scratched the side of her face. And all the time she cried, talked, interrupted and made the same pleas over and over again in a desperate hope that somehow what she was saying would turn out to be the truth, and what she was refusing to hear would dissolve and disappear.

AT SOME POINT, if she is lucky, Jenny will be pushed by the external reality of Bram's physical absence from her life to re-examine her own inner reality in the light of what he has told her, and what action he has taken.

She may be forced to reconsider her conviction that he could not get along without her; that they needed to do everything together; and that marriage is forever. She may come to see that those had been her hopes, and not a shared reality. This insight will undoubtedly bring her grief, yet it is a grief that arises from the truth she has probably spent huge amounts of energy avoiding and evading through much of her marriage.

There is a famous statement by Spinoza, in his *Ethics*, that is often quoted in psychological texts concerned with life's meaning: 'Emotion, which is suffering, ceases to be suffering as soon as we form a clear and precise picture of it.' *Ceases* may be a little too optimistic, but certainly suffering takes on a different quality when some truth has been salvaged from the pain. Or, as Merlin the Magician said to his pal King Arthur, 'The best thing for being sad is to learn something.'

In his supremely inspiring book *Man's Search for Meaning*, Viktor Frankl cites a clear example of this from his own psychiatric practice: 'Once an elderly general practitioner consulted me because of his severe depression. He could not overcome the loss of his wife who had died two years before and whom he had loved above all else. Now how could I help him? What should I tell him? Well, I refrained from telling him anything, but instead confronted him with the question, "What would have happened, Doctor, if you had died first and your wife would have had to survive you?"

'"Oh," he said, "for her this would have been terrible; how she would have suffered!" Whereupon I replied, "You see, Doctor, such a suffering has been spared her, and it is you who have spared her this suffering; but now, you have to pay for it by surviving and mourning her." He said no word but shook my hand and calmly left my office.'

Frankl did no more than point to the truth, but the consequences were profound.

FACING THE TRUTH of her relationship with Bram, however demanding that proves, Jenny is likely to be able to reclaim some of that uselessly expended energy for herself, and begin not only to recover from the acute pain of her failed marriage but also to more fully reclaim her own self. For it is only facing that truth, with all its attendant feelings of sadness and anger and maybe even betrayal, that will tell her something *about herself* that is essential for her to know. As long as she doesn't know it, she is in danger of continuing to project those beliefs either into the vacuum left behind by Bram, or onto her next partner, if she dares to trust again.

Knowing that those beliefs belong to her, and were perhaps only ever partially and temporarily shared by Bram, she can also make some decisions as to how useful they are, whether they reflect the outward reality she is struggling to create, or if they could be modified and softened by more trusting and loving beliefs about herself, life, and what it should bring her.

Following the line of Frankl's thought, it may even be that if Jenny comes to see that Bram actually is happier now that he is no longer living with her, or perhaps because he is no longer living in a conventional marriage, she may have a way out of pain. If she has loved him as she claimed, and not just wanted him or needed him, then however hard it is to do without him as a husband, *her own happiness for him* could be a genuine consolation, as well as the means by which she can move forward into her own future without bitterness.

OPENING UP TO the truth of who we are, and of what love is, has profound, far-reaching social as well as personal consequences.

When we love people primarily because they are doing what we want, our love is compromised.

When we behave cheerfully or charmingly to people only because they have something that we want, or we want them to do something for us, our goodwill is compromised.

When we pretend to be someone we are not, or feel ashamed of who we are, our capacity to feel fully alive is compromised.

This is not a problem of individual narcissism only. It is a problem of socially approved inauthenticity that separates us from a truthful, loving relationship with ourselves, and keeps us from having positive, trusting and trustworthy relationships with other people. This can be lonely; it can also be extremely dangerous.

Feeling real and acting truthfully are essential to personal and psychological good health. There are also dire social consequences when people remain locked in with their delusions, or unconscious of their projections. As the famous analyst D. W. Winnicott has pointed out, 'In the community it is the ill members who are compelled by unconscious motives to go to war and to attack as a defence against delusions of persecution, or else to destroy the world, a world that annihilated them, each one of them separately, in their infancy.'

THAT IT IS through suffering that we may find at least part of our way out of unconsciousness into a more truthful way of living does not mean we have to make a special plea for suffering, or look for suffering. No life is free of suffering; just as no life will fail to end in death.

The knowledge that we all inevitably suffer, and will die, is what should allow us to recognise each other, even when we are total strangers. We can be so extraordinarily possessive about whatever it is that brings us happiness. We can behave as though happiness is indeed something *to* possess. But suffering strips away the superficial differences between people, even those differences we may have built our lives on.

It is suffering that teaches us more than anything else about our common fate. To look into the eyes of anyone who has suffered deeply, or is now suffering, is to find yourself moved into at least a momentary relationship with them that is immensely tempering of your usual self-absorptions.

Perhaps glimpsing that 'suffering will bring its own rewards' is enough to loosen the stranglehold of fear that most of us have when we contemplate even the idea of suffering, often without realising that such fear itself is creating suffering and holding us at some distance from living fully.

In *Dialogues with a Modern Mystic*, Mark Matousek tells this story: 'We're not instructed [in Western society] that suffering is a door to wisdom, that grace often works through loss, and that these are direct opportunities to grasp our true nature. There's a strange account of a woman telling the great saint Anandamayi Ma a terrible story about her life. Ma laughed and laughed until the tears flowed down her face. The woman was shocked and asked her why she was laughing about her misery. Anandamayi Ma said, "Because you are being shown the end of misery through the cracks that this misery is opening in your heart. Through them you can see the sun of the Self shining.'"

THIS STORY – effective *because* it is startling – can tell us a great deal about the value of practising restraint. Our first reaction to one woman laughing at another's grief is likely to reflect our distaste or even abhorrence. 'How could she?' But then comes our chance to pause, the moment during which we can sink beneath or rise above the conventional response, the 'normal' response. *It is in that pause, that briefly held moment, that we have a chance to reflect and thus to call out of the story the message it is intended to convey.*

Reflecting, we may choose not to judge.

Reflecting, we may choose not to speak.

Reflecting, we may deepen our listening.

Reflecting, we may remember how to endure our own uncertainty.

Reflecting, we may choose to speak lovingly, rather than bitterly.

Reflecting, we may remember that not reacting can also be an action.

Reflecting, we allow ourselves to be surprised.

WHAT THE MEANING is in any of the many stories that not only reflect but create our lives is rarely uncovered at first glance. Often, we owe it to ourselves, as well as to others, to go beyond that first glance. In laughing at another woman, Anandamayi Ma shocked her, and she shocks us. Shocks can be painful, but they can also most usefully ruffle our habitual responses. Taking time to consider, we are likely to discover that Ma is not mocking the other woman; she is loving her, taking her seriously, trusting that she can take a little pain and distress in order to reach an appreciation of life that is seasoned, ripened and reflective.

Our first reaction to Ma's response arises out of habit. It is not a reaction that we have chosen out of the many possibilities available to us. It is simply what is closest to hand. In any situation, from the most banal to the most extreme, it is only by letting that habitual response rise, rise, and then fall again and settle, that we can move beyond it to discover what we think, freshly, in this new moment. What is most helpful, *in this moment*. What is most true, *in this moment*.

USING RESTRAINT TO carve out this space for us, to free us from the tedium of stale or habitual responses, to give us a chance to appreciate the freshness of each new moment, to remind us that we continually have choices, we gain a vital chance to grow into the fullness of who we are: muddled, stubborn, frequently foolish and wrong-headed, but also complex, creative, imaginative – and more than capable of seeing 'the sun of the Self shining'.

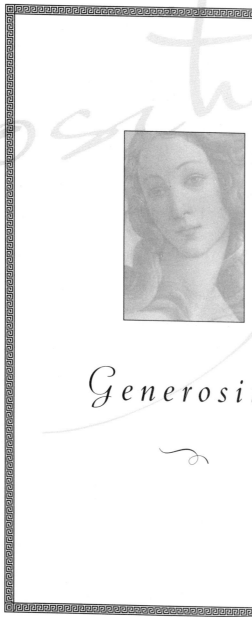

Generosity

It is in giving that we receive;

It is in pardoning that we are pardoned; and

It is in dying that we are

born to eternal life.

ST FRANCIS OF ASSISI

*G*enerosity builds human spirit. Every act of generosity – the willing giving of your time, interest, concern, care, understanding, humour, loyalty, honesty – expresses and nourishes love. And every missed opportunity to be generous erodes your experience of love, connectedness and spirit.

In giving, it rarely matters whether the love that is expressed is personal or impersonal. Giving to someone you know is wonderful. It can intensify your feeling of connection with that person and your appreciation of them. Giving to someone you don't know may be less immediately rewarding, but it expresses your awareness that *other human lives matter*, and that the extent to which they matter is not determined only by their proximity or usefulness to you, or your intimacy with them.

IN THE STORIES that come from all the corners of the earth about how it was in the beginning, before there was life in any way as we know it, there is always the making of something out of nothing. There is creativity. There is wonder and there is giving.

IN THE HINDU scripture, the Rig Veda, we can read: 'There was neither death nor immortality then. No signs were there of night or day. The *One* was breathing by its own power, in deep peace. Only the *One* was: there was nothing beyond.

'Darkness was hidden in darkness. The all was fluid and formless. Therein, in the void, by the fire of fervour arose the *One*.

'And in the *One* arose love. Love the first seed of soul.'

FROM NEW ZEALAND comes this account of how thought was created and, later, light. It is part of a lengthy and magnificently poetic genealogical chant, which would end with the names of the speaker's own ancestors, reminding listeners of where they, too, come from, and how interconnected life is:

From the conception the increase,
From the increase the thought.
From the thought the remembrance,
From the remembrance the consciousness,
From the consciousness the desire . . .

From the nothing the begetting,
From the nothing the increase,
From the nothing the abundance,
The power of increasing,
The living breath;
It dwelt with the empty space, and produced the
     atmosphere which is above us,
The atmosphere which floats above the earth . . .

IN GENESIS, THE first book of the Hebrew Bible, we can read this version of how light was made: 'In the beginning God created the heaven and the earth. And the earth was without form, and void; and darkness was upon the face of the deep. And the Spirit of God moved upon the face of the waters.

'And God said, Let there be light: and there was light . . .

'And God called the light Day, and the darkness he called Night.'

When light and darkness, sky and earth, and lands and oceans had been created, we discover that God said: 'Let the earth bring forth grass . . . Let the waters bring forth abundantly the moving creature that hath life, and fowl that may fly above the earth . . . Let the earth bring forth the living creature after his kind . . . And God said, Let us make man in our image, after our likeness . . . And God saw every thing that he had made, and, behold, it was very good.'

THE MOST PSYCHOLOGICALLY healthy individuals in our communities are those who are able to give without feeling diminished by giving. They are least trapped by the illusion that giving something away freely leaves you with any less. They are least likely to live as slaves, guarding their own private horde of treasures. They may also be least tricked by the illusion that material possessions, and the time and energy it takes to create those possessions, are something that you can 'own' on a permanent basis, and look to for safety.

GIVING IS AN expression of freedom and abundance. It's a celebration of sufficiency. When done with love, it is connective, enriching, uplifting. Through their mother, babies feel the generosity of the world. Breast milk – and the milk of human kindness – flows into them as they suck. The infant's first experience of wanting and getting is intense, physical, passionate, oral, greedy, satiable.

Later, things become more complicated. (Sometimes they become more complicated too early; sometimes, too late.) The world is not only generous. It can be withholding, even cruel. Some needs cannot be satisfied. Desire splits into various realms. Intellectual, physical, spiritual and emotional needs compete within a single being. One realm is deaf to the other. One realm starves another.

The mother has already been similarly fragmented for most of her life. When things go well after the birth, or well enough, the intensity of feeling she has for her baby unites her temporarily within herself, and, differently, within the mother–baby dyad. Often this unification within herself, and within her relationship with her baby, is more intense and more satisfying than anything else she has ever experienced, even though she is simultaneously tired, uncertain, fraught, frazzled. If she is lucky she will know that she is free to say, 'Now I am beginning to understand what love is.'

She is propelled by her emotions, and the hormonal and physiological changes of earliest maternity, into a state of intensified self-sacrifice. It doesn't feel like sacrifice, though. It feels awesome, like a privilege. Through her innumerable daily acts of generosity to her infant child, she draws on and lives out the archetype of the good mother. She has never been less 'herself'; she has never been more herself.

When she is lucky, nothing pulls her out of this state too soon. She and the baby can remain absorbed in each other, attuned to every tiny detail that passes between them. When she is lucky, the new mother has a partner mature enough to be generous to her, however briefly unrecognisable she has become. And mature enough to be as reluctant to intrude into this changed, elevated, integrated relationship with herself, and her consuming, selfless relationship with her baby, as a bull would be to enter a china shop . . .

If he is absent, or is a baby-man himself, perhaps she is emotionally held by the generosity of her own mother, or her women friends. If she is emotionally held by a woman lover, then that lover – whatever her own needs, questions and uncertainties – must be just as patient and sometimes just as inconspicuous as the bull . . .

If none of those people is present, if there is no husband, woman lover, close women friends or her own mother to hold her emotionally and keep her feeling safe, then the new mother's abundant, passionate generosity towards her baby may be curtailed. The archetype of the good mother may fail to take hold. Perhaps the archetype of the wounded child takes its place. Then the mother may feel compelled to search much too soon for some generosity from the baby itself.

GENEROSITY IS ABOUT being present in the given moment, mindful of it, attentive to what's needed. For the new mother to be present *for her changed self*, as much as she needs to be present for her baby, other things must be allowed to disappear, sometimes for good, sometimes just for a few months.

It is not possible to be fully present to someone else who needs you utterly – as a new infant does – and in those same moments also call your stock broker, plan menus or an ad campaign, check up on interest rates, run over your latest brief with a colleague or correct a manuscript. I want to find some useful analogies. I want to suggest that to do so is like trying to meditate with the television on; or like trying to learn to swim with bricks hanging off your feet so that, no matter how hard you try, you never float. But those analogies don't begin to touch the significance of being present in the presence of a new life. Of not mixing the media of earliest motherhood and worldly concerns.

For all babies after the first, of course, there is the bedlam of other children, pets, meals, washing, school, doors slamming, basketballs being dunked, more washing, more meals, arguments, laughter, tears, exhaustion and more exhaustion. But that's different. That's still swimming in a single stream: the stream of love.

TOWARDS THE END of *Paula*, Isabel Allende's exquisite, heart-breaking account of the months of her young adult daughter's dying, she writes: 'How simple life is, when all is said and done . . . In this year of torment, I had gradually been letting go: first I said goodbye to Paula's intelligence, then to her vitality and her company, now, finally, I had to part with her body. I had lost everything, and my daughter was leaving me, but the one essential thing remained: love. In the end, all I have left is the love I give her.'

IN THE BEGINNING, and at the end, that willingness and capacity to be wholly attentive is what love can give us and what love asks of us. Between times, there will also be the generosity of *things*, of money, objects, big and small parcels, actual or symbolic, gorgeously wrapped, containing who knows what and costing heaven knows how much. Those moments of giving, of passing something from me to you, have their value also. They can arise out of and express moments of sparkling creativity: 'I have chosen this – this, and nothing else.' They may provide healing and humour. They may provoke wonder. They may express authentic care and interest. But they cannot replace a willingness to be present: to listen, to watch, to touch, to think, to talk, to pause, to care. They cannot replace a willingness to give time, and to be present in that time with an open heart: 'In the end, all I have left is the love . . .'

GENEROSITY IS BUILT and expressed through the most mundane moments as well as the most profound. It is an acknowledgement of our common humanity, a recognition that we are all part of humankind. Generosity can be sombre, serious, life-changing; it can also be playful, humorous and imaginative. Generosity arises out of an intention to care way beyond the limits of one's own self or the group to which one is immediately attached. It is expressed in these and a thousand other ways.

Paying attention to what someone needs, not what you think they need.

Always giving the benefit of the doubt.

Taking responsibility.

Not blaming.

Being courteous.

Bringing beauty to all tasks.

Letting your mistakes go.

Giving more than is necessary.

Appreciating your dependence on others; appreciating their dependence on you.

Not keeping tabs on what you have given or what you are owed.

Allowing others to give to you.

Receiving gracefully.

Not using power to wound, undermine or abuse.

Giving others emotional and physical space for their sake, not for yours.

Curbing your demands.

Taking an interest in others' interests.

Making room at your table and in your home for any guests, however unexpected.

Giving extra attention to avoid a feeling of hurt.

Giving all the time you have promised – and more.

Honouring your obligations as a privilege of relationship.

Treating a new experience as a new experience – and not an affront.

Paying attention to who is feeling left out, and redeeming that situation.

Refusing to pass on hurtful gossip.

Praising lavishly.

Expressing gratitude.

Letting past hurts slip away.

Welcoming compromise.

Giving something up for the sake of someone else.

Doing without what is acquired at others' cost.

Extending your borders between 'us' and 'them'.

JAMES J. LYNCH is author of *The Broken Heart: The Medical Consequences of Loneliness* and a leading specialist in psychosomatic medicine. He writes movingly about the dependence we all have on 'dialogues of love'. These are the verbal and non-verbal exchanges that bring us close to other people, and close to a feeling of being understood and cherished by those people. When these dialogues are disrupted or eroded, significant increases in disease and death follow, with obvious social costs as well as great personal loss.

Keeping your capacity for loving dialogue alive demands a willingness to be generous, flexible and tolerant. 'An individual can only receive to the extent that he gives,' Lynch points out, 'and, in that sense, dialogue is a mirror of his personality.'

When you engage with another person, whether this is at work, within a love relationship, with a member of your family of origin or a neighbour, you rarely explicitly promise to be generous. Yet the presence of generosity within that relationship (or dialogue), or its absence, can utterly determine the quality and longevity of the connection.

SOMETIMES MONEY AND time are given, but they are given for the sake of the donor, and not because they are what the recipient wants. That's only too easy to understand, but it doesn't support a loving dialogue and often it's not especially rewarding either. Generosity involves two parties, at least, and flows two ways. It is often subtle, and demands that the donor has the capacity to pay close, mindful attention to whoever else is involved in the interaction.

The rich, work-obsessed businessman who breaks down and weeps when his wife leaves him, and cries 'But I gave her everything she wanted!', is not so different from the rest of us. We all learn early on to substitute things for time, and flattery for close attention; to build up labyrinthine, self-serving excuses as to why we can rarely be mindfully available and attentive even to those we claim to love best. Yet what others long for from us is also what we ourselves can feel most starved of: the giving and getting of time in which love can be cherished, nurtured and expressed.

Dr Lynch again: 'In the most ironic fashion, marital separation and divorce stand as mute testimonials to the Platonic idea of the nonmaterial nature of human dialogue. Few individuals who leave their mates ever gain materially from the separation. Why then do they leave? What are they escaping from? What are they searching for? What do they hope to get in return? Why do people who have comfortable material existences and physically stable environments suddenly abandon it all? It seems that what they sense is that they are being slowly choked to death in their current environment, that their very existence is being threatened. Dialogue has deteriorated below a certain critical threshold, until one of the partners can no longer tolerate the isolation.'

GENEROSITY USUALLY INVOLVES listening and 'tuning in', rather than imposing, and a willingness to enter into the life of another human being as an honoured, respectful guest, not as an invader or coloniser. This can be most difficult of all between members of the same family where unconscious 'debts' may tangle with equally unconscious 'requests' that often emerge in ways destined to get you almost any result but the one you want.

A painful and repetitious scenario like this was true for Rose's mother, whom I only ever got to know indirectly. Rose is a pretty woman in her mid-thirties, full of humour and kindness. Despite her attractiveness, and although she is valued at work, she is unusually shy and struggles with painful doubts about her own self-worth. Her mother has been intermittently depressed through most of Rose's life and rarely allowed the family any quiet time together. Her strategy to distract the family was to have loud music or the television on at almost all times, precluding the possibility of conversation, much less intimacy.

While her three children were still living at home, Rose's mother rarely shopped for them, but after they left she began buying things for them almost compulsively. She frequently turns up at Rose's apartment to leave what she always calls 'a little something', which is usually quite an expensive but inappropriate gift. Sometimes these gifts are clothes that are always far too large for Rose, and anyway are not to her taste. Sometimes they are knick-knacks for the apartment, but the kinds of things that Rose can't bear, never displays, and usually gives away to local thrift shops.

Rose has long ago ceased to be amazed that her mother does not seem to notice that she never wears the clothes, and that the knick-knacks are not displayed. She is far more concerned about whether she should be honest and say to her mother that she feels these gifts are wildly misdirected – that they neither suit her, nor are wanted by her – or whether she should continue to suffer in silence, feeling more and more invisible to her mother, while nevertheless noticing that her mother is making these painful, misguided efforts to give to her and maintain some loving contact.

Listening to Rose talk about her mother, it is impossible not to feel the sadness of both women. Rose's mother wants to give to her daughter, but the person she is giving to exists only in her imagination. If she could look at her daughter, sit with her and say to Rose, 'How can I help you? Is there anything you want?', what she would be asked for would be markedly different from the too-big clothes and the ornaments. And what she would receive from that direct heart-to-heart contact would also be very different because sensitive Rose is only too aware that her mother, too, feels unrecognised and unrewarded.

By conventional standards, both these women are generous. Yet both are unhappy in their relationship with each
other. The image that springs to my mind is of Rose's
mother, blindfolded, helplessly trying to pin the tail on the
donkey of her genuine concern for Rose, yet unable to get
anywhere near the mark. And my image is of Rose-the-
child, as well as Rose-the-woman, jumping up and shouting
'Here I am! Here I am!' to someone who can neither see her,
nor hear her.

A FAILURE TO be generous in the way that someone else
wants or needs may be so acute it can feel like a failure to love.
In her novel *Other Women*, Lisa Alther gives a marvellous
description of generosity that's gone to seed. The two women
Alther is describing are both nurses: good, kind, intelligent
women suffering from a surfeit of selfless love.

'The relationship wasn't working, they finally concluded,
because each had an equivalent need to be needed. In relationships with men, each had been exploited to her heart's
content. But with each other life was a constant struggle to
outnurture. The cabin filled up with their greeting cards.
Banks of flowers were always dying on the tables. Each put on
ten pounds from the candies and pastries the other brought
home, which were dutifully devoured to please the donor.
During lovemaking each would wait for the other to climax
first, until both lost interest altogether. They fought over who
got the most burnt toast, or the lukewarm second shower.
They would have fought to be the last off the *Titanic*, or the
first off Noah's Ark. Eventually they were compelled to address

the issue of what to do about two people in whom thought-fulness had become a disease.'

WE LIVE IN a grossly materialistic society. Writing in *The Sibling Society*, social philosopher and poet Robert Bly was pessimistic enough to say: 'Consumer capitalism's dependence on stimulating greed and desirousness has changed something fundamental inside the human being.'

Any personal and collective resistance that we can make to that change is worthwhile. So is every revolt we can encourage within ourselves and others against the 'laws' of greed and desirousness. Yet it is inevitable that our ideas of kindness, giving and generosity are bound up with our ideas about money and objects, rather than with our ideals about time and attention. Learning how to give other people material objects is easy: any mail-order catalogue will teach you. Learning how to give people the attention *they want* requires tremendous patience, persistence and subtlety. And so does learning to discover whether your actions and 'gifts' are loving or demanding.

Most of us do hope for a good return for our efforts. If I am kind to you, I am more than likely to hope that you will be kind in return. If my thoughtfulness is met with your ill-temper and selfishness, I may feel quite entitled to be aggrieved. And we are, indeed, on perilously thin ice here because being consistently kind or generous to someone who could be kind in return, *but chooses not to be*, is clearly a way of being markedly unloving to yourself.

Yet sometimes the clash of agendas is much more subtle than that. If you are pleasant to me, buy me a gift, take me to dinner perhaps or even to the opera, does this mean I should listen to your complaints about your father, sleep with you, *marry* you? Or if you were marvellous to me twenty years ago when we were both young, does this mean I should now open my house to you, even though you have become self-pitying and drunken? Sympathy and generosity go hand-in-hand; but sympathy and a sense of traded obligation may become disastrously entangled.

Giving freely does not begin or end with the act of giving. What precedes the act of giving is at least some awareness that generosity is an expression of love. And what needs to follow is a sense of letting that act go, detaching from it, moving on into the next moment, not hanging around for a reward, a prize, or even thanks, necessarily.

This flow of loving, giving, moving on, is difficult for most of us to live out. Years later we are still hanging onto our weighty bags of memories of past hurts and injuries; to moments when we were overlooked, misunderstood or belittled. How many of us give that same degree of passion to the memories we have of being given to adequately? Or to our even rarer memories of the perfect moment, the *sufficient* moment?

'We look before and after' wrote Shelley in his famous poem 'To a Skylark', 'And pine for what is not.'

Coming back into the present moment, and attending to nothing but that, is always the most direct route to generosity – and to happiness.

Giving with the expectation of a reward, or of establishing a debt that the other person will then owe you, is a painfully compromised form of generosity. In the face of such a demand, one could even question whether this is generosity at all. Surely the only authentic expression of generosity is to act, or be present for someone, *and not expect to make them pay*?

The Bhagavad Gita affirms this: 'A gift is pure when it is given from the heart to the right person at the right time and at the right place, and when we expect nothing in return.

'But when it is given expecting something in return, or for the sake of future reward, or when it is given unwillingly, the gift is of the Rajas, impure.

'And a gift given to the wrong person, at the wrong time and the wrong place, or a gift which comes not from the heart, and is given with proud contempt, is a gift of darkness.'

WOMEN FREQUENTLY COMPLAIN – and often with good reason – that in order to get something for themselves (time away, some rest, a meal cooked) they must 'pay' their male partners before and afterwards with extra attention or sex, and that if they don't do what's expected they will be punished with complaints, sulking or threats that such 'generosity' won't be so readily available in the future.

And some men also complain with great bitterness that when their capacity to provide generously is diminished, they are cast aside, no longer loved, and left with a sense of betrayal and confusion as to whether they themselves were ever loved or only what their money could buy.

How we are able to receive what is given to us, whether we can take this genuinely or not, whether it builds trust and love or not, will profoundly determine the quality or even the presence of the dialogue of love. When any two people are in an intimate relationship they will want to feel that they are able to give and receive freely, equally and fearlessly. But this demands that each thinks deeply about what love means, and that each consciously challenges the inner fears and barriers that can thwart a love relationship and turn it into a battle for control and power. For women, especially, this is treacherous territory. Women's sense of obligation can so easily be confused with their deepest sense of self: who am I if I am not giving, if I am not *nice*?

Yet in giving, there should not be fear, or a sense of emptying yourself out, even for the sake of someone else. It is vital to know when you are depleted, or besieged; when it is time to say, 'Enough!'

Giving to others, or emptying out your own needs for the sake of others, can be an addiction, a means to avoid facing your own fears of loneliness or emptiness. But each one of us deserves better than that. The experience of giving and receiving can teach us so much about subtlety and discernment, about the interplay of light with darkness and darkness with light. If giving and receiving are severely out of balance, and giving continually wears you down, it is time to take stock. Time to ask: 'What do I need? How can I replenish myself? In what ways am I showing love to myself also?' It may also be time to ask: 'How could I give *more* generously, without feeling that I am creating a sense of burden, debt or obligation?

Could I give with less attachment to the object or the outcome – and perhaps receive with less attachment in return?'

The Sufi teacher Hazrat Inayat Khan turns us sharply away from the sentimentality and self-absorption that can encourage us to hover over our disappointments and discolour our experiences of kindness. He suggests: 'The one principle to be remembered in the path of sympathy is that we should all do our best with regards to the pleasure of those whom we love and whom we meet. But we should not expect the same from those whom we love and whom we meet. For we must realize that the world is as it is, and we cannot change it; we can only change ourselves. The one who wants others to do what he wishes will always be disappointed . . . He should remember that self-pity is the worst poverty. The person who takes life in this way, who considers his poor self to be forgotten, forsaken, ill-treated by everybody, by the planets, even by God, for that person there is no hope; he is an exile from the garden of Eden. But the one who says, "I know what human nature is, I cannot expect any better, I must only try and appreciate what little good comes from it and be thankful for it, and try and give the best I can to the others," has the only attitude which will enable him to develop his sympathetic nature . . . Life's reward is life itself.'

YOUR WILLINGNESS TO develop the capacity to hold the needs of others *and* yourself in your mind is the only way out of narcissism, the self-protective delusion that your life is more – or less – in need of care and attention than anyone else's. Generosity frees us from this trap and opens up the channels of consciousness that allow us to receive as generously as we give, and to experience how giving and receiving support each other so that one could never say that the water the flower needs is more important than the flower itself, or the flower more important than the water.

Siddha Yoga master Gurumayi Chidvilasananda speaks eloquently about the ways in which we can learn to do *what needs to be done*, regardless of whether it's what we most feel like doing, and she warns against doing 'the right thing' for the sake of our ego only.

'When it comes to helping others, you have to be especially careful. You have to reflect on your motives and your interests. Are you doing something because it is gratifying to you, or because there is a reward of some kind? Or are you doing it because you really want to help? You have to do a great deal of self-inquiry to be able to tell; you have to contemplate every ripple of thought that goes through your mind . . . To be compassionate, you must learn to think well of yourself and others. Therefore a bleeding heart, which sees other people as helpless, is not a sign of compassion.'

FEW OF US give as freely to strangers as we do to our own family. Nevertheless, it is possible to suggest that the more expansive our awareness, or consciousness, is generally, the less we will be gripped by limiting notions of 'family', 'nation', 'race', 'sexuality' or 'religion'. When we are relatively unshackled by divisive thinking, we can continue to refine our vision of family until it embraces all living creatures and the planet itself.

It is also possible, on the way, to learn that we can sometimes give more easily to strangers *because* we are less tied to them by bonds of guilt or obligation. Learning from that more impersonal giving, we can bring an easier, less obligated and probably much less attached kind of giving back into our personal relationships. And, in the marvellous rhythm that such giving and receiving inevitably sets up, as we become less obligated and tight within those conventionally intimate relationships, we have yet more to give outside them.

Mark's Gospel tells the story of the woman willing to give all that she had: 'And Jesus sat over against the treasury, and beheld how the people cast money into the treasury: and many that were rich cast in much.

'And there came a certain poor widow, and she threw in two mites, which make a farthing.

'And he called unto him his disciples, and saith unto them, Verily I say unto you, That this poor widow hath cast more in, than all they which have cast into the treasury:

'For all they did cast in of their abundance; but she of her want did cast in all that she had, even all her living.'

Commenting on that teaching, William Johnston writes: 'Her mite contributed little; but her loving sacrifice – this shook the universe and the universe is still shaking under its impact.' Elaborating on that thought, he adds that it was her faith and love – exemplified through her willingness to give 'all her living' – that 'gave birth to spiritual vibrations which will always remain'.

DEEPAK CHOPRA, IN *The Seven Spiritual Laws of Success*, writes that he taught his children not to focus on doing well in school, or on getting the best grades or finding their way into the top colleges. Instead, he taught them to focus on the question: *What am I here to give?*

To discover what they are here to give, Chopra's children – like all children lucky enough to know they have something to give – had to discover their unique talent and way of expressing that talent.

Discovering your talent and expressing it is, according to Hindu teachings, the second part of the threefold Law of Dharma.

The first part is the crucial recognition that we are, as mystics from all the spiritual traditions have taught, not human beings on a spiritual path, but spiritual beings living (and learning) on the human plane.

The second part is the discovery and expression of your talent.

The third component, says Deepak Chopra, is 'service to humanity – to serve your fellow human beings and to ask yourself the question, "How can I help?"' He goes on, 'When you combine the ability to express your unique talent with service to humanity, then you make full use of the Law of Dharma.'

Finding your talent does not mean struggling to sing like Kathleen Battle or to write like Doris Lessing. I believe it means bringing your own imprint to what you do: *making it your own in the way that you do it.* If you can also find something to do (and this may not be the work for which you are paid) in which you can totally lose yourself at least some of the time, then you are probably expressing and developing your talent for being alive.

Equally, service to humanity need not necessarily mean taking up a conventional job that directly involves helping others, such as teaching or nursing. It means, I believe, *examining the intention you bring to whatever you are doing.* It means asking the question: am I doing this only for myself, or do others benefit also?

It is possible, for example, to be a bank teller and to deal with your customers each day in such a way that they feel lifted by their brief encounter with you. You have acknowledged each of them as a human being, rather than as one transaction among many.

A wonderful example of how intention can transform the most simple interactions came my way recently when Carolyn, a philosophy graduate in her mid-thirties, drove my daughter and me home from an out-of-town function. During the hour-long drive she spoke with tremendous sincerity and warmth about her work as front-of-house manager in a leading restaurant. It would be easy to miss seeing such a job as one of service in the deeper meaning of this word, but Carolyn believes that with each person she comes into contact she has the chance not only to ensure they have a pleasant evening out, but to extend to them something of her awareness of that person's uniqueness and value.

'Many of those people would never go to an ashram or spiritual centre,' she explained. 'Yet I can behave towards them with the same respect as if we were meeting in such a centre.'

I am lucky enough to have a Chilean friend who has been coming to help me each week with my housework for the last eight years. Cleaning someone else's house could be regarded as demeaning. Instead, Erika brings to her work dignity, creativity and pride in beautiful work well done. What's more, whenever she comes to my house she is giving me something generous and precious. We can both acknowledge that. Like all generous people, one of her most striking characteristics is that she always gives more than is absolutely necessary, so she leaves behind not just a clean house, but one subtly infused with her innate sense of beneficence and harmony.

Generosity arises from a person's own nature and, like every other gift, some people have more of it, some less. But as an act of love, it is also something that can be learned or refined through observation, through the most simple analysis of what is pleasing and what is not; through a willingness to leave oneself behind at least sometimes, and make room in one's vision for others.

IN THAT INVALUABLE guide *Life and How to Survive It*, family therapist and writer Robin Skynner talks about what good business sense it makes to be generous. 'Everyone knows about the large Japanese firms' policy of lifetime employment,' Skynner writes, 'but there are many Western firms . . . which go to enormous trouble, apparently contrary to their immediate financial interest, to protect the workforce from redundancy. Companies like these see the need to provide new jobs for people who would otherwise become redundant, *as a reason for diversifying their operations* [that is, their generosity runs alongside their capacity to exercise flexibility and creativity]. In addition they look after their employees in an astonishingly wide number of other ways, from health schemes and providing help with housing, right through to sports and social facilities that seem to have almost no bearing whatsoever on making the company more profitable. The effect of all this is to generate a high level of loyalty and commitment in the workforce, so that everyone contributes more towards the success of the firm.'

Skynner usefully describes companies that work this way – taking into account human and social factors as well as economic realities – as 'healthy'. Such companies, he says, 'take it for granted that honesty, giving good value, and providing good service are all worthwhile things *in themselves*'.

TWO TRIVIAL ANECDOTES from my own life as a shopper demonstrate the differences between a generous and a not-generous company. About eight years ago I bought a Smeg oven. It was bottom of their range, but nevertheless expensive. After about four years, the multi-purpose clock stopped working. As it is essential to the efficient functioning of the oven, I tried to replace it. When I was told the cost of a new clock and installation, it represented half the original price of the oven and not much less than the cost of a new local oven.

I was appalled, and wrote to the managing director to complain. Not only did he respond, he came and installed a new clock for me himself, charging me only the wholesale cost of the item. Such service, and kindness, one would not forget.

In contrast, last year I bought two Mexican tin picture frames from a shop in a suburb near my home. It's a stylish, quirky gift shop and I had often bought items there. When I got home, I discovered that the glass was missing from one of the frames. I immediately called the owner to let him know, assuming he would suggest I bring it back for a replacement.

Instead the owner said, 'You must have broken it.'

'No,' I replied, more than somewhat taken aback, 'I didn't. If I had broken it, I wouldn't be calling you now.'

'You must have broken it,' he said. 'Those frames all had glass in them.'

'This one didn't,' I said, between tightly gritted teeth. 'That's why I am calling you. I have just got home, unwrapped the parcel, and one of the frames has no glass.'

'You must have broken it,' said the man . . .

I have not forgotten that exchange either.

These two stories demonstrate, I hope, not just that one man felt that he could afford to be generous, while the other man did not, but that our lives are made up of a whole trail of similar encounters, every one of which has its effects. It's a sobering thought. No matter how powerless or insignificant we may feel, our encounters inevitably leave their impressions, affecting others as well as shaping who we are.

THAT FEELING THAT you are willing to give something extra
is essential to the practice of generosity. You may not always
feel that you have something extra to give, but in giving it
anyway, that mysterious 'something extra' has a chance to
burst into existence.

David K. Reynolds, therapist and author of a number of
books, is just one of many teachers who have talked about this
ancient practice in terms of 'walking the second mile'. You are
asked (or ordered) to walk one mile for someone else's sake;
the second mile you walk because *you have chosen to do so*.

You are asked to help clear up for an hour after a neighbour's house has been burgled. Instead, you work with your
neighbour until the clearing up is finished.

You are asked by your boss to do a task you loathe. You do it,
and voluntarily do something else you dislike almost as much.

You are fed up with your partner's habit of sitting in a chair
and calling out to ask if you are thinking of putting on some
coffee. You are ready to shout, 'Put it on yourself!' Instead, not
only do you make coffee, you put the pot and mug on a tray,
with a plate of biscuits, and flowers in a vase.

What is happening in each of these scenarios – and your
own life will present you with dozens most days – is that you
are exercising free will. You will almost certainly feel stronger
for doing so.

It helps to know that you are not 'walking the extra mile'
for the other person's sake only, although to do so can be a
powerful expression of respect or love or concern. You are
walking that extra mile to express that *you can make choices* –
that the quality of your life is in your own hands – and that

you are choosing positively, rather than negatively. Every
choice that expresses love is a positive choice. Every choice
that recoils from love is negative. *Experiencing* this through the
appropriate giving of time, money, concern, is an utterly direct
and uncluttered way to gain a sense of centredness and power
within your own life.

Reynolds' unusual therapy is Zen-based, but in this teaching he is drawing on the example of Jesus Christ, who urged
his followers to carry the Roman soldier's pack not only for a
single mile, as Jews were then obliged to do, but to carry it for
just as long again – this time free of the weight of duties, orders
or obligations.

In Matthew's Gospel we learn more about this therapeutic
tool: 'Ye have heard that it hath been said, An eye for an eye,
and a tooth for a tooth:

'But I say unto you, That ye resist not evil: but whosoever
shall smite thee on thy right cheek, turn to him the other also.

'And if any man will sue thee at the law, and take away thy
coat, let him have thy cloke also.

'*And whosoever shall compel thee to go a mile, go with him twain*
[my italics].'

REYNOLDS GIVES TWO examples of 'walking the second mile'
that may seem extreme on first glance. In *Constructive Living*,
he writes: 'A young teenager complained about his stepfather's
disinterest and strictness. I suggested he shine his stepfather's
shoes twice a week. A middle-aged woman wondered how to
get her wealthy brother to return thousands of dollars he had
owed her for years. I advised her to send him still another fifty

dollars along with a letter of apology for pressuring him to return the money all these years.'

Commenting on those suggestions, Reynolds says: 'Servitude and subjugation were the farthest things from my mind . . . Service and voluntary self-sacrifice are quite different matters from servitude and subjugated passivity. One who walks a second mile *may* change the person whose load he carries. That result would be fine. But he is certain to change himself. That result is dependable. Control returns to his own hands. He frees himself once more.'

Then Reynolds asks: 'Do you see why *choosing* to be a slave makes one free? Why *choosing* to throw good money after bad makes one rich?'

MY ANSWER – which is not David Reynolds' answer – is that at such a moment I am transcending the grasping, limited rational mind, which wants to insist stridently on my *rights*. It wants to tell me that I have every *right* to be furious with my stepfather, and every *right* to be outraged at the meanness of my rich brother. Instead, I am moving to the broader perspective of the self, which lets me experience that in not acting primarily to protect my ego I am achieving two vital things.

First, I am freeing myself as well as the other person from the uncomfortable grip of my outrage.

Second, I am showing myself that I do not need to be bound by negative circumstances created by another human being.

All the ingredients of generosity are present in such a moment: humour, creativity, richness, awareness, wonder. It is not possible to 'choose to be a slave'. A slave is, definitively, someone without choices. As Reynolds wisely shows, in the exercise of freedom of choice, all traces of slavery slip away.

SUBVERTING THE USUAL behavioural moves in this way (your stepfather does not expect kindness; your brother does not expect generosity), you may well collapse old patterns and find that you and an old adversary have discovered a refreshingly new way of relating.

Or you may not!

The point of these acts of goodwill and generosity is not to bring you a specific result. It is to free you to know and express your true nature: the nature of compassionate love.

I PUT MY hands into the sink. It is filled with greasy dishes. It's late. I am tired. In the course of a lifetime, haven't I already done more than my share of dishes? I would like to be in bed, reading. If only my children would help more. If I had been clearer and firmer about domestic obligations, they would want to be helping me. In twenty years' time they will still be at home. I will still be doing their dishes. All because I have failed now. The light is poor above the sink, which is tucked into an obscure corner of the kitchen. I blame the architect for that. Only a man could fail to light a sink properly. I can't see well enough to check the plates. My legs ache. My back aches. I feel round-shouldered and old. This is what my life has come to: standing in the half-dark, by myself, muttering over a sinkful of dishes.

I put my hands into the sink. Slowly, very slowly, I wash a plate clean. With great deliberation I place it in the draining sink. I bring my attention to the next plate. I watch the plate, and my hands moving to make it clean. When other thoughts intrude, I simply wipe the plate, round and round, continuing to make it clean. Then the next plate. The saucepans are very greasy. I take a long time to clean them. This is my meditation. At the end of my meditation, I have much to thank Zen teacher Thich Nhat Hanh for, because it was he who taught me to meditate in this way. At the end of my meditation, I also have clean dishes.

TEACHINGS ON COMPASSIONATE love are at the heart of all the world religions. The failure, in the name of religion, of massive numbers of individuals to practise compassionate love does not diminish the simplicity and power of those teachings. But I do think that one could truthfully say that the teachings on compassion reveal their value *only* when they are put into practice, when they are acted upon, and experienced.

In the Mahayana Buddhist tradition the practice of *dana* (generosity) involves responding to a situation of need without asking: 'Is this my business? Are you anything to do with me?' As provocatively, it demands that you allow yourself to be aware of the situation in the first place.

Thich Nhat Hanh explains this with characteristic simplicity: 'When you hammer a nail into a board and accidentally strike your finger, you take care of the injury immediately. The right hand never says to the left hand, "I am doing charitable work for you." It just does what it can to help – giving first aid,

compassion, and concern . . . We do whatever we can to benefit others without seeing ourselves as helpers and the others as
helped. This is the spirit of non-self.'

REFLECTING THAT SAME spirit of 'non-self' – which elimin-
ates the distinctions between you and others, and transforms
what 'generosity' between you and others could or should
mean – priest and author Henri Nouwen writes, 'It is my
growing conviction that my life belongs to others just as much
as it belongs to myself and that what is experienced as unique
often proves to be the most solidly embedded in the common
condition of being human.'

ANY ACT OF selfless giving expands your world outwards. It is
a gesture of solidarity with other human beings. It makes connections. It breaks the illusion of your aloneness. It takes your
attention away from yourself, even momentarily. It changes the
atmosphere you create around you. It affects the crevices of
your mind.

Yet in the face of constant, overwhelming and legitimate
need from the world's poorest people, we may understandably
feel defeated. How many Third World children can we spon-
sor? How many different charities can we support? How many
protests against human rights violations can we give time to?
How often must we remind our politicians that we really do
care about the most basic issues of human decency?

Taken *en masse*, those issues inevitably overwhelm us. Even
as we think about them, they grow larger and we grow
smaller. Yet it is also true that each time we choose to make a

meaningful gesture that expresses our care for others, and our willingness to go some way to meet their needs, we generate change. We align ourselves with the forces of good and grace. In doing that, we ourselves are changed. We move from fear about how out of control poverty is on our planet, to a position of love that reminds us that each time one person chooses to make a difference, there *is* a difference.

Group Captain Leonard Cheshire was the most highly decorated pilot of the Second World War, a man who had every opportunity to gain personal fame and fortune. Instead, he has spent his life in the service of others and with his wife, Sue Ryder, founded the Ryder-Cheshire Mission for the Relief of Suffering. His suggestion is that in response to the enormity of the world's pain and suffering we do not turn away, or even ask 'How do we solve that problem?' He suggests a much simpler question: 'What can I do?'

Cheshire's belief is that God speaks to us through other people, as well as through the books we pick up: 'Our work, our relationships, everything we do is all part of our co-operation with God's creation of the new Heaven and the new Earth.' Equally, Cheshire believes, we can be God's 'spokespeople', God's hands, God's energy, and the messengers of God's love. 'If all I can do is save one life,' said this man who has saved hundreds if not thousands of lives, 'I must do it. Saving one life to that person is as important as if I've saved ten million lives.'

IN TIBETAN BUDDHIST practice a compassionate meditation (Tonglen) is taught that allows meditators gradually to take into themselves the pain and suffering of an increasing number of people, and to transform that pain through the power of compassionate love. Tibetan teacher Sogyal Rinpoche describes it like this: 'In the Tonglen practice of giving and receiving, we *take* on, *through compassion*, all the various mental and physical sufferings of all beings: their fear, frustration, pain, anger, guilt, bitterness, doubt, and rage, and we *give* them, through love, all our happiness, and well-being, peace of mind, healing and fulfilment.'

There are strikingly similar practices in all the major religions. I remember that as a Roman Catholic child I was encouraged to 'offer up' to God my sufferings for the benefit of those who could not help themselves. The goal was to see my suffering as a source of relief for others: as something I could 'give'.

In the more complex Tonglen practice the reminders are stark that those who are suffering and those who wish to relieve their suffering are in this realm together. The negative feelings that lead to suffering are experienced by all; the positive feelings that lead to happiness are also experienced by all. Whatever non-material differences exist between any of us are marked only by the emphasis we give to what we believe will make us happy, and what we believe will free us from suffering. (You may believe that nourishing the righteousness of your rage will relieve your suffering. I may believe that taking on your rage, and visualising clearing it and cooling it with the light of joy and wellbeing, will ease your suffering – and mine. This difference is not an abstraction only. It will reverberate through our actions, thoughts, physiology and our essential wellbeing.)

Responding to the inevitable question as to whether taking on others' suffering could harm you, Sogyal Rinpoche says: 'The one thing you should know for certain is that the only thing that Tonglen *could* harm is the one thing that has been harming you the most: your own ego, your self-grasping, self-cherishing mind, which is the root of suffering. For if you practice Tonglen as often as possible, this self-grasping mind will get weaker and weaker, and your true nature, compassion, will be given a chance to emerge more and more strongly. The stronger and greater your compassion, the stronger and greater your fearlessness and confidence.'

IT IS IMPOSSIBLE to imagine that such practices can be done in a wholehearted way without leading the practitioner also to take part in some appropriate social action in the outer world. But the change that can be achieved on the inner level through meditation, prayer, or simply by thinking with a different purpose, is certainly of no less value. Step into the presence of just one person who radiates love, and effortlessly you, too, are positively affected.

Giving fearlessly of your time, money or prayers – giving in whatever ways most truthfully express your particular means to give of yourself to others – may bring you that same quality of love that you would feel in the presence of a loving person. But whether or not such a 'reward' emerges is probably irrelevant. *Choosing* to act in this way is a vital opportunity not just to know but to experience what love means, and to experience how the absence of love also feels.

I AM STANDING in a pharmacist's, waiting to buy something to relieve the headache that has my scalp in a fiery bind. I have about eight minutes left to me between clients. I am scolding myself that it is so hard for me sometimes to bring a session to a close in good time. I feel bad for my clients if I seem to be hurrying them. I feel bad for myself when I run over and have no time to collect myself for the next intense encounter. I have been scolding myself about this for years. I am bored with the subject. Today, I am also hungry, hot and thirsty. I would feel better, of course, if I didn't also have this splitting headache. And I would feel better if I could already have taken an analgesic, but the old woman in front of me is insisting on engaging the young sales assistant in a long discussion about her working hours, and how hard it is for the old woman's daughter to manage *her* working hours with two young children to care for. This conversation is taking place at a snail's pace. I want to scream. I don't want to know a single thing about these people's problems. I want them to shut up, hurry up, get on, go away. I look at the old woman. She is wearing a long, sleeveless cotton dress. I see her arm, inches from my eyes. It is ancient. Sagging flesh, long ago drained of its bounce, hangs unevenly from the bones. Her flesh gathers thickly at her elbow. I feel revolted and afraid. That will be my arm soon, I tell myself. If I am lucky enough to live that long. If I don't drop dead first of impatience, heat, frustration, or this damned headache.

NOTICING HOW UGLY my thoughts are towards that woman, how much fear they express about my own concerns with ageing, pain and mortality, I could berate myself. Tell myself what a dreadful person I am. I am tempted to do so. It would be easy and familiar to do so. But it won't change me, or help her. If self-laceration and self-criticism provided a route to enlightenment, I would have reached the Pure Land years ago.

Instead, I must struggle back to the basic teachings of love, without which there is no point whatsoever in thinking about generosity. I need to remind myself that I am projecting onto that woman my own self-dislike. Taking that back and attempting – however inadequately – to be a little kinder to myself, it is impossible for me not to be kinder to her also. This woman, whom I will probably never see again, is not separate from me. How I think about her arises from the presence or absence of compassion within myself. What's more, allowing myself the time, patience and generosity to gaze at her with compassion, rather than impatience and contempt, returns me, too, to a state of love.

THAT PRECIOUS, UNIFYING cycle of giving, receiving, receiving, giving sounds so simple, doesn't it? Yet it is usually beyond us to stay in touch with the paradoxes within us and without us simultaneously.

In *Goodbye to Guilt*, Gerald Jampolsky writes, 'The law of love teaches us that giving and receiving occur at the same time, and the more we give, the more we reinforce the reality of love's presence in our lives.'

It is possible constantly to *monitor your own inner state of compassion* and generosity *by the reactions you have to other people.*

It is also possible to bring yourself back into a state of equi-
librium and love *by giving love to others*.

And it is possible for you to bring compassion into your
attitude towards others by *quietly loving yourself*.

I LEARNED MORE about this talking to Helen, a woman who
has lived with chronic pain for more than ten years. It will
never get better. It can only get worse. She is a regular medi-
tator and has thought deeply about the relationship of her
mind to her body. Yet for all her intellectual and spiritual
insights, Helen was unable to love her body as it is, and was
unable to avoid wondering what she had done to 'deserve' the
body she felt was her greatest cross.

'I think my greatest mistake was trying to be high-minded
about what was happening to me. Because of my particular
turn of mind, that meant an elaborate kind of intellectualis-
ing wrapped up in a few "spiritual" ribbons. I'd learned that
every crisis is an opportunity and I could laugh that my
entire life had managed to become such an "opportunity",
but actually I was totally pissed off about it. There were many
days when I wanted to scream with frustration and many
nights when I really thought the only way to get through the
night was to plan how I could kill myself if the pain got
worse by even one degree.

'I am telling you this as though it is all in the past tense. That's
only partly true but there has been a change. I had the same
dream several times over a period of a couple of months. It was
just a fragment of a dream, really, but the repetition certainly got
me to sit up and take notice. In the dream, a mother mouse was

nudging her infants into a safe place. That was all. Nudge, nudge, babies in a safe place, and then the dream was over.

'I don't even like mice and I happen to know that female mice can be shockingly unreliable mothers! That's not the point. The point is that I saw, again and again, like a repeated image on film, this primitive little brown furry creature protecting her blind, raw-skinned, ugly little babies because it was the right thing to do. She was following her instincts and no thoughts were there to get in her way.

'That made me consider how my attacks on myself are *led* by my thoughts. When I am asleep, I am so much freer than I am in the daytime. Even when I am meditating I am not that free because I often need to dissociate myself from my body in order to keep meditating despite being in pain.

'Now obviously I can't stop thinking, and I don't want to. What I can do, though, is use my thoughts to associate myself more closely to my body. That mother mouse and her babies were in a kind of huddle together. I needed not to draw away from my body, but to get closer to it. I needed to be inside it and to concentrate on it very deeply indeed in order to find its own peculiar beauty.

'You have been asking me about generosity. I think I could say that I have had to learn to be more than generous to myself about my body. Not to see it only as an opportunity to learn compassion, or as a vehicle through which I can learn compassion, but as something that exists, here and now, and that, here and now, I can look at with disgust and regret, or with the same kind of instinctual protectiveness and care that mother mouse was showing to her babies.

'If you look into almost anything deeply enough – a rose, a hand, a piece of cloth – you can see something in it that pierces your kind of everyday dumbness and arouses tenderness.

'That's the way I have learned to look at my body. Not as something to avoid, but as something that I want to contemplate deeply in order to penetrate its mystery and its ordinariness.

'In terms of the transitory nature of everything I can say, "It's just a body and a hundred years from now and maybe ten years from now, it won't exist." Or I can say, "In the present this body has its wonders, as all of nature does. And I can care for those wonders. And wonder at them!"

'Would you call this being generous? I don't know. It is certainly not generous, however, to live in a dualistic or even dissociated relationship to one's own body, to chide it with one's mind, or allow one's own thoughts to become the whips that cut it to shreds.

'I won't cut myself to shreds any more. I will do whatever I can for this body of mine. And I've learned to make allowances. I've learned to give myself credit for what I can achieve. I've learned to look very deeply indeed into my flesh. I know it much better now. What that means, of course, is that I know myself much better. And you, too!'

FOR MANY WOMEN, a lack of generosity begins with the way that they think about their own body. To be punitive, untrusting and ungenerous about one's own body is so automatic and habitual for most women that it can seem self-evident, even natural. That literally millions of thin or emaciated girls and women look into a mirror and see a fat girl or woman

reflected back at them tells us how easy it is to become dissociated from the precious reality of our own body; how easy it
is to see a grotesque embodiment of what we fear, rather than
the mirror image of what we treasure.

Even for those of us who are not suffering from such an
extreme disjunction between who we are and what we see, it
is all too easy to look into a mirror and see only what is
wrong. Women (and some men) will undergo the trauma and
risks of surgery to rearrange their features by the most fractional amounts. Would those fractional flaws even be percep-
tible if they were able to regard themselves as a whole? If they
were able to see how they themselves, in their entirety and in
all their tiny details, reflect nature's wonders, as Helen has
learned to do?

Mary Pipher is the author of *Reviving Ophelia*, a book that
describes how the undermining demands and false values of
contemporary society are wreaking havoc in the lives of female
adolescents. She writes: 'In all the years I've been a therapist,
I've yet to meet one girl who likes her body. Girls as skinny as
chopsticks complain that their thighs are flabby or their stomachs puff out. And not only do girls dislike their bodies, they
often loathe their fat. They have been culturally conditioned
to hate their bodies, which are after all themselves. When I
speak to classes, I ask any woman in the audience who feels
good about her body to come up afterward. I want to hear
about her success experience. I have yet to have a woman
come up.'

Unlike Mary Pipher, I have met women who feel happy
about their bodies, who explicitly relish their strength and

vitality, and the psychological as well as physical health that comes with that. But they are rare. Most women, and I am among them, have cultivated a habit of ingratitude towards their bodies that is the absolute antithesis of generosity. Clearly, it is crazy to absorb oneself in what is thought to be wrong with one's own body (size, age, colour, capacity to allure, some detail that is less than a sales-driven notion of perfection), and even more crazy to do so at the expense of observing what is absolutely right with it (that it is the living, physical expression of who you are). This craziness is where our failure to be generous to ourselves displays itself most rampantly, and our failure to be faithful to who we are and to what matters.

Even thinking about the way the word 'generous' is used in relation to women gives me the creeps. The phrase 'a generous-sized woman' should be a compliment. Yet it is not. We should hear the voluptuousness in the phrase, the roundness, the softness; picture the gorgeous sensation of leaning against full breasts and belly. But we don't. I sit here, typing these words, knowing that in my forties I have become a 'generous-sized' woman. I also know that if someone were to come into my office waving a magic wand, offering me the chance to be the same size I was in my twenties, I would take it. Would I be happier? Would anything other than my vanity be gratified?

When I was in my twenties, and able to wear clothes that now look extreme in their skimpiness, I also worried about my weight, and believed that I would be more attractive if I were even thinner. I wasn't happier then. I wanted to make my way in the world. I passionately wanted women to take up more

political and social space, and more physical space too.
Yet through those most intensely politically active years,
I remained concerned about my physical appearance and
critical of it.

IN THE UNITED States, according to Mary Pipher, 'eight million women have eating disorders'. In every rich country, as
you read this, women are looking at each other, silently
commenting if their friend's weight has noticeably increased,
complimenting her with a smile if it has noticeably decreased.

'You look great,' we routinely say. 'Have you lost weight?'

I am not ignoring the fact that millions of people in the
richest countries are unhealthily fat. If a fat person eats well,
exercises sensibly and pleasurably, and loses weight, it is a legitimate reason to celebrate. But when a woman has not been fat,
why are her intelligent, insightful friends rushing to congratu-
late her on her new thinness?

What makes these customs especially bizarre – and distressing – is that our ungenerous, enculturated obsession with thinness co-exists with our knowledge that one and a half of the
world's five billion people are classified by the United Nations
as 'desperately poor'. This means a totally inadequate diet, no
permanent shelter, perhaps no clean water or firewood, certainly no sewerage, and little feeling of safety. We know this,
yet do less and less about it.

With the exception of the nations of Scandinavia, we in the
West are turning our back on the involuntarily thin. In 1994,
half the countries in the Organisation for Economic Co-
operation and Development cut their foreign aid budgets.

(This was done despite the fact that 'foreign aid' is increasingly linked to trade, and spent on aid programmes that employ substantial numbers of workers from the donor countries.)

The world's richest and most politically powerful country, the United States, gives 0.1 per cent of its gross national product in overseas aid. The United Nations recommended figure is 0.7 per cent. In 1996, an international declaration on hunger was adopted at the UN World Food Summit held in Rome. The summit affirmed 'the right of everyone to have access to safe and nutritious food, the right to adequate food and *the fundamental right of everyone to be free from hunger* [my italics]'. In response, Washington stated, 'The United States believes this is a goal or aspiration to be realised progressively, *but does not give rise to any international obligations* nor diminish the responsibility of national governments towards their citizens [my italics].' The US government also said that it did not accept the summit target 'for countries to provide 0.7 per cent of their annual economic wealth in overseas aid'.

Also in 1996, the newly elected Liberal (conservative) government in Australia cut its aid to 0.29 per cent of GNP, a new low in Australia's history of overseas aid. There was virtually no public outcry. And despite the fact that the world's poorest people live in Africa, less than 8 per cent of Australia's overseas aid is directed there. Is it too cynical to suggest that this is because Australia's trade links with the nations of South-East Asia remain far more vital to Australia's own economy than those with any African nation?

The generosity we are failing to show to the 'desperately poor' is not only shameful, it is short-sighted and stupid. The

World Bank, which itself has had a fairly bleak record for worsening the economic situation of some of the world's poorest and least politically sophisticated countries, issued a warning in 1995 that the cuts in aid from rich to poor countries would 'seriously undermine global stability'.

IT IS NOT a very big jump from the lack of generosity we show to ourselves – the pettiness, self-absorption and irrelevancies that consume us when we contemplate our own appearance – to the lack of generosity we show to those whose physical conditions legitimately demand our most urgent and unstinting concern.

Would it be too absurd, then, to suggest that if we could release ourselves from a punitive, judgemental relationship with our own bodies, we could take much more seriously the plight of those whose bodies are continually under threat? If we were able really to love our physical bodies, honour them as expressions of our individual and shared natures, cherish them as houses of our spirits, rejoice in them as miracles of creation, then surely we would find it much harder to remain indifferent to the fate of the children, women and men with whom we share our most wondrous and vulnerable planet.

YOU MAY, OF course, be responding immediately to what I am suggesting by correctly pointing out that it is still largely men who make and implement the political and bureaucratic decisions that reflect a nation's willingness to be generous or not. And that men are less tormented in their relationship to their bodies than women are.

But surely that is only partly true? While dramatically fewer men suffer from the severe eating disorders that plague women, and while men in general are much less harshly judged by their looks than women are, men also suffer. Who knows if they suffer more or less. That's immeasurable and I think irrelevant.

My observations suggest to me that many men also suffer from a dualistic, distancing relationship to their own bodies ('I can "master" my body and do what I want with it'). Ten minutes on the corner of a busy street in any major Western city will show you hundreds of men rushing by who are overweight, underweight, grey with fatigue, tense, anxious; men who are breathing shallowly, heads tilted forward so that their brain can arrive at wherever they are going nanoseconds before the rest of themselves has a chance to catch up.

Men may not need to stay young and beautiful in order to attract the opposite sex (not if they replace youth and beauty with power and money, anyway). But this doesn't liberate them. Men far too often use their bodies brutally as a means to an end: to work longer and longer hours; to win sports events in virtually inhuman conditions; to express or retain power; to prove to themselves or other people that they have 'what it takes'.

The man who is driven by his own ambitions or fears to continue to work when he should be resting is unlikely to be in touch with either his physical or his instinctual life. The man driven to run when he should walk, to 'fuck' when his spirit is crying out for a cuddle, or to 'carve out' yet another deal when his wife is waiting at home on their son's birthday, has not learned to care for himself lovingly, tenderly. And the man who drops dead in his early forties from a heart attack is also unlikely to have had a close, knowledgeable relationship with his own precious body.

LEARNING TO BE generous to ourselves is quite different, I think, from protecting our inner sense of fragility through acts of self-indulgence. Those acts of self-indulgence often involve excessive amounts of food, drugs, alcohol, tobacco, gambling, shopping, sex. They may involve excessive amounts of work. They may also be expressed through inactivity, such as social withdrawal or lying in bed feeling too weary, bored or nihilistic to get up, or even through a relentless round of 'self-development' projects. All too often, however, the satisfaction we are is seeking is fleeting, incomplete or totally absent.

Yet the urge towards such excess is, itself, instructive. It describes a need and hunger that may have arisen precisely because we are starving ourselves of the love and compassion that fuels, and is fuelled by, authentic feelings of generosity. This same lack of simple kindness, ease and generosity leads us to berate ourselves for our own failures, and to blame ourselves unmercifully for our own disappointments. It refuses to allow us to give ourselves the benefit of the doubt. It dwells disproportionately on what has gone wrong, and what might never be.

It may equally lead us to feel invaded, unworthy, insufficient and extremely uncomfortable when something positive is offered. The thought may arise: 'I am not worthy of this', or 'I could never match what is being offered to me. I could never repay it', or 'I may grow to like this. And then it will be taken from me.'

Generosity is the best possible corrective to such self-punishing attitudes. It reminds us how much wisdom and resilience can be gained through apparent failure; that our ego or rational mind does not always know what is best for us; and that we can rarely foresee the larger and perhaps quite unexpected picture while we are feeling overwhelmed by a painfully disappointing detail.

Stepping back from fear and anxiety, self-criticism and despondency, we discover that there is spaciousness in generosity's view, and many shades of meaning between what we first perceived as white and black.

THE CRUCIAL DECISION to cultivate generosity towards oneself cannot arise from will alone. To transform thought into action we need will: the conscious awareness that we have a choice about our reaction in any situation *and are capable of exercising it*. But the impulse to generosity must arise from something more, from something that is as near as any of us can get to unconditional love.

This does not mean suspending judgement or discernment about our actions and behaviour. It does not mean coddling ourselves like a spoilt baby. Unconditional love is much bigger than that, much tougher and more truthful.

Unconditional love is a commitment to go on loving *for love's sake*; to go on appreciating the gift of life *for life's sake*; to go on believing that there is good in humankind, *despite* the failures, disappointments, tragedies and mysteries that are part of every human existence. '

IT'S A SUBVERSIVE virtue, generosity. It undermines solemnity. It allows connections to be made between the most unexpected people. It lends itself to small gestures as well as large. It flies in the face of greed, arrogance and desire, and can undo them all. It does not depend on learning, privilege, status or riches. It is ignorant of nationality, class, colour and gender. It is as vital in the boardroom as it is in kindergarten. It is impossible to manufacture, measure, sell or waste. It springs from a conscious intention for good, and it involves the body and mind as much as spirit. Generosity can be shy or assertive, memorable or fleeting. Without its presence, we would scarcely know what love feels like or looks like; how love smells or sounds; how love survives and what miracles love allows.

In every impulse that restores or celebrates our faith in humankind, there generosity is. In all our finest moments, our most transcendent, tender or illuminating moments, it's also present. And so it is when disaster strikes at our communities, and we face that together.

HAZRAT INAYAT KHAN suggests the reward of life is life itself. There is no other way to discover what life is, and what our purpose is, other than through embracing it: the griefs and the glories, the raging disappointments and the precious, fleeting moments of perfection.

It is seductive and all too easy to mistake life for objects; to confuse meaning with goals, schedules, agenda. Cultivating a sense of trust that *you do now have enough*, and that, in giving where giving is needed, *you will have no less*, leads to an experience of freedom and of love that is beyond riches. This is what generosity can teach us.

'Love deeply and strongly,' urges Piero Ferrucci, 'so that the heart stops looking for satisfaction in illusory possessions. Face death in all its aspects and possibilities, thereby banishing all greed.'

Letting go of what we believe we must possess leaves us free: free to reach out to others without grasping; free to be reached towards without experiencing loss or intrusion.

If every one of our lives is to be worth living, and if we are to come to realise in time that our planet is worth saving, it will be because we have allowed ourselves to discover the radiant power and ease, magic and beauty of generosity: the spaciousness of it, the joy of it, the colour and wonder of it; the immensity of it, the infinity of it.

It is in giving that we receive/It is in pardoning that we are pardoned; and/It is in dying that we are born to eternal life.

Tolerance

True love and prayer are learned in the moment

when prayer has become impossible and

the heart has turned to stone.

THOMAS MERTON

olerance is not a neat and tidy virtue. In its bonsai forms it certainly allows people to be nice, compliant, patronising, pleasant, hypocritical, blind, unreal and half-alive. But where it lives and breathes, sweats and weeps, grows and soars, it is anything but nice. It is confronting, flexible, blatant, humorous, sometimes harsh, always encompassing, truthful, demanding – and real.

TOLERANCE LIVES – or dies – first in our own minds. Forget, for just a moment, thoughts about others that lead to the establishment of attitudes, beliefs, convictions, and sometimes to peace or war. Stay with the rivalries, the contradictions, the perplexities, paradoxes, ambiguities, elisions, obsessions, certainties and ignorances that exist within your own thought processes.

Tolerating this untidy, writhing heap is not easy. It demands at least a partial awareness that you are not the predictable unity you might like to imagine. You may not be wholly good, kind and reasonable. Tolerance demands that you face that. It demands that you can bear your own interior chaos and clashes; that you are willing to be utterly surprised not by others only, but by yourself; that you can sometimes live with prolonged uncertainty about who you are, what your life means, where you are heading; that you can come to understand times of bleakness as well as joy; that you can accept in the spaciousness of your own mind thoughts and their accompanying feelings that you might well prefer to assign somewhere far outside yourself.

What this adds up to is that you are able – as your life progresses, and you learn from it – to take yourself on in your entirety, and not just in the bits that fit with others' ideas of you, or your regularly polished illusions about yourself.

'Taking yourself on' makes it hard for you to disown your actions that cause others pain or harm. It makes it hard for you to see yourself as separate from other people, and markedly better or worse than they are. It makes it impossible to rest on any certainties, not least those that accompany the labelling we give ourselves – and allow others to give us – when we believe we are in the process of creating a life. (I am a woman, middle-aged, middle-class, white; a mother, a writer; liberal-minded; fond of friends, books, music, gardens, food; somewhat restless, impatient, ambitious . . . and so on.) Such labelling always dwarfs us, and can only be, at best, a perilously circumscribed version of the truth.

Tolerance – especially for what is raw and untried, confronting and unfamiliar – means taking ourselves or allowing ourselves to be taken to the outer limits of our potentials, even if this means risking encountering the perils of ecstasy or hell. And not taking ourselves in a single direction only. Facing what we may prefer to ignore, repress or disown may feel dangerous, even crazy. Contemporary culture discourages us from venturing into these tricky realms. We are supposed to *consume* extreme experiences, but not risk living them. Risking them might turn us into nations of artists, warriors for peace, internationalists, nature lovers, protectors of children and old people, mystics, storytellers, perpetual students hungry to know more, employees who want our work to add up to something.

Nothing in our education or public culture encourages or prepares us to live like that. Too many of our experiences have become synthetic: other people's lives and fantasies mediated to us through movies or television. Yet authentic experiences remain always close at hand. They are not available for rich people only, or for special people only. They could include witnessing the majesty and beauty of the sun sinking down low behind an ocean and spreading colour as it does so; the timeless wonder of staying close through the transitions of birth or death; singing or dancing with no goal other than pleasure; participating in a solemn, meaningful ritual; refusing to be diminished by other people's ideas about what is right or appropriate for someone of your age, size, colour, gender, sexuality, talent, education, looks, family background or beliefs; raging against the desecration of our living, breathing planet in the name of multinational business; activating your protest that the United Nations Security Council is dominated by armament-producing nations; acknowledging how many of the five billion people on our planet live starved of the most basic resources necessary for existence, and doing everything you can to change that.

TOLERANCE CANNOT BE a private virtue only. It has profound ramifications in the public arena. And there its shadow forms – resignation, passivity, lack of action, ignorance – are most strikingly evident.

It is apathy not tolerance that we demonstrate as forests fall, soil is salinated, rivers clog or dry up; as many basic crops become increasingly difficult or impossible to grow; as chemicals, landmines and nuclear waste penetrate and pollute the earth; as some species die out forever and others live in horrific, threatening conditions; as gaps in the ozone layer increase, and as the temperature of our planet rises. It is surely apathy and not tolerance that allows us to stand by as children are sold into industrial slavery and prostitution, used in wars, traded between countries, denied the most basic human right: that of safety.

And in the West, where distance cannot be our excuse, we 'tolerate' the production and sale of increasingly violent movies and electronic games, products that seem quite 'normal' to our children, that turn violence into a game and confuse them about what is real and what is not. Simultaneously, we 'tolerate' or accept that most people, including our own children, are largely ignorant of what violence actually expresses and achieves. We teach them far too little about the political, cultural and social realities that led to the cataclysmic violence of the concentration camps, of the Gulag, of the decimation of the American Indians and Australian Aborigines, of Southern African apartheid, and that now extends to 'no-go' areas within some of our own cities. We teach them far too little about the causes of the current horrific wars within and between nations, where fear, hatred, bitterness and violence rage unchecked by meaningful international care. We teach them far, far too little about how peace and justice could be achieved. Our children don't know – but should know – that none of the 'action' is or was ever a game. They don't know – but should know – that we defame the dead as well as the living when we 'tolerate' violence being used as yet another commodity for profit.

In one of those extreme paradoxes that tell us so much about the profound inconsistencies within human nature, we want to see and vicariously experience increasingly horrifying violence while refusing to listen closely to the stories of people who are truly suffering the effects of violence. We fail to learn from what they have learned and could teach us. What has emerged from real experiences, we ignore. Yet, doing that, we do not push violence away. On the contrary, we invite it in and give it a home. We fear violence, but a version of it may be invited into our homes through our television screens on most evenings. We fear violence, but line up to see movies that offer nothing but violence, unredeemed by kindness, insight, beauty or genuine grief.

Susan Griffin captures that paradox powerfully in an anecdote in her book on war, *A Chorus of Stones*. The anonymity and relative lack of specificity in the story sharpen its truth somehow. It could be told by any of us, and about any of us.

Susan Griffin: 'In a famous short story written about the bombing of Hiroshima, a man who is poisoned with radiation returns home to his village. He tells his family and friends what he has seen. No one believes him until news reports arrive. Then they listen to his story with shock and grief. But after a time they no longer want to hear his story. *He is condemned to repeat what he has witnessed over and over to those who do not listen* [my italics].'

To tolerate listening, even when the hairs on our backs stand on end, our mouths dry, our stomachs heave, is the least we owe to those who suffer. To tolerate listening is also the only way we will begin to feel sufficient rage to cry out with conviction: 'Such horror must stop. We must do whatever we can to prevent it. *I* must do all that I can to prevent it.'

Honing such tolerance, which arises from compassion for humanity and expresses love, *allows us to bear listening and to face what is real.* Only such compassion and knowledge can prevent us from colluding with fake versions of tolerance that say 'It is not our business', and turn us away, in indifference.

Still close to home – and of course writing this brief catalogue, and reading it, is not easy – we claim, as individuals and as a society, to be horrified about child abuse and especially child sexual abuse as it is increasingly reported. We rail against the individuals who are caught abusing our children. We vilify and demonise them. Yet our 'tolerance' of their actions is actually made tremendously clear through our reluctance to pay additional taxes, or to enforce a different allocation of government expenditure, so that as a community we could more adequately educate and support the families and individuals among us who are in need, and adequately educate, value and remunerate the adults upon whom children must depend for their safekeeping: teachers, kindergarten teachers and childcare workers, social workers and child protection workers.

And while abuse and violence cuts across all social groups and classes, it is self-evident that 'People cannot think clearly when they are ill, hungry or afraid.' Does it make any sense, therefore, that we 'tolerate' increasingly widespread unemployment and poverty, even when we know that, as Gandhi taught us, 'Poverty is the greatest violence of all'?

TOLERANCE, ESPECIALLY WHEN it slides into apathy, has this fearsome shadow side. But that does not make it any the less valuable or powerful. It is a law of nature that the brighter a light is, the darker its shadow. That is true for this virtue as we see it practised (and defiled) socially, and as we experience it within ourselves.

It may be, however, that it is only when we are up against the limits of what we believe we cannot bear, or could never bear, that the sleeping tolerance within us can come awake and, as it does so, waken love and wisdom. This is certainly my own experience. Only through tolerating what had to be faced, as well as the range of feelings that erupted around that, could I come slowly and erratically to a point of recognition of my own inner strength.

Looking back at the unendurable that I have, inch by inch, endured, I can see how tolerance has emerged, inch by inch: tolerance for the situation I was in; for the uncertainty of its outcome; for my own insufficiencies in dealing with it as well as I might have wished. I could have discovered nothing about that experience in prospect, and even looking back I feel

extremely tempted to say, 'I could never do that again.' Yet I am
a stronger person because I did see those situations through;
because, despite my feelings of dismay and helplessness, I did
tolerate them, endure them, and survived.

What's more, when I look around at the people I know, and
think about the many, many people whose lives have met mine
through their books, I know that psychic, emotional and spiritual survival is no small thing. It may even be that conscious
survival – surviving *and* reflecting upon it – is our greatest
source of wisdom.

Nancy Mairs and her husband, George, were foster parents
in the late 1970s to an adolescent who had been dumped,
betrayed, ignored, pushed around, and who eventually landed
in their home. A decade later, writing not only about the
experience of fostering this young man, but about her experience of life, Nancy said: 'People have asked me often whether
I regret taking Ron in, whether I'd do so again if I had to do
it over. Hard questions to face, the answers risky to the ways I
like to think of myself.

'Because I did regret taking him in, many times. I lack the
largeness of spirit that enables someone like George to transcend daily inconveniences, lapses in behaviour, even alien values, and to cherish a person without condition. I often judged
Ron harshly, by standards inappropriate to his peculiar situation; I was often grudging of approval and affection; I made
him work too hard for the privilege of being my son. He suffered, I'm afraid, for my regrets. And no, I think, I wouldn't do
it again, knowing what I now know. But then, I wouldn't have
Anne and Matthew again either. Might not even marry

George again. Such ventures seem now, in the wisdom of hindsight, to demand a woman of more than my mettle. *That's how we get wise, by taking on in ignorance the tasks we would never later dare to do* [my italics].'

And the answer to that stark question: did Nancy regret taking Ron in?

'No. Yes.'

SOMETIMES, OF COURSE, we must tolerate what we ourselves have not taken on. We must tolerate what has been forced on us by what are often called, passively, neutrally, 'historical' or 'social' circumstances. Yet in refusing to tolerate the inevitability of such 'circumstances' it seems vital to remember that torment, torture and murder do not arise neutrally; they are created and enacted by individual human beings *who could always say no.*

Looking back from the safety and peace of contemporary Australia, over the breach of fifty years, into the heart of what is arguably the most profound tragedy of the twentieth century, Australian Holocaust survivor Abraham H. Biderman writes: 'When I recall the days behind the electrified fences, I often wonder how I went on living. So many times I nearly gave up: when hunger pangs punished my body; when rain and frost chilled the marrow of my bones, and my fingers and toes were paralysed by the cold. Many of my comrades froze to death in temperatures that dropped to twenty, sometimes twenty-five degrees below zero; yet I continued to struggle to stay sane and to stay alive. Half-naked and frozen, I would cry with pain, but my tears simply froze on my cheeks. Every so often, I thought how much easier it would be to touch the high-voltage electrified fence than to go on living. Just one split second and it would be over. But somehow I did not. I could not. Driven by a force beyond my own reason, beyond logic, I had to go on. I found that I wanted very much to live and one day to fulfil my mother's last wish.'

JUST AS TOLERANCE itself has a shadow side – allowing us to turn away from people or events in fear, indifference or apathy – so, too, in the realm of our most personal experiences, in the inner home of the self, it is precisely what we fear or cannot tolerate that becomes our own shadow.

That shadow is the basement of our home, or maybe the ignored, unfamiliar and potentially eruptive wing. What we can't tolerate out in the open, in the light of conscious awareness, becomes our unconscious: the realm of our own experience that is hidden from us. Everything within the unconscious is not 'bad'. Far from it. Much of it is dazzling; too dazzling for us easily to own. To acknowledge our own dazzle, and live it, we would need to give up some of our self-pity, some of our hope that others may take care of us, or dazzle for us. Giving up our self-pity and illusions of powerlessness is as difficult for most of us to do – perhaps more difficult – as it is to acknowledge that some of the ugly beliefs we have about other people speak volumes about what we fear in ourselves.

Few writers have gone hunting the elusive shadow more skilfully than Robert Bly. Here he describes the personal

shadow, which can never usefully be understood separately
from either the collective or social shadows that it is fed by –
and that collectively it also creates: 'When we were one or two
years old we had what we might visualize as 360-degree personality. Energy radiated out from all parts of our body and all
parts of our psyche. A child running is a living globe of
energy. We had a ball of energy, all right; but one day we
noticed that our parents didn't like certain parts of that
ball. They said things like: "Can't you be still?" Or "It isn't nice
to try and kill your brother." Behind us we have an invisible
bag, and the part of us our parents don't like, we, to keep our
parents' love, put in the bag. By the time we get to school our
bag is quite large. Then our teachers have their say: "Good
children don't get angry over such little things." So we take our
anger and put it in the bag. By the time my brother and I were
twelve in Madison, Minnesota, we were known as "the nice
Bly boys". Our bags were already a mile long.'

Towns, cities, nations: they all have their shadows. So does
any organised group, from the local Rotary Club to psychoanalytic associations to the Catholic Church. When the group
has only conscious, rational aims – like winning at soccer – it
is less likely to be affected and infected by its shadow than
when it has ideological or transcendent aims. Such aims are
not in themselves wrong; on the contrary. But the higher the
aims of any group, the more watchful the individual members
need to be of where the shadow is falling.

Look closely at how 'exclusivity' is maintained by an individual, group, collective or nation; at who is excluded and on
what basis; at how criticism is fought off or denied. Look at

what is most feared, reviled, envied or disparaged and you will have a rapid insight into what is 'in the bag' – what is the intolerable shadow.

BLY SUGGESTS THAT most of what has to go into the bag is put there before we turn twenty. That gives us the rest of our lives to pull things out. Tolerance is a virtue that ages well. And we age much better when we practise it. A broad, rich, flexible, curious, tolerant *old* mind, open as much to what is still to be discovered as to what has been discovered and contemplated, offers the most splendid defiance possible to a world that fears ageing and the elderly.

Tolerance can certainly be taught to the young and, more usefully still, modelled for them. But for tolerance to flourish in our hearts as well as our minds, we may need to experience a whole series of fairly violent jolts and realisations that we can't order the world in the way we want to. Or that we can order the world until we are breathless, but our orders must compete with those of all with whom we share this planet.

The analyst and writer Marie-Louise von Franz, a colleague of Jung, had a refreshingly accessible way of describing how we can learn to catch sight of our shadow in daily life: 'Whenever we are tired or under pressure, another personality often breaks through. For instance, people who are very well-meaning and helpful suddenly become ruthlessly egocentric. They push everybody else aside and become very nasty. Also, when people have the flu or are ill, you suddenly see their shadow side coming through . . . There's a sudden change of character. That's the breaking through of the

shadow. It can take on a thousand forms. Let's say you have
a very good friend and you lend him a book. Now, it's just
that book that your friend loses. It was the last thing
he wanted to do, but his shadow wanted to play a trick on
you . . .

'We all have our favourite enemies, our best enemies. They
are generally our shadows. If people do some harm to you,
then it's natural that you hate them. But if somebody doesn't
do special harm to you and you just feel so madly irritated
every time that person enters the room that you could just spit
at him, then you can be sure that's the shadow. The best way,
then, is to sit down and write a little paper on the characteristics of that person. Then look at it and say, "That's me." I did
that once when I was eighteen, and I blushed so that I was
sweating blue in the face when I had finished. It's a real shock
to see one's shadow.'

WHEN UNDERSTOOD AND used skilfully, with love and some
humour, tolerance allows us to embrace our own shadow. This
is never an abstract matter. It means watching out for those
'sudden changes of character' that tell you your persona is
cracking and your shadow is emerging. It means listening with
your mouth closed when others accuse you of something. It
means hesitating long and hard before you assign fault. It
means owning up to your own divisive thinking. It means
refusing to believe or cultivate myths of your own powerlessness. It means checking out your simplistic assumptions against
the complex realities. It means acknowledging the differences
of opinions, needs, wishes, desires that exist within your own

mind – and recognising how these mirror the conflicts that you may despise that exist outside yourself.

Such hesitations, reflections, acknowledgements and incorporations also bring the flexibility, mobility, expansiveness and depth that characterise an interesting mind. In relationships, too, the outcome of bringing light to the shadow can be markedly uplifting. Marie-Louise von Franz again: 'When people learn to know their shadow and to live their shadow a bit more, they become more accessible, more natural, more roundly human. People without shadows, who are perfect, inflict [project] an inferiority on their surroundings, which irritates others. They act in a manner superior to the "all-too-human". That's why one is so relieved when something nasty happens to them. "Aha!" we say. "Thank God, he's only human."'

YOUNG CHILDREN AUTOMATICALLY rush to blame others when accused of some wrongdoing. They are right to do so. Through most of childhood, their egos are more easily crushed than the most transparent eggshell. They are also (and for much the same reason) so easily invaded by hot words and even mild accusations that they feel compelled to push the barrage of your words away with fierce defences of their own.

Even older children have little capacity to distinguish between your disapproval of something they have done, and your disapproval of their entire being. Accused of almost anything, they will shout, protest and blame. You *must* be wrong. They *don't care*. With their words, they will do everything they can to let you know that you are coming too close and that they are compelled to push you away.

As we get older, we continue to try to push away unpleasant truths, especially when these disrupt a view of ourselves to which we are particularly attached. We do this through denial (failing to recognise the nose on our face) and through the somewhat more subtle but no less drastic processes of projection: projecting outwards onto someone else thoughts and feelings that belong within ourselves but which we do not want to 'own'.

Because of the mix of positive and negative that is tucked away in our unconscious, some of what we project is our goodness or strength. That's more or less what is going on whenever we idealise someone. More often, though, it is our least attractive tendencies that we pass along like the hot potato we don't want to touch, never mind recognise or take responsibility for.

A man has sexual thoughts about his fifteen-year-old
  daughter. He accuses her of behaving 'like a bitch on heat'.
A woman spends years refusing to tell her husband why she's
  silent, then accuses him of deserting her when he finally
  leaves.
One business partner accuses another of wanting to ruin
  him, then walks like a lemming into a trap of his own
  making.
A disgruntled lover shouts at his girlfriend that she is
  uninterested in their relationship.

A mother feels powerless to intervene positively with her
teenage children, and tells her husband that everything he
tries is hopeless.

A man pursues the 'secret' bank accounts of his ex-wife.
They don't exist. What do exist are shady financial
dealings on his side.

A child comes into a room where her brother is reading. She
pokes him, then takes his book. When he protests she asks,
'Why are you in such a bad mood?'

In all these situations there is an unwillingness on the part
of accusers to ask themselves: 'What's happening here? What is
it that I am finding hard to face? *How can I help?*'

THE DISTRESS OF these banal, everyday dramas goes beyond
the pain caused by denial and projection. That is bad enough,
and sometimes tragic. But when you accuse someone else of
what you cannot face in yourself, you also lose a precious chance
to reclaim something from the shadow, to haul something back
out of the bag, and to know more about who you are.

Only by risking knowing how complex and contradictory
you are, and owning up to who that person is, can you discover
that actually you can tolerate your own uncomfortable desires,
needs and emotions and no longer need to believe they are
happening elsewhere. This process is called 're-owning your
projections'. It probably involves learning some relatively
unpalatable truths about yourself, though oddly enough this
makes your life feel not more precarious but safer, in part
because it is then more securely based on the ground of truth

rather than on the shaky foundations of wishful thinking. Knowing who you are, *feeling responsible for who you are and what you do*, it is possible to tolerate most of what life brings you, and to feel increasingly confident you can do that.

Unfortunately, however, because we live in a historical moment that encourages 'victimism', aggressive passivity and blaming others, and discourages reflection and self-responsibility, these psychologically vital tasks of 'owning up' and 're-owning your projections' are too rarely achieved. 'Most people,' writes Jungian analyst June Singer, 'feel no particular need to make these projections conscious, although by refusing to do so they place themselves in an extremely precarious state.'

This, too, is a matter of social gravity.

Singer again: 'The person who will be most effective in his strivings toward social justice is the one who is most critical of himself, who takes care to differentiate his own flaws and to take responsibility for them before he goes out to correct his neighbor's. He will make his impact more effective by setting an example than by bludgeoning his opponent into submission. The person who commits himself to a life of continuing confrontation with the unconscious within himself will also confront the unknown in the world at large with an open mind, and what is more, with a heart of wisdom.'

What we relegate, repress or disown is not silenced, but usually emerges indirectly, mostly through our attitudes towards others. And, as a rule of thumb, the less conscious we are of what we are doing internally, the more intolerant we will be of difference externally. This is not a question only of having little patience, or of being fretful, irritated, dismissive or critical. Such behaviour is unpleasant and often unnecessary. But the poisonous reach of intolerance can go much further.

Weak, intolerant people need to hold unusually strong and narrow views. They may also be unusually insistent on broadcasting them, and condemning of people who object or disagree. They may be excited and gratified when their racism, sexism or homophobia allows similar bile to be released in others; when the 'fence-sitters' get the permission they were waiting for to attack and denigrate those they perceive as different and somehow enviable or disgusting in that difference.

Weak, intolerant people always seek an enemy on whom to project their own negative or destructive feelings. This is the only way that they can keep their own illusions of 'purity' and 'righteousness' intact and prop up a flimsy, unreliable sense of self. History is littered with tragic examples of this psychological and moral failing. Contemporary media offer ever more.

Men who turn on other men because they fear their power, their weakness, their sexuality, their colour; men who feel justified in controlling the lives of women; women who arouse race or gender hatred, especially in their own children; white people who turn on black people; heterosexuals who condemn and seek to control gay people; political groups that murder those whom they believe stand in their way; religious groups who revile or kill other religious groups: these are just a few of the gravest examples that arise when people disown some of their own fears or feelings and project them in extreme and degraded forms onto other human beings, with tragic consequences.

Within communities, there are tremendous dangers when political, social or religious leaders collude with the unconsciousness of those who believe themselves to be injured and unheard and are righteously blaming. Such leaders most profoundly betray the privilege of leadership, as well as every woman, man and child who is directly or indirectly affected, when they give tacit or explicit permission to any section of the population to unleash its latent feelings of intolerance, to bring those feelings out from the private places of shame and guilt into the open and express them through acts of verbal or physical abuse.

Tolerance expresses and supports maturity. As tiny children grow, so does their world view. As important as learning to talk and walk, to listen and look people in the eye, are the lessons they must soon learn about how their behaviour affects other people, and how they are affected by them. If they are lucky, they will become truly conscious of how each of us plays our part in creating what we call society; they will know that their social, outward-looking responsibilities and their personal, inward-looking responsibilities are never separate; that they are one.

A mature population knows that it is not possible to injure one section of that whole without injuring all. When any section of the population shows signs of forgetting this, a mature leader needs to carry that knowledge for them, and remind them of it, both through explicit words and, more importantly, through overt, persistent refusal to tolerate or condone any lies that set one group of the population against another; that blames a single group for general social ills; that seeks to isolate any group through hatred, envy, shame or fear.

Such maturity is, however, all too often lacking. Leaders arise from groups that are themselves massively self-interested. With rare and precious exceptions, politicians demonstrate through their actions a striking lack of tolerance and maturity because they flourish within a system where posturing, blaming, lying, goading, defaming, egotism and lack of personal responsibility can bring success. To listen to politicians elaborate their refusals to take responsibility for actions that were ill-advised or even stupid, *and to hear how the fault lies always somewhere else*, is to hear the language of profound immaturity and lack of tolerance, which is also, all too often, the language of our communities and even of our homes.

Singer quotes Jung commenting in 1928 – eleven years before the start of the Second World War – on just how inflammatory this process can be of 'disowning' what is unacceptable to one's conscious mind. 'The psychology of war,' said Jung, 'has clearly brought this condition to light: everything which our own nation does is good, everything which the other nations do is wicked. *The centre of all that is mean and vile is always to be found several miles behind the enemy's lines* [my italics].'

Decades later, despite a massive popularisation and dissemination of psychological and psychoanalytic ideas, the processes of disowning, and the cults of demonisation, continue. And we tolerate that.

RECOGNISING THAT MUCH of what we need to tolerate is within ourselves and not in other people only, it is useful also to recognise that there is a tendency in most of us to over-simplify much of what is not in the least bit simple. We tend to cluster certain kinds of attitudes together, assuming some are 'ours' and others are 'theirs'. This is what leads to the facile categorisations of people as 'like us' and 'not like us', which is what tolerance absolutely asks us to rethink and question.

Of course it is true that there are people we feel immediately at home with, and others whose views or attitudes leave us extremely cold. But so automatic are our processes of categorising that we may think that our tolerance is sufficiently expressed by the degree to which we are judgemental about 'people not like us': people whose lives apparently express a set of attitudes that we largely disown. Yet such simple divisions go no way towards reflecting the infinite diversity of human life and the contradictions that exist within each person's experience.

Tolerance drags you away from the temptation to think you can learn anything significant at all about a person by asking the conventionally reductive questions that pass for information-seeking in our impatient society: 'Are you gay or straight? How old are you? How much money do you make? How many children do you have? How many lovers have you had? Do you sleep on the left side of the bed or the right?'

Tight little definitions, whether they are the ones we give ourselves or those that others give us, convey nothing much and achieve nothing much. And they can be dangerous. For the giving and receiving of definitions, however involuntarily, has allowed and led to the oppositional thinking that is at the heart of all prejudice.

Tolerance recognises difference, subtleties and inconsistencies that cannot be measured or categorised – that emerge only partially through people's dreams, desires, imaginings, and conscious and unconscious actions – and supports your capacity to accept them. Speaking about this, my friend Pam Benton said: 'The best part of me is the sense of connection I have with a diversity of people; not having only good, left, feminist, right-on friends. I have a huge range of friends that I can still connect with at the level of the important human values that they live. They don't live a life that I would want to live, and there are many things about which I would disagree with them, but I can still connect with parts of them that seem to me immensely valuable as human beings. And there's a sense that many [politically] left men have a puritanism, a sense that there's only one right way to be, and you cut off or are very dismissive of people who don't live up to that standard of rigour, commitment – who are just ordinary lapsed human beings!

'Connection's also about how it's possible to be social human beings: the possibility of social life rests on the ability to forgive, to tolerate, to allow – *to see yourself in other people.*'

Tolerance thrives on the unexpected. Tolerance knows there *are* white male judges who are actively feminist. There *are* feminists who are vile to their mothers. There *are* environmentalists who invest brilliantly on the stock exchange. There *are* left-leaning men who espouse feminism and cheat on their wives and children. There *are* gay fundamentalist Christians. There *are* homoeopaths who smoke cigarettes. There *are* liberals who are invasively controlling of their own children. There *are* conservatives who are open and accepting of theirs. And such statements describe these lives only in their broadest strokes, not in any of their myriad details.

That we have been clustered, and cluster ourselves, according to a few dominant traits or attitudes, suits town planners, the advertisers of products, the producers of television shows, and the publishers of newspapers. It does not necessarily reflect reality, nor does it aid our communities.

IT IS DEMANDING to try to understand people who engage with life very differently from the way we do. But it can also be fascinating and hugely instructive. Why do we read books, travel far from home, shop for exotic items, see movies, listen to music, have friends, lovers, neighbours? Isn't it so that we can see through thousands of eyes, and not just our own? Hear with thousands of ears, and not just our own? Listen to thousands of voices, and not just our own?

Indeed, it may be one of the great gifts of the unsettled, demanding life so characteristic of these times that it does sufficiently disrupt our certainties to force us to recognise that a fully human life can be lived many different ways; that rapid judgements are rarely helpful; that it is possible to be tolerant in ways that go far beyond mindless acceptance, or the kind of patronising sentimentality that many of us can fall into when we contemplate lives that seem less 'lucky' than our own.

A Mother's Disgrace is a tender, thoughtful autobiographical account of a man in early mid-life being pushed by curiosity and circumstance to re-examine his most fundamental labels. In the book, writer Robert Dessaix tells the story of meeting

Fazil Iskander, a novelist from Abkhazia, part of the former Soviet Union.

'I first met him in his Moscow flat in one of those apartment blocks on Red Army Street reserved, in Soviet times at least, for writers. Over tea the talk veered round to religion. Abkhazia is partly Christian, partly Muslim, although the dominant ideology was in those days atheist. So the topic was bound to come up. I asked Fazil if he was Christian or Muslim. "Oh, I'm a non-believer," he said, using a much less strident word [in Russian] than "atheist" with its overtones of Soviet dogmatism. "But I don't want to rid the world of believers. There will always be believers and there will always be non-believers. I like it like that. I'd hate to live in a world where there were no believers."'

Robert then reflects on the richness not just of a pluralistic society, but of a pluralistic mind. He goes on: 'In saying that, hardly noticing he'd said it, he'd inadvertently prised open some fuggy, boxed-in part of my brain . . . Sitting right there on his sofa, staring at the blue-and-gold teapot, I thought seriously for the first time of letting the believer inside myself talk to the non-believer, letting the knowing part converse in good humour with the mystified and the credulous with the sceptical. It was a wicked feeling.'

This is an inspired piece of writing, and I had my own 'wicked feeling' of delight reading it because it so pointedly captures the way in which most of us censor the possibilities for rich exploration and cross-fertilisation even within our own minds. Yet it is really only when the believer within our own mind no longer needs to shun the non-believer, who is also within our own mind, that we can begin a true dialogue with the believers and non-believers alike who live in the near and distant lands beyond ourselves.

EXPANDING YOUR SENSE of who you are, and simultaneously expanding the inner ground of your self, is an achievable human enterprise. Indeed, there is no mystery about how to re-own your projections. You do it as you would any other shadow-redeeming activity, by paying attention: by listening to what you say and how you say it; by watching for the discrepancies between what you profess to believe and how you live; by looking for the gaps between your rhetoric and your behaviour. You do it above all by pausing when the temptation arises to accuse others, *tolerating your own uncertainty about what's going on*, and asking yourself: 'What is my part in this drama? Why am *I* feeling angry, accusatory, upset or self-righteous? What's going on with me here?'

I AM AT the local swimming pool, waiting for my daughter. Two boys are talking next to me. I listen with increasing interest.

'You shouldn't be rude to your mum,' one says.

'But you're rude to your mum,' the other replies.

'That's not the point,' the first boy valiantly persists. 'You are *very* rude to your mum.'

'You're rude to your mum, too.'

Later, thinking about this conversation, I could again sense the first boy's frustration with his lively, intelligent friend who was quite unwilling to take on that the topic under discussion was not the first boy and *his* mum, but the second boy's behaviour towards his own mum.

The persistence with which the second boy deflected the potentially uncomfortable focus of the conversation is totally understandable in a child. Unfortunately, it is also typical of adults who are unwilling to look at aspects of their behaviour for which they should be taking responsibility. This kind of exchange is not something children will simply grow out of, no matter how intelligent. The majority will, as adults, continue to deflect comments about their behaviour or attitudes in remarkably similar ways.

'It really upsets me that you are so often late for appointments.'

'You're often late, too.'

'I try to let you know when I'm going to be late. But I have told you so often that it really bothers me when you are late and don't let me know . . .'

'I am not late any more often than you are.'

'It worries me when you are late . . .'

'Well, that's your problem, then. Nothing to do with me . . .'

IT TAKES MORE than intelligence to attend closely to what other people are saying to you, and not to hear every potentially critical remark as an attack. It takes self-awareness, flexibility, commitment to self-responsibility, and self-love, too, I think, to stand your emotional ground, and to learn something about yourself, instead of rushing in with defences or defensive accusations.

This implies, too, of course, a readiness to face reality, which is not always an attractive proposition. As Wallace Stevens observed, in 'Reply to Papini':

The way through the world
Is more difficult to find than the way beyond it.

Yet, plainly, when we can struggle to forego the quick satisfactions of defending ourselves through the expression of anger or contempt, or of proving someone else wrong, or of telling other people how they should think, it becomes much easier, and certainly more rewarding, to relate in an open, even affiliative way. Such relating opens up the possibility of a rich sharing of ideas and experiences, without the cost to yourself as well as others that always accompanies violent and destructive feelings, no matter how they may be justified either by the 'correctness' of your position or the flagrant 'incorrectness' of the position held by someone else.

KATY IS A close friend. Observing her over the last year has given me a marvellous example of how this process of projection, and re-owning one's projections, can work. She is an oncologist in her late forties and had not been in a sexual relationship for some years when she fell (cautiously) in love with Isabelle, also a physician, with whom she feels there is a real possibility of a life-long commitment.

Katy explains: 'Because I hadn't been sexually intimate with anyone for so long, and had not exposed myself to how I am in a close-up, committed intimacy, I could observe with a rather painful clarity how my own moods utterly colour how I perceive Isabelle. When I feel self-critical I certainly notice small faults in her. When I feel self-loathing because I am over-tired, or fretful about my work or getting older or whatever it happens to be, any small frailties in her fill my vision. They don't replace my self-criticism, I might say. They add to it. There were several anxious weeks when to be honest I thought that this would mean I couldn't continue with the relationship – not because of her, but because I so much dis-liked my own sourness and pettiness being revealed to me in this way. Then I decided this was my last chance to have the kind of love I believe is possible. I took myself in hand and resolved to use those perverse "revelations" about Isabelle as a barometer of my own feelings of self-love or self-loathing, and to do something about it. The outcome has been confronting, but invaluable. I know more than I used to about myself. I feel more open to Isabelle than I thought possible. For the first time in years I am experiencing what a wonderful teacher an intimate relationship can be.'

DREAM THERAPIST SALLY Gillespie also powerfully described to me the rewards of taking time to observe what is happen-ing within ourselves, and between ourselves and others. She has particular sympathy for those who do indeed try to be tol-erant, good, even virtuous, but continually fall short of those high ideals.

'It's really interesting for those of us who get into spiritual striving that we can fall out of tolerance for our full nature and for the fact that we can be at times petty, mean, depressed or many of the things that we feel at a spiritual level we should be "above". And yet life is extremely gruelling, and our natures are *human*. I think I have had to learn a great deal because I have wanted to leave my human nature behind very often – and it has only created larger shadows in doing it.

'In my dreamwork groups, week after week, people come in with all kinds of stories of their weeks and, sitting there, us being tolerant of each other, and tolerant of what's going on in our lives, we find that we can work with that substance rather than reject it and then be left with nothing to work with. When we do that – when we say that nothing that has happened to us is of any importance – we are only left with emptiness.

'We need to tolerate the fact that we repeat our patterns over and over again, but that each time we repeat that pattern and see ourselves doing it – something that feels destructive in some way – that is actually the time that we can work with it. It is like the herpes virus! You only get to work on it in the body when it's active! When it is most obstructive, it is also most instructive. And if we can be tolerant of that and say, "Look, here it is again. This is a time yet again for me to look at this and work with it", then we get back to the dance [of our life]. If I can dance with my difficulty instead of abusing myself or life that it has happened, and if I can bring a little humour into it, a little bit of play, then the tolerance can become quite natural and easy. It doesn't take enormous

self-discipline or will to be tolerant. It just takes edging ourselves out of the black hole to be able to work *and* play with
whatever we discover.

'It's part of humanness that we are not perfect at every
moment of the day. We need to find a way to see our faults,
accept that they're there, and then find a way to work with
them. And see that life has not ended because we have cheated
ourselves or others – *and* that we don't have to repeat that.'

PEOPLE RAISED IN more or less tolerant households have had
that tolerance of difference modelled in the actions and attitudes of their parents. However, for tolerance to take hold,
there has to be an act of will, a choice *for* tolerance, rather than
just a putting on of a raincoat because it happens to be hanging on the family peg.

Tolerance may arise quite naturally in some people, but for
most of us, it develops out of an everyday series of humbling
or tempering experiences that demonstrate to us that, for all
our longings to be different, 'special', or unsullied by the
defects we so clearly see in others, we are in fact much more
like other people than we are unlike them.

'A life of ease,' wrote Jung, 'has convinced everyone of all
the material joys, and has even compelled the spirit to devise
new and better ways to material welfare, but it has never *produced* spirit. Probably only suffering, disillusion, and self-denial
do that.' This is a painful lesson to learn. We want spirit. We
want zest, warmth and sufficient insight to live life fully and

generously. But we certainly do not want to suffer. Zen teacher
Charlotte Joko Beck points this out in pithy Zen fashion: 'We
imagine that we will be able to be nice to others without it
being inconvenient.'

Whatever our differences in class, gender or beliefs, most of
us occupy a kind of middle ground between kindness and
indifference. Or, if we broaden our view to take in greater
extremes, between lives of luminous generosity and compassion for others and an inner bleakness exemplified by gross acts
of violence towards others.

Out of laziness, or awe, most of us would feel we could
safely leave it to Mother Teresa to be Mother Teresa. With
probably much the same degree of certainty, we generally
assume that murderers, rapists and terrorists inhabit an inner
world that is equally different from our own. This may be true,
although only in a matter of degree. Mother Teresa was once a
little girl who surely had moments of murderous rage. And
each rapist and murderer, no matter how foul in adulthood,
was once a baby who raised dinner-smeared cheeks for someone to wipe clean and then perhaps kiss.

Buddhism draws our attention to something else that
Mother Teresa and the most violent person share. Both want to
be happy, both want to avoid suffering. And so do you and
I. That one of them goes about it in a way that makes sublime
good sense, and the other goes about it in a way that makes no
sense at all, does not diminish what they share.

IN HER NOVEL *Before and After*, Rosellen Brown carefully and
credibly describes a decent, tolerant family who raise a beloved

son apparently capable, at the age of seventeen, of bashing his girlfriend to death.

Ah, you might say, here are the ways in which his family is unlike ours. The father is an artist – mercurial, boyish. The mother is a paediatrician – restrained, intelligent, dedicated. Could the combined frailties of these parents be fairly said to be any greater than those of most other families doing their best?

As you consider this family's situation – and Rosellen Brown's measured writing allows you to do precisely that – tolerance may prevent you from rushing to judge them. Holding back from condemning these parents and their child-rearing does not excuse what the son has done. Tolerance simply warns you: there is a vast range of human behaviour that exists at least potentially in each one of us, *which makes the issues of choice, will, self-responsibility and care for others all the more vital and all the more urgent.*

Analyse Mother Teresa's DNA and that of a mass killer. What makes them different would not be revealed. Those differences can only be measured through the effects of their actions. One acts with love. The other is driven by anger, hatred, fear.

Yet life can seem less stark and more complicated than that. In *Before and After*, Brown has presented us with a well-educated, loved, middle-class boy who is capable of killing his girlfriend and, as it turns out, of stoning a dog he had tied to a tree. Not nice. Yet this same boy is also widely known in his small town to be kind, courteous, thoughtful. A boy almost like any other.

TOLERANCE IS NOT just a good idea; it is a highly dynamic virtue. As an idea only, it is soggy liberalism at its least appealing. Put into practice, however, tolerance has an immediate effect.

Like all the other virtues, the practice of it depends on love – for oneself, for others, for the universe. It is most powerfully practised from the perspective (the depth and spaciousness) of the self, not from the ego. This poetic, inspiring definition of the self supports that vision. Writing in *Mystery of Mandalas* – mandalas are themselves infinitely varied symbols of the self – Heita Copony calls the self 'the secret, immortal centre of the personality'.

When we actively remember that not only do we ourselves have such an 'immortal centre', but so does every other human being, it softens how we can think about tolerance. Copony has written, 'When we see beyond the outer appearance of another person, through the eyes of love and from the heart, then the true secret and the beauty of that person's soul is revealed to us.'

Intolerance is symptomatic of fear, ignorance, bitterness. It can also express envy and even rage that someone has what you do not. If tolerance towards others is going to exist relatively free of those negative, destructive emotions, it must be based on the conscious cultivation of tolerance towards yourself. This need not mean making excuses for yourself when you behave like a fool or a sadist. On the contrary, the practice of tolerance would make foolishness or sadism much less likely, or certainly much less habitual and automatic.

Tolerance allows you to develop a frame of mind that is neither clinging nor condemning; that is neither mechanically self-sufficient, nor empty; that avoids the pitfalls both of self-inflation and of debasement; that acknowledges fear, and speaks to it with love.

Tolerance helps you to accept yourself – no easy task – and allows you to extend to others the precious, spacious benefit of the doubt. If that is met with hostility or suspicion, it is tolerance that will allow you to respond resiliently, aware that in betraying your trust, the person is expressing their own angry, guilty or defensive world view, which may have little or nothing to do with you as an individual human being, and in no way predicts the success or failure of any future encounters you will have with other people.

It is also tolerance, as well as flexibility, that supports you in the search for a creative way to meet the reality of constant change. The more psychologically healthy people are, the easier it is for them to accept that because life itself is dynamic, change is inevitable. They can face knowing that, and move with the results. They may even find opportunities in those changes, while still appreciating what is established and familiar.

The person who is less flexible, less tolerant, and probably more fearful, will resist change. This can, when carefully observed by writers and actors, make for hilarious comedy, and a great deal of situational comedy actually is based on only minimally exaggerated versions of how a character can be stuck with an emotion or set of responses long after they have ceased to be appropriate. In real life, however, such paralysis is usually less amusing.

A MAN IS unable to get work. This is a painfully common story these days, but this particular man has excellent qualifications in an area of the building industry where work is still available, yet he is unable to face – something. Sometimes he complains to his wife and friends that he would be bored by his colleagues. They are all fools, greedy, or crass. Sometimes he says he has been out of his field for too long, or is too old to spend a lot of time outdoors.

Clearly something *is* wrong. The man does suffer, not least from the increasing boredom of his own company, but also from anxiety that he is asking too little of himself.

A year goes by, then another. The man disallows any mention of his inability to return to work. His family must creep around the topic in the same way that the family of an addict will creep around the truth of that family member's addiction. The power of his own avoidances silences everyone.

His reluctance to find work is a matter of central importance to the whole family but because that cannot be spoken about – because he himself cannot tolerate speaking about it or hearing it spoken about – family members are silenced on almost everything else that matters. In the midst of a crisis, they are reduced to platitudes and half-truths. They are drained of energy, because it takes so much energy not to burst out with what should be said.

The man continues to be silent and unyielding on this matter, but in speaking about others, *he is as critical and intolerant of their human frailties as he is unconsciously critical and intolerant of himself.*

The man is frequently self-denigrating. He thinks that it is honest to turn his considerable wit against himself. But his behaviour speaks of self-pity, not of insight. It makes other people uncomfortable and resentful. Realistically, not much will change until the man is willing to look at the effects of his own behaviour. Perhaps he will have some chance of discovering what keeps him angry, fearful and immobilised. Perhaps somewhere in his psyche a war is raging between the defeated 'good husband and father', who genuinely does want to make some contribution to his family's wellbeing, and a sulky, self-absorbed adolescent figure who is saying that he is not going to go out the door before he is ready, and that meantime he doesn't give a damn what anybody thinks because maybe today he is not actually feeling bright enough or safe enough even to get out of bed.

IT IS OFTEN within the hothouse of our own family circle that we exhibit our own most intolerable behaviours, and weigh up whether we can accept the intolerable judgements or behaviours of others. Sometimes these behaviours arise out of rage; sometimes out of disappointment.

How we tolerate the parents we have, rather than the parents we might have wished for, or the adult children we have, rather than those we believe we deserved, may be the litmus test of our tolerance. For can there be much merit in practising this virtue for faceless groups of people whom we will never meet if we cannot bear being in the presence of our own parents or accepting our adult children as they are?

Sitting in a room, perhaps a room that is redolent with memories, *hating* being there with someone who is related to you by the closest ties of blood, is an exceptionally grim experience. It is also one that arouses strong defences.

'He was always vile to me. Why should I care about him
    now?'
'I did everything I could and got no thanks for it.'
'I'd have to be a fool to go back there and have them tell me
    where I've gone wrong in my life.'
'Mum's only ever cared about her boyfriends. Never about me.'
'He never asks me how I am. He just goes on and on about
    my brothers. He never even asks me about my kids. I just
    don't exist for him, no matter what I do.'

In every story of rage and separation between adult children
and their parents there is tremendous pain. Sometimes that
pain is so great it is literally impossible for those people to be
in physical proximity. Could this be because the potential
between parents and children for love and trust to develop is
so exceptional that when it fails it leaves a chasm to be filled
with misery, cynicism, rage and disappointment?

Edward is a thirty-five-year-old farmer who has always had
an uncomfortable feeling of being an outsider in his own
family. He left home at the age of seventeen and, for a long
time, lived in a predominantly Maori area of New Zealand, but
he has kept in intermittent touch with his parents and brothers and sisters, all of whom now live in Australia. In just the last
year, these familial relationships have shifted significantly.

'Members of my family at times express very racist views.
I've been through tremendous arguments. I came to learn
that arguments weren't getting anywhere, but I couldn't
respect myself if I let it all totally go either, so I had to find a
point where I can make a few comments to make it clear that

I don't agree with what is being said, but at the same time, not go into a useless crusade to try to change their opinions. Then also I realised that we have had this argument for years and that what is under it really is that they weren't going to accept the indigenous people of Australia or New Zealand *and they didn't accept the indigenous me either.* Everyone had to be "civilised". Underneath that was all my hurt and bitterness that they couldn't accept me. And they can't accept their own "indigenousness" either. They have striven their whole lives to live this "civilised" life, a "reasonable" life, and had enshrined in their value system a lot of very good values, but these other ideas, too. So much of my hurt was that they were rejecting me along with this. But having seen this – and I have only come to see it relatively recently – now I can be so much lighter about it. I can have some humour about it. The arguments are different for me. All these layers have been stripped off. Now it's become easier to see what my parents have gone through themselves. I am more admiring of them even if our views are very different on some quite crucial issues.

'We are so much into being nice, agreeable, charming. At the ego level. But I can now see that we find it very hard to know how to experience ourselves when something threatens to disrupt that. When there is something in ourselves or others that we can't tolerate.'

YOUNG CHILDREN'S TOLERANCE for their parents is usually boundless, even in extreme situations. Their need to idealise their parents and forgive them for their failures, even for their cruelty, is compelling because as long as children's own ego-development and emergent sense of self depend at least in part on their positive identification with their parents, they cannot afford easily to give up their illusions or hopes that the 'good-enough' parent continues to exist within or alongside the parent who may truly be failing them. When young children are openly angry with or critical of their parents, or physically attack them, it is usually within a context of relative safety: they can trust that their parents will tolerate the attacks and will not attack them in return – or die or abandon them – and can eventually set limits. This is not to say that these children may not then grow up affected by the feelings of rage, envy or jealousy that they have experienced towards their parents. Probably all children experience such feelings or their effects, and whether they learn from the 'aftershocks' – whether these increase their resilience to disappointment and contribute to their capacity to cope with life creatively – is central to the ongoing processes of maturation.

If young children are largely forgiving, tolerant and idealising, however, adolescents present a very different picture. And sometimes that reactive period of adolescence – that moment when we 'compensate' for our earlier idealisations by cutting our parents down to half their size, by letting them know how *unlike* us they are – is where we stay. We may become capable of bringing sympathy, insight, wisdom, patience, tolerance to a huge variety of people and circumstances, yet never truly accept the disappointment that lines the gulf between our idealised parents and the flesh-and-blood human beings who were or are our actual parents.

Of her own father, the writer Doris Lessing has said, 'We use our parents like recurring dreams, to be entered into when needed; they are always there for love or for hate; but it occurs to me that I was not always there for my father.'

All art forms, but perhaps most obviously writing, are rich with overt or covert examples of how painfully unfinished most parent–child relationships are, and with what difficulty an adult moves beyond the stages of idealisation and blame to something that is more genuinely accepting, and that allows the dead, as well as the living, greater peace. Yet that lesson, too, is part of tolerance.

John Fowles is the author of a number of successful, elaborate, passionately written works of fiction, which include *The Magus* and *The French Lieutenant's Woman*. With a considerable sense of loss for what might have been, he reflects on his life as the son of a highly constrained father.

'Successful artistic parents seem very rarely to give birth to equally successful artistic sons and daughters, and I suspect it may be because the urge to create, which must always be partly the need to escape everyday reality, is better fostered – despite modern educational theory – not by a sympathetic and "creative" childhood environment, but the very opposite, by pruning and confining natural instinct. (Nine-tenths of all artistic creation derives its basic energy from the engine of repression and sublimation, and well beyond the strict Freudian definition of those terms.) That I should have differed so much from my father in this seems to me in retrospect not in the least a matter for Oedipal guilt, but a healthy natural process, just as the branches of a healthy tree do not try to occupy one another's territory. That they grow in different directions and ways *does not mean that they do not share a same mechanism of need, a same set of deeper rules* [my italics].'

Years after writing those lines, Fowles reflected, obliquely, on the difficulties of tolerating even the knowledge that one may love a parent in such a way that the possibility to express it in any direct or disinhibiting form becomes tragically unavailable. 'I realise now,' he writes, 'that he severely pruned me by telling me so little of himself, in part obeying his own intense hatred of any exposure and over-intimacy . . .

'Over twenty years ago I wrote a poem about my father, which, very typically, I never dared show him. Both our sadness and our mystery lay less in what I did not say (I loved him) than that I could not. That great cultural glacier, which I think of now as the last and perhaps most fatal bequest of the British Empire, froze so many others besides us, and not only in the middle classes. I hope a thaw has now begun, and pray the future will not too contemptuously mock our choked, self-murdered spirits.'

HOW YOU THINK about tolerance depends in part on where you stand between two divergent versions of reality. On one side is the version that says you're a separate human being who interacts through a finite lifetime with a number of other human beings, each one of whom is living their own independent existence. On the other side is the version that tells you that you're part of a greater whole. Proponents of this version may talk about energy fields, the cosmos, or reflections of the Divine. Either way, it adds up to a view of life that emphasises unity rather than separateness.

Albert Einstein, no mean mind, held the latter view. He explained it memorably: 'A human being is part of a whole called by us the "Universe", a part limited in time and space. He experiences himself, his thoughts and feelings, as something separated from the rest – a kind of optical delusion of his consciousness. This delusion is a kind of prison for us, restricting us to our personal desires and to affection for a few persons nearest us. *Our task must be to free ourselves from this prison by widening our circle of compassion to embrace all living creatures and the whole of nature in its beauty* [my italics].'

My own experience has taught me that thinking, taking action, living is best done collectively. (Perhaps it can only be done collectively; the issue is one of awareness.) This is a strange thing perhaps for a writer to be saying. After all, I work alone, and need to spend time alone in order to think, write and intellectually and emotionally survive. But when this 'aloneness' feels good, it is because I am in touch with that part of myself that can respond to ideas that fascinate me, to people whose thoughts nourish me, to a sense of where I am in nature (awake to the weather, to the sounds around me, to the feel of my cat's fur when he jumps on my desk, to the rumblings of my stomach, to how good food tastes when I eat, to some thought as to where that food has come from), to an awareness that what I do, *how I am* affects others, and that *how others are* affects me. In none of that am I any more alone than when I can sink into meditation and leave the confinement of my rational mind and enter the spaciousness where mind ends and Mind begins.

In none of that is there loneliness, but there are, of course, other periods when I do feel alone. Whether or not I am with other people at such times does not substantially affect how alone I feel. And at those times I am probably most touchy, least tolerant: of my own human frailties as well as those of others.

Then the wheel turns again. Unity comes back into view. I am 'more of a piece' within myself, more at peace within myself; and, outside myself, I can again at least glimpse that sacred 'circle of compassion'. As Zen master Suzuki Roshi taught: 'Everything is perfect. But there is always room for improvement.'

IN HER SUPREME novel *To the Lighthouse*, published in 1927 after the devastating losses and social upheavals that accompanied the First World War, but before those produced by the Second, Virginia Woolf looked for ways to use words to express the unity or perhaps the unifying nature of love that I am trying to describe.

'Directly one looked up and saw them [the family], what she called "being in love" flooded them. They became part of that unreal but penetrating and exciting universe which is the world seen through the eyes of love. The sky stuck to them; the birds sang through them. And, what was even more exciting, she felt, too, as she saw Mr Ramsey bearing down and retreating, and Mrs Ramsey sitting with James in the window and the cloud moving and the tree bending, how life, from

being made up of little separate incidents which one lived one
by one, became curled and whole like a wave which bore one
up with it and threw one down with it, there, with a dash on
the beach.'

YET INTO THAT idyllic landscape, where, as in an Impres-
sionist painting, no single thing is given more weight in the
observer's vision of it than anything else, bursts the painful
awareness of someone who has hurt you or others you love;
someone who has behaved outrageously or cruelly; someone
whose actions you have every right to despise, condemn and
should never tolerate.

Zen teacher Thich Nhat Hanh points out that tolerance of
such a person – though not of their actions – arises only
through understanding. 'We have to understand why he is that
way, how he has come to be like that, why he does not see
things the way we do. Understanding a person brings us the
power to love and accept him. And the moment we love and
accept him, he ceases to be our enemy. To "love our enemy" is
impossible, because the moment we love him, he is no longer
our enemy.

'To love him, we must practice deep looking in order to
understand him . . . When we understand another person, we
understand ourselves better. And then when we understand
ourselves better, we understand the other person better, too.'

This depth of insight, and of compassion, cannot be
achieved through an act of will only. Nor, when you are
affected deeply, can it be achieved rationally. Our rational mind
will scream in protest at the very idea of looking deeply into

the mind of our personal enemy, whether it is a solitary person
or a group of people.

So, in the wake of suffering, or in the face of continuing
injustice, *for tolerance to exist in your heart as well as in your mind,*
it is necessary to call on your heart's depths, to look steadily
through the eyes of our common soul and not your individual ego; and to call for help from the most profound forces
of love.

In Matthew's Gospel, Christ says, 'Love your enemies, bless
them that curse you, do good to them that hate you, and pray
for them which despitefully use you, and persecute you; that ye
may be the children of your Father which is in heaven: *for he
maketh his sun to rise on the evil and the good, and sendeth rain on
the just and the unjust* [my italics].'

This passage describes unity in its highest state of perfection, while also conveying a boundless lack of discrimination.
But it, too, must be approached and understood as a lesson that
asks us to relinquish our defences and sacrifice some of the
comfort of our rage.

All acts of intolerance express discrimination: a sense of difference between you and me that is great enough to allow me
to treat you badly, believing that I can do so and not hurt
myself, or allow you to treat me indifferently, ignorant that the
heartbeat of my life and yours functions as one.

So painful, terrifying and mysterious is that difference, it can
only be a great virtue, a virtue that is expressive of love, that
will move to bridge it. 'There are four kinds of people who are
good,' Krishna tells Arjuna and us in the Bhagavad Gita, 'and
the four love me, Arjuna: the person of sorrows, the seeker of

knowledge, the seeker of something he treasures, and the person of vision.

'The greatest of these is the person of vision, who is ever one, who loves the One. For I love the person of vision, and the person of vision loves me.'

However delicately, however tenuously, tolerance reaches out from the heart and says: 'I loathe what you have done. I despise what you have done. I will never tolerate your actions, or condone them. Yet I must also acknowledge: *we are in this life together*. The suns rises on you, no less than it rises on me. The rain falls on you, no less than it falls on me.'

Christ's teaching rebukes the outrageous prejudice that runs through much organised religion proclaiming that some people are more deserving of God's love than others. Yet as distasteful as that prejudice is – and *wrong* – it is what we emulate and cultivate when we, too, feel free to judge, convict, condemn, almost always in complete ignorance of the mysteries that lie buried in another person's heart.

Speaking of the men who in 1986 raped, tortured and killed his daughter, twenty-six-year-old Anita Cobby, Garry Lynch said: 'In the early stages I wanted Anita's killers to suffer, and if I wanted to go back to that mentality I'd say, "No, they didn't get adequate punishment. Let's get hold of the bastards and tear them, slowly, limb from limb. Let's flagellate them, peel their skin off in small strips while they are still alive." But you can't do that.'

Garry Lynch, with his wife, Peg, not only became a support person and advocate for other families of murder victims, he also spent five years as a member of the Serious

Offenders Review Council. But has he forgiven the men who stole life from his daughter and happiness from his family, and were seemingly incapable of expressing the slightest remorse for their actions? 'I do not excuse the five people who murdered Anita, or what they did, but I forgive their souls. I believe their soul is another part, it belongs to another region.'

Reading Lynch's autobiography, *Struck by Lightning*, I was repeatedly moved by his insight and persistent courage. Among many memorable moments in the book, one particularly held me, perhaps because it so directly expresses this elusive notion of unity, and does so without preciousness or sanctimony. Writing about the 1950s, when he must have been a rare Australian man indeed to be reading the Upanishads and learning to meditate, Lynch describes an out-of-body experience: 'I remember this total awareness of the fullness of being, of feeling gloriously uplifted, and saying quietly to myself, "So this is what it's all about." Then I came back down gently into my body, gave it a little bit of a shake, and a sigh, and for the next three months I don't think my feet touched ground. Everything, even a little dog turd on the footpath, looked good to me. *Everything was nature.*'

HERE IS THICH Nhat Hanh again, speaking about the person whom we may feel justified in condemning: 'If we visualize ourselves as being born in his condition, we may see that we could become exactly like him. When we do that, compassion arises in us naturally, and we see that the other person is to be helped and not punished . . . Suddenly, the one we have been calling our enemy becomes our brother or sister. This is the true teaching of Jesus.'

And if we cannot visualise being born in that loathed person's condition, if there is nothing in us that allows us to imagine the inner desolation and confusion of being that mass murderer, rapist or abuser, and to know that in imagining this we are denying neither the sorrow of their victim, nor the abhorrence of their acts; if we are quite unable to separate our loathing of the 'sin' from the 'sinner', then this may be a failure of our own imagination.

Sri Sathya Sai Baba offers a universal teaching when he says: 'Whatever acts a good or bad person may do, the fruits thereof follow him and will never stop pursuing him . . . When you are invaded by anger, practise silence or remember the name of the Lord. Do not remind yourself of things which will inflame your anger more. That will do incalculable harm.'

TOLERANCE IS AN act of love, a commitment to the belief that none of us has a life more precious than another's, and a vital articulation of our common humanity. To learn the value of tolerance, one does not give up making judgements about what is right or wrong; about what will bring happiness or take it away. The practice of tolerance does not mean condoning behaviour that robs other people of their freedom or their happiness. On the contrary. It frees us to be very clear indeed about what we must be aware of within ourselves and what we are powerful enough to be aware of in others. Tolerance simply says (or not so simply says): these actions are human actions. They belong within the realm of human experience. They are committed by members of the human family. *And I am part of that family also.*

In our efforts to understand this, the fourteenth-century mystical poet Kabir helps us out:

> Here is Kabir's idea: as the river gives itself into the ocean,
> what is inside me moves inside you.

When we ration our love, hoard our compassion, and barricade ourselves behind our valid reasons why this person deserves our tolerance, but that person does not, why this group's actions can be tolerated, but that group's cannot, why this part of ourselves is acceptable, but that is not, we defy that crucial teaching. We are forgetting the sacred, healing, universal knowledge that God's sun (in psychological terms: warmth, the power of reason, thought, speech, Logos) rises on 'the evil and the good', and his rain (moisture, growth, cleansing, emotion, Eros) falls on 'the just and unjust', between whom the difference may be just a sliver.

Forgiveness

The holiest of all the spots on earth is where an ancient

hatred has become a present love.

A COURSE IN MIRACLES

Forgiveness, as an act of love, is felt, not achieved. It can be given, but it may not always be received. It cannot be bestowed as either a triumph over another person, or as the means to secure their humiliation or acquiescence.

It is most healing, most profound when it grows out of humility and realism, a hard-won sense that, whether you are entirely to blame in these events and I am blameless, there is in each of us insufficiencies and imperfections that can be our greatest teachers.

You may not recognise forgiveness even when you have experienced it, for what we are seeking to know better is subtle, difficult to define, multi-layered and contains an element of magic. You will, however, feel it in your body. Something – very nearly a 'thing' – has left you. You are no longer carrying the load you were; you have put it down. Anger may have given way to sorrow or regret. Rage may have flattened out into indifference or pity. Into what seemed black and white has crept a little grey.

The muscular tensions that you had come to assume were normal are eased. You are less vulnerable to infection or to far more serious illness. Your immune system lifts. Your face muscles let down. Food tastes better. The world looks better. Depression radically diminishes. You are more available to other people and a great deal more available to yourself, yet you think about yourself less, and less anxiously.

Forgiveness does not lead to forced reunions. There may be some people whom we are better never to see, to hear from, or even to think about for more than a few moments at any time. Letting people go from our thoughts, releasing them from any wish that we could harm them or that they will be harmed, brings us cleansing, sometimes exhilarating, freedom.

Forgiveness can be discovered in a moment, but more often it takes weeks, months or sometimes years. It is something we can open to, invite in, think about and desire. It rarely goes one way only. We may need to learn how to forgive ourselves before we can accept others' forgiveness of us for the ways in which we have hurt them, or before we can offer our forgiveness, silently or face to face, for the ways they have hurt us. The ancient Chinese text the I Ching teaches, 'You cannot overcome the enemy until you've healed in yourself that which you find despicable in them.'

'That which you find despicable' will not be neatly mirrored in individual acts. It is simply the painful, unwelcome recognition that we are somehow, however mysteriously or even unwillingly, in this world together, facing constant choices: that we can be part of the world's brutality or that we will do what we can to relieve it. Glimpsing the meaning in that paradoxically bestows an ease and release that hatred and division never can.

'Forgiveness is a lifetime aim,' said one woman I spoke to. She is someone who has spent most of that lifetime regretting, blaming and grieving. But now she is able to say, with fire and feeling and delight: 'In ultimately forgiving, one can release life. One can go into death singing because one has released oneself from the chains of life, from life's lessons, from the chains of love, from the people you've got here. It's that ineffability of forgiveness. When it comes, your soul leaps.'

FORGIVENESS DEEPLY OFFENDS the rational mind. When someone has hurt us, wounded us, abused us; when someone has stolen peace of mind or safety from us; when someone has harmed or taken the life of someone we love; or when someone has simply misunderstood or offended us, there is no reason why we should let that offence go. No reason why we should try to understand it. No reason why we should hope for enlightenment for that person. No reason why, from our own pain and darkness, we should summon compassion and insight for that person, as well as for ourselves.

To grope our way towards forgiveness, we may need momentarily to circumvent the rational mind, or transcend it. Yet the rational mind is the known ground that we share. There is no easy way to talk of circumventing or transcending it. And there is certainly no easy way to put forgiveness into practice.

As challenging and single-pointed as it is, forgiveness may be the supreme virtue, the most virtuous of the virtues, the apotheosis of love, for it declares: 'I will attempt to go on loving the life in you, or the divine in you, or the soul in you, even when I totally abhor what you have done or what you stand for. What's more, I will attempt to see you as my equal, and your life as having equal value to my own, even when I despise what you do and everything you stand for.'

This is, of course, awesome to translate into practice. In emotional terms, it is Everest without oxygen; Wimbledon without a racquet; La Scala without a score.

In the Bhagavad Gita, the most profound of the Hindu scriptures and one of the greatest spiritual teachings of any tradition, we can find a refreshingly straightforward recognition of how difficult the practice of forgiveness is. In the Gita, it is clearly stated that 'loving-forgiveness' is expected only of the Brahmin: 'The works of a Brahmin are peace; self-harmony, austerity and purity; loving-forgiveness and righteousness; vision and wisdom and faith.' The Brahmin were the highest social caste in India. I believe, however, it is possible to understand this instruction not in the tragic context of gross social privilege, but as it speaks to a heightened level of awareness that allows us to embrace the profundity of loving-forgiveness, and extend it also towards ourselves so that from all our innumerable failures to be loving, powerful and forgiving we draw increased determination and renewed insight.

BECAUSE FORGIVENESS IS, in its raw forms, a virtue that is as disturbing and confronting as it is healing and uplifting, it is important to be very clear indeed that there is no confusion between forgiving and condoning. The stark lack of sentimentality of this stance is reinforced and strengthened for me by author and therapist Dawna Markova when she writes: 'Forgiveness in no way justifies the actions that caused your wounding, nor does it mean you have to seek out those that harmed you. It is simply a movement to release and ease your heart of the pain and hatred that binds it. It is the harvested fruit of a season of darkness, followed by a season of growth, and very hard work.'

So, if I am able to forgive you for the harm that you have done to me, this is not because I am weak or masochistic. Nor am I saying that what you did or are continuing to do no longer matters. In forgiving you, I am not denying what you have done, minimising it, or making excuses for it. In fact, in disentangling myself from you in the ways that forgiveness allows, I may even see what you have done more vividly and clearly and have even stronger feelings against it.

Perhaps I will always be disgusted by what you have done. Perhaps I will never want to understand it. Perhaps I will never find myself able to be in a room with you, or to speak to you, or to acknowledge you. Yet if I have even set the intention in train to forgive you, I am acknowledging two crucial things.

The first is that I am capable of learning from my suffering.

The second is that I am willing to acknowledge that you are no less and no more deserving of love than I am.

Of course the rational mind rushes to tell me how crazy this is! Surely a good person is more deserving of love than some-one who is bad or evil? Surely a bad person is more deserving of harm than someone who is good? Yet I can find no evidence of that. What I do find is plenty of evidence to suggest that the 'bad' person, the 'evil' person, feels very little love, and often feels very little.

THE NEED FOR forgiveness begins with an act of betrayal, cruelty, separation or loss. Sometimes what is lost is trust or safety. Sometimes it is the actual presence of a beloved person. Sometimes it is a feeling of certainty about ourselves; about who we are, how we are seen, and what we stand for.

The suffering that precedes the need for forgiveness is never welcome. It may well be the dross in our lives that we will eventually and agonisingly turn into the gold of insight, but we are usually dragged towards this knowledge only with the greatest reluctance.

Jungian analyst Polly Young-Eisendrath captures this: 'When I look back over my development as a person and a therapist, I realize that nine-tenths of what has been important or essential was related to pain and suffering in some way. On the surface perhaps it sounds morbid, but I often value what's negative and difficult more than what is easy and comfortable. And I'm not a masochist. It's just that our difficult circumstances and negative emotions keep us awake [conscious, alert] far more fully than any pleasures do.'

Suffering pushes us to expand our emotional repertoire even as it pulls away the security of what is familiar, forcing us to consider and then re-consider what our values are and how they can support us; what meaning we dare to assign to events; what strengths we dare own up to; and what strengths we need rapidly to acquire. All of this is far too bracing to be in any way consoling, yet, as Young-Eisendrath points out, 'When suffering leads to meanings that unlock the mysteries of life, it strengthens compassion, gratitude, joy, and wisdom.'

THE STORY OF Demeter and Persephone tells us something useful about suffering and reflection, and offers a comfortingly partial version of forgiveness. You will probably remember that the goddess Persephone was young, free-spirited, beautiful and naive. This is a dangerous combination for a woman. It made Persephone vulnerable, and it made Demeter, her mother, afraid.

Persephone adored her mother, but she also wanted to be loved by a man. In fact, what she longed for most was to be swept off her feet into the realm of the 'other'; to trade the familiar ground of her own reality for the excitement of the unknown. The sweeping in her case was done by Hades (who was also known as Pluto, Lord of Riches). He was powerful, rich, clever, decisive. An ideal husband, you might think. The only problem was, the territory where he ruled was the underworld, the world of the dead, a place we might also think of as hell. Some families might find this acceptable, or might anyway be willing to overlook the ugly details of how his money was made and his power secured because there was so much money, and there was so much power.

This was not true of Demeter. She was a formidable goddess in her own right. Without her attention and blessing, winter could not come to an end, and the sun could not warm the earth. Without sunlight and warmed earth, no crops could grow and the people could not live. She was, literally, what stood between the people and death, between them and the far underground kingdom of Hades.

When Persephone had gone to the underworld with Hades, Demeter found herself lost and frighteningly alone in a state of rage and despair. 'How dare he take my daughter?' she shrieked, over and over again. 'How dare he!'

Weeks went by. Then months. Demeter remained as angry as she had ever been. Her anger was fed by her grief, and grief fed her anger.

That was about all the feeding that was going on as the people grew hungrier and hungrier without their crops, but Demeter was deaf to their misery. Her own misery was so great that she was lost in it. She had always been extraordinarily compassionate and generous. But now nothing else mattered to her except the loss of her daughter. Demeter's previously rich, abundant world had shrunk to a few monotonously repeated, compulsive images.

'If I had brought Persephone up to be less gullible, more discerning . . . this might not have happened. If only I had insisted that she stay home more; study harder; have a career of her own . . . this might not have happened. Perhaps if I had been less successful as a goddess, more like ordinary women, less engaged with helping others . . . this might not have happened. Perhaps she needed a father or a couple of brothers to help her to see that men are fallible, weak creatures and rarely the answer to a virgin's prayer . . .'

These lamentations did not help Demeter any more than her rage had.

Persephone, meantime, was enjoying life with Hades, but she missed her mother dreadfully. Hades offered her what her mother couldn't; her mother understood and loved her as Hades clearly wouldn't. Sometimes Persephone would wake in the morning, after a night of uneasy dreams, and she would be crying.

Although far away from her, Demeter could feel those tears on her daughter's cheeks. They touched her as her own rage and self-blame had not. They gave her fresh energy and the resolution that however impossible everyone said it would be to go to hell and return, she would risk going wherever necessary to find her beautiful, vibrant, hopeful daughter and fetch her home.

When Demeter finally reached the underworld, however, she discovered that Persephone did not want to come home. Certainly, she longed to be free to visit her mother, but not to leave Hades altogether. Demeter was outraged and freshly wounded. She blamed Hades for confusing Persephone and unduly influencing her, but no matter how she tried, she could not persuade her daughter to leave Hades forever to come home; nor could she persuade Hades to release her. Even her careful explanations, showing him that if the entire human race were wiped out Hades would have no fresh manpower in the underworld, could not dent his stubborn resolution.

At this terrible point, Demeter had to reach beyond the righteousness of her feelings. All of life depended on it. With great reluctance, she suggested that Persephone should come home for six months of the year only. With great reluctance,

Hades agreed that Persephone could go to her mother, but for not more than six months of each year.

To celebrate this victory, as partial as it was, Demeter returned with her daughter to earth and ended the long, long winter of terror, pain, injustice, helplessness, darkness and cold. In its place came spring: a time of renewal, warmth, light, planting, growth, sustenance, hope.

No one ever asked Demeter if she had forgiven Hades for seducing her beloved daughter and carrying her off. Certainly no one dared to ask her how she felt about her daughter's collusion with those events. (Some people believed that Persephone had not gone willingly, anyway. They believed she would never have left her mother voluntarily; that she had been seized, raped, dishonoured, blinded, and then mesmerised by Hades; and that might have been true.)

What people could agree on, however, is that life on earth could not have continued without Demeter facing the darkness of her righteous fury; without descending into the underworld; without opening herself to the reality she found there, as unpalatable as it was; without asking clearly for what she needed; without going beyond rage, self-pity, grief, even while that defied her sense of fairness and justice; without accepting that life would never again be as it once was; without adjusting herself to a changed reality; without acknowledging her continuing feelings of sadness as well as partial relief. Most significantly of all, Demeter could not have been part of earth's spring without allowing new life in herself also to begin.

THOSE CHANGES THAT took place within Demeter were exquisitely echoed by the changes that took place in the outer world: winter became spring.

You may feel, however, as though you are stranded in a place where even the first stages of forgiveness are beyond you. Let's suppose those first stages go something like this: forgetting about the matter some of the time; not actively wishing the other person harm; feeling that you are able to be patient with yourself. That may not sound like much to someone who is happily ignorant of the agony of having been profoundly betrayed or wounded, but for someone in the depths of suffering, any one of those first steps can seem far out of reach.

The seriousness of this is captured well by Jungian analyst and writer James Hillman in his famous essay 'Betrayal': 'We must be quite clear that forgiveness is no easy matter. If the ego has been wronged, the ego cannot forgive just because it "should", notwithstanding all the wider context of love and destiny. The ego is kept vital by its *amour-propre*, its pride and honour. Even where one wants to forgive, one finds one simply can't, because *forgiveness doesn't come from the ego* [my italics]. I cannot directly forgive, I can only ask, or pray, that these sins be forgiven. Wanting forgiveness to come and waiting for it may be all that one can do.'

It is my personal experience, and something that I have observed with many other people also, that waiting is a crucial stage in forgiveness. It is almost as though one has to incubate events, let them settle; unconsciously as well as consciously sort out what really matters and what does not, and then, slowly, and having achieved at least some distance, return to them, find the learning in them, *take from them what they can give*, and begin to look forward to moving on: although never to life as it once was.

It may also be that this settling allows the issue of forgiveness to move from the head to the heart, which is where it belongs. In conversation with me, writer Lindel Barker-Revell said, 'Forgiveness is a state of grace. It can't be applied as a concept. Compassion can rise up, but forgiveness is God-given, spirit-given. It must not be muddled up with judgement: who's right and who's not right. That separates us off from the healing power of love and I think that forgiveness is the greatest of the healing powers of love. It is an ineffable feeling.'

False forgiveness – forgiving because it is the decent thing to do, or is in some way advantageous – does not bring healing. It adds to the original injury and cannot resolve it. Resolution begins and ends with truthfulness, with a genuine expression of feeling, and the change this allows.

The question of whether it is ego that has been wounded or a deeper sense of oneself is also at best a tricky one. It is not self-evidently wrong to protect your ego. Sometimes it may be healthy and life-enhancing. However, it is extremely useful to be able to distinguish between protecting your ego and taking on board new information that may be difficult to assimilate but will support the broader vision of the self.

Certainly when one feels *offended* that is likely to be a question of one's ego reeling from a blow. Something like this occurs whenever you are in some way sidelined; when you are overlooked for a promotion; not invited to a party; ignored at a public function; receive a thoughtless comment about your work; are mistaken for someone else; are judged hastily and impersonally. Depending on what else is going on in your life – whether it is draining or supportive – and whether you generally enjoy feelings of health, wellbeing and optimism, those ego blows may either bounce off you lightly or bring you to your knees.

Wounding to your sense of self is of a different order. This is dead-winter territory where it may seem that you must now learn to live without trust, safety, mercy, love, and with no prospect of spring. Worse, although you may never have felt more alone, there is something horribly intimate about being wounded at this level. You may feel bound negatively to the person who has hurt you. This may be someone you once believed you knew well, perhaps someone you believed was capable of loving you and caring about you. But you were wrong. Or it may be someone you had never met before an isolated, tragic event brought your lives into a hideous collision.

OFFENDING GOES ON within most relationships, which does not in itself redeem it. Some offending is unintended: the result of genuine misunderstanding, ignorance, or a misreading of a situation. It is rarely useful to make too much of that, and even when there is a little less excuse, it is frequently possible for the sake of someone else to overlook a personal offence or to give up the brief satisfaction of pointing it out. It may, however, in other circumstances, be just as loving to say what is getting in the way, especially when the traces of a pattern are appearing, and if it can be done without adding the twin corrosives of self-pity and other-blaming.

Cartoonist and social observer Michael Leunig has discovered the benefits of waking up to what's going on, including offences, and feeling free to point them out. And free to receive some pointers in return.

Speaking to broadcaster Caroline Jones, he said: 'I got terribly depressed about ten years ago; deeply, deeply depressed, quite seriously depressed over a period of a couple of years. I think that depression was just having avoided and denied a lot of things that had happened to me, a lot of hurt. I didn't go into it. I didn't want to know about the pain and I somehow switched off. I understand now that it's better to be angry when you're angry and fight when you want to fight, and if you love something you love it, you express it . . . It seems that men suffer more from this than women. They don't know what it is they're feeling. They think they're feeling one thing . . . they get hurt and they pretend they're not hurt and they joke it away. They're hurt deep inside but they don't even recognise it, they're so removed. I think I was a bit like that, saying, "I can tough this out. I can bear this . . ." Say someone's just insulted me – "I don't care." But it hurts . . . it hurts. Now I tend to challenge – if someone hurts me maliciously I'll say, "Why did you say that?" It causes trouble; you become something of a troublemaker, but it's better for all in the end . . .

'There's something miraculous in it; it brings you into relationship with the other. And I'm talking about an honest exchange and a frank and emotional exchange, and to love you have to learn how to exchange, and you have to learn how to give it and to take it. And you've got to learn, I suppose, to hear the other. If you want to be heard, you've got to hear the other.'

Offending can lead to a real burst of understanding. You know more about how the other person sees you; you know something more about yourself. And if that 'something' is somewhat unpalatable, all the better. You have a chance then to transform what you are doing, or drop it. There is vitality in that, and power in its most attractive forms. The benefits of offending are lost, obviously, when offences can't be discussed openly; when someone clings to the fantasies that it is not 'nice' to be truthful; or to the illusion that you or they will crumble under the assault of honest talking. Yet a relationship will always be significantly strengthened and supported where there is a commitment between people – and this is as likely to be implicit as explicit – that they can lovingly and truthfully say what is on their minds without fear of tantrums, withdrawal, attack or retaliation.

In the healthiest relationships such open communication can be assumed. There is an affiliative understanding that each person will be actively supported in their psychological and social growth by the other, and is not in need of protection from reality. And I am not thinking about sexually intimate relationships only. Friendships, family relationships, political or social groupings, colleagues in a workplace: all of these connections are enhanced when the individuals have sufficient consciousness to refrain from voluntarily undermining another person *in any way*, and sufficient trust to be able to speak frankly when that is necessary.

In several of the long-term relationships I have admired most for their liveliness as well as their lovingness, a specific and overt commitment exists between the partners not only to clear and truthful communication, but to forgiveness. There is, in those relationships, a realistic assumption that sometimes there will be conflicts of interest or need, confrontation, differences of opinion, flashes of selfishness or outbursts of negativity. But when hurt occurs, each party is willing to ask the other for forgiveness, and to give it; is willing to discuss how that person feels distressed and not rush into a tangled tale of defensiveness and denial; is willing to make amends; is willing to negotiate changed patterns of behaviour that will better suit both people, and not just one.

Such graciousness assumes, I guess, that each person has separately made at least some progress in their own struggle with feelings of self-defeat. Because it also seems true that when someone is avoiding that fairly universal battle, they are likely to project their own negativity outwards so that the other person carries the 'bad bag' and they are left snow white. 'Wrong cannot afford defeat,' poet Rabindranath Tagore warns us, 'but Right can.'

The art of yielding for the sake of love is precious. So is the art of expressing sorrow for the pain you have caused – and meaning it. Both arts can be learned just as all other psychological arts are learned: by watching, reflecting, and choosing how you will act.

Perhaps one of the most mindless phrases that ever came into widespread use is from the 1970 movie *Love Story*, a saccharine tale of two beautiful, barely adult lovers torn apart by

cancer and untimely death. Ryan O'Neal and Ali McGraw –
then two of the world's most famous beautiful people – did
their best, but neither they nor we were well served by a line
that came to be closely associated with a bizarre version of selfless love. 'Love,' murmured Ali, as she edged towards the Great
Horizon, 'means never having to say you are sorry.'

On the contrary, Ali. Love allows you not only to say that
you are sorry, but to *be* sorry – and to rise again.

The sheer ordinariness of this is wonderfully captured by
Michael Leunig: 'I find that there is a crucifixion and a resur-
rection every day; in some sense or other there seems to be lots
of little crucifixions and occasionally some big ones, and if it is
gone into and almost embraced, if possible . . . when you're
truly, truly broken – and sometimes you think you're broken and
it hasn't begun, it gets worse sometimes – it never seems to end
in a futile . . . it always seems to be enriching ultimately. But you
don't pursue crucifixion, obviously; it comes to you. And it
comes to all, that's the other thing: nobody escapes this.'

BETWEEN FORGIVENESS AND responsibility exists a tense and
intense relationship. Forgiveness comes to life not through our
capacity to see the failings in others and to judge them, but
through our willingness to own up to who we are, to know
what we have done, and to acknowledge without self-pity
what we are capable of doing.

It demands that we take responsibility for ourselves, with all
the discomfort that may imply. And that we take responsibility

for all other living creatures and our planet. None of that is easy, but forgiveness asks for more. It asks us to think about what kind of society we are creating through our actions, and with our attitudes and illusions, our excuses and desires.

Here is an extremely important statement from the Vietnamese Zen teacher and writer Thich Nhat Hanh: 'Our enemy is not the other person, no matter what he or she has done. If we look deeply into ourselves, we can see that their act was a manifestation of our collective consciousness. We are all filled with violence, hatred, and fear, so why blame someone whose upbringing was without love or understanding?'

I have read those few lines many, many times. I agree totally with him that the negative emotions arising from fear that are in our collective consciousness do indeed manifest through their eruptions within individuals. Sometimes those eruptions are small: you yell at me because I use the wrong disk in the computer. Sometimes they are grave: you tear my house apart because I won't give you what you want. Sometimes they are catastrophic: you maim or kill because you have confused your victim with the persecuting pain you feel inside.

However, there is also a point where I must part with Thich Nhat Hanh. 'Why blame someone whose upbringing was without love and understanding?' he asks, assuming, it would seem, that only such people are erupting with 'violence, hatred, and fear'. I don't believe that this is so.

In my own limited experience I have come to learn that there are many adults in our society who have been loved, who have grown up in positive-thinking, child-loving homes, who have had an excellent education, who are capable of at least some insight, and of kindness and humour, yet who are also capable of acts that range from awesomely selfish through exploitative to sickeningly sadistic.

They may be the elegant, high-achieving fathers who want to push their fingers into the vagina of their tiny daughters. They may be pillars of the parish who beat their sons often and for trivial matters. They may be husbands who relish the mind-games that strip their wives of confidence and self-esteem. They may be new wives who make it their mission to impoverish their husband's former family. They may be mothers who envy and pollute their daughters' youth. They may be parents who steal their children's childhood from them so that their illustrious achievements will enhance the parents' prestige and status. They may be parents who find it amusing to play one child off against the other, disrupting the children's chances for sibling love and solidarity. They may be lovers who delight in deception and subterfuge. They may be managers or bosses who knowingly undermine their most vulnerable members of staff. They may be solid citizens who actively campaign to take benefits and assistance from the most vulnerable members of our society. They may be high-minded churchgoers who incite racist misery and divisiveness.

All such behaviour – and the variations on the theme are infinite – exhibits a deficiency of empathy, probably an inner sense of insecurity, and a capacity to cause or take pleasure in another's pain that is difficult to describe as anything but sadistic.

Yet, with every possible respect to Thich Nhat Hanh, I believe it is simplistic and incorrect to assume that all such people are behaving as they do because they were brought up without love and understanding. Even if this were so, it would ignore the reality that in all but the most bleak lives there are figures outside the family offering some kindness and care. It would also ignore the mystery as to why some people grow up in genuinely emotionally deprived circumstances, yet become adults who are capable of expressing tremendous compassion for humanity.

It is my hard-won view that throughout every life there are innumerable moments of conscious choice, moments when you know that you are choosing between behaving positively or negatively, between harming or helping, between treating another human being with care or with contempt. Surely what you make of those moments of choice through your conscious lifetime is every bit as important as whether your parents were as consistently loving and understanding as the ideal parents should be?

As the twentieth century has progressed, we have been increasingly flooded with theories to explain why someone would make the negative choice. Depending on the psychological rhetoric we most favour, we could say they are in the grip of their shadow; that they are stuck at the schizoid phase; that they are unintegrated; that they are sociopathic. And certainly it would be incorrect to assume that there is not some pathological disturbance in people who demonstrate through their behaviour that they can find satisfaction in causing others a loss of trust, safety or wellbeing.

But such pathology is only ever part of the story. I am talking about something that ranges from contempt to carelessness about other people's lives that moves right across race and social class. Those same people may be capable of working as doctors, nurses or lawyers; as teachers, sales assistants or bankers. Like the rest of us, they are bombarded with psychological information. At no time in human history has it been easier to peer into other people's lives through documentaries, talk shows and written personal accounts, and to draw some conclusions at least about what reasonable behaviour between human beings involves. And at no time in human history has it been easier to take one's own personal mysteries and talk about them to someone in a confidential setting, without any threat of the listener's judgement or contempt.

Many therapists would say that such people feel too vulnerable to seek help. Or are unconscious of what they are doing. Or that they protect themselves with grandiose notions of their invulnerability and their disdain for therapy, therapists and the 'psychobabble' that may contain clues to their own behaviour.

Some of that may be true. One can easily envision that the challenge of openness would indeed be uncomfortable, distressing, maybe even frightening to people who lack empathy, or who are driven by the desire to exploit, hurt or humiliate other people. However, whether such people are generally unconscious of what they are doing seems to me arguable, at the very least. After all, the sadism within them is satisfied only when they can see *exactly* what they are doing, and witness the effect their behaviour is having on the person or people suffering from their active or passive aggression. Even if the reward for the 'victory' of exploiting, humiliating or causing distress to other human beings is self-righteousness rather than sadism, that too is something the perpetrators usually seek and witness within themselves with at least some degree of satisfaction.

It seems to me hopelessly pessimistic to presume that such pathology arises from poor parenting, or that where there has been poor parenting, the results of that inevitably roll on throughout a lifetime.

Crucially, in pathologising inhumane, cruel or sadistic behaviour (calling it sick; considering only what harm has been done to the perpetrators and not what good has been done for them; mournfully aggrandising that harm through our attention to it), I suspect that we ourselves collude with those perpetrators in ways that are personally and socially unhelpful or even dangerous.

By playing into the notion that their behaviour is inevitable, stemming as it does from a history that cannot now be changed, we lose touch with an almost embarrassingly simple idea: that those of us who are not genuinely psychopathic or psychotic are capable of using our minds to perceive what we are doing. More than that, using our minds, witnessing who we are and what we are doing, we know (even when we don't want to know) that we *remain responsible for all our actions*, whoever our parents were, and (almost) whatever they did.

AS A SOCIETY, we are far more comfortable talking about pathology than we would be talking about, say, sin. 'Pathology' has a kind of hip, contemporary feel to it. 'Pathological' is a word you could push across the table at a dinner party and no one would drop their spoon. Whereas even the idea of sin has fallen right out of fashion except in fundamentalist circles, where neither the pathological nor the complex social and economic factors that undoubtedly do contribute to wrongdoing are given sufficient credence.

I have absolutely no interest in resurrecting the idea of sin. I am actually quite uncomfortable linking it to this discussion about forgiveness. But it is difficult not to think about sin when what I am doing here is considering the kinds of actions that put victims of those actions into a terrible dilemma about whether or not they can forgive. This is not a trivial matter. If your life has been mauled and torn apart by another human being, and then you are mauling and tearing apart your own conscience about whether or how you should forgive that human being, this is absolutely not a trivial matter.

Part of my own distaste for the idea of sin arises from my awareness of how *flexible* the arbiters of sin have always been. Priests murdering the women they called witches while preaching against the sin of murder; priests condemning women seeking abortions while millions of children already born starve to death; priests and clergymen condoning the killing or slavery of minority groups; religiously affiliated businessmen stealing from their employees, or sacking their employees in order to increase their profits – these are just a few of the most obvious examples of an excessively *flexible* attitude towards sin that organised religion has always maintained.

So the whole concept of sin itself has a dire past. However, it is impossible not also to be aware that in the days when sin was regarded with some seriousness, people who committed those sins were largely held to be accountable for what they did. And we can assume, I think, that they held themselves as accountable also.

THE IDEA THAT human beings are capable of distinguishing between right and wrong, and that doing wrong should disturb and arouse their conscience, is as old as humanity.

In reading the story in Genesis of poor old Adam's banishment from Eden, we find these bleak lines: 'And the Lord God said, Behold, the man is become as one of us, to know good and evil . . .

'Therefore the Lord God sent him forth from the garden of Eden, to till the ground from whence he was taken.'

In the Dhammapada the message is as clear as the surface of a deep lake: 'Do not what is evil. Do what is good. Keep your mind pure. This is the teaching of Buddha.'

And in the Bhagavad Gita, we can read: 'Desire has found a place in [humans'] senses and mind and reason. Through these it blinds the soul, after having over-clouded wisdom . . . They say that the power of the senses is great. But greater than the senses is the mind.'

WE CONTINUE TO regard the mind with great respect. Certainly as a society we value intellect over emotions, and intellectual intelligence over emotional intelligence. Yet for all that, I am wondering if it is possible that we have also allowed a new 'cloud' to descend and block our minds, a cloud we call pathology, a cloud that misdirects and confuses us about the uncomfortable business of personal responsibility.

Just in case it is necessary, let me repeat: I am fully aware that some asocial actions are the result of serious pathological disturbance. I do know that such a disturbance, while always being multi-factorial, can certainly be dramatically influenced by inadequate or non-existent parenting, and is also dramatically affected by living in a society that is harsh, violent, sexist, racist, unjust, and profoundly disruptive.

But for all that, is it not also possible to say that there were some significant benefits that arose from a less cluttered view of wrongdoing? A view that saw wrongdoing as something that the wrongdoers themselves needed to acknowledge, with such acknowledgement being followed by expressions of remorse, acts of reparation, and then – and only then – petitions for forgiveness. Is it not possible to say that this is what we all need in our interactions with each other? And that society as a whole needs if we are going to unravel and reweave the tattered threads of social responsibility that bind us, one to another?

OF COURSE, THIS potentially revisionist (and easily misunderstood) view comes loaded with all kinds of assumptions. Central to these is that the person is capable of recognising that they have done something wrong. For many people whose defence mechanisms are more highly developed than their conscience will ever be, this alone would be a huge stumbling block.

What is also assumed is that wrongdoers *could themselves benefit from this process* of recognising the seriousness of their actions. That they could move through these several stages with increasing awareness of their free will to make that critical choice between right and wrong, and with some confidence that they would have the insight to choose more positively in the future. And while it is also appropriate – and I believe psychologically healthy – to feel remorse for the pain one has caused, it would be important that they did not get stuck at the remorse stage, buckling under the weight of shame and guilt, rather than moving on from that rather self-involved stage to the moment when they can become more aware of the person who they have hurt than they are of themselves, and ready themselves to ask that person for their forgiveness.

HOW ON EARTH am I assuming that such a switch in attitude could ever be achieved, even supposing that it is in fact desirable? It would be a move away from an assumption that history determines pathology, that pathology underlies most serious wrongdoing, and that in cruel or hurtful acts it is the pathology speaking rather than the wrongdoer doing wrong, towards an assumption that whatever their history, most people are capable of exercising free will, of distinguishing right from wrong, of feeling at least some remorse, of making up for what they have done, and of asking the person they have hurt for their forgiveness.

To answer that question – how could this be achieved? – I want to go back to Thich Nhat Hanh: 'For us to achieve results, our enlightenment *has to be collective* [my italics].'

In other words, what I am talking about does not involve much of a distinction between wrongdoers and their victims. It is not a cry for a return to the days when 'criminals' were placed in the docks, and the righteous were free to throw their rotten vegetables or stones in blissful ignorance of their own complicity in humankind's ills. It is not a cry for more rigorous 'punishments' for those people unfortunate enough to be victims themselves of judicial proceedings. Nor am I suggesting that it would benefit wrongdoers or victims for anyone to be forced to confess to something they are incapable of acknowledging, or to apologise for something from which they feel dissociated.

This is not the time in history to impose any more rules, or even any more theories. It is, instead, a time to take on, in a most committed and creative way, personally and socially, *what we are responsible for*, and find, in a most committed and creative way, *what we can do about it*.

It was Jung who pointed out that 'Only an exceedingly naive and unconscious person could imagine that he is in a position to avoid sin.'

We need to think about how we ourselves can and should 'own up' to what we do, or what we fail to do. We need to think daily, with clarity and positive intent, about how we treat each person with whom we come in contact. We need to model a willingness to acknowledge our part in wrongdoings, as well as what we fail to do, even (and especially) with our children and with those people we want to think well of us, such as our bosses or spiritual teachers. I think we need to be clean and clear about acting and not wallowing. And I believe we need to take notice of how our behaviour affects the physical as well as the emotional environment we are creating all around us.

How can we atone to the planet for the excesses that we have thoughtlessly taken, squandered, and not replaced? How can we atone to the natural habitats as well as to the peoples of the Third World for all the bargains we have enjoyed at their expense? And for those of us who are of European descent, and who live in countries where the aboriginal populations suffered so wretchedly at the hands of our forebears, how can we create opportunities to acknowledge that, while also finding ways to live and raise our children to honour what those cultures can teach us?

Perhaps it is not so difficult after all. 'Looking deeply at our own mind and our own life,' says Thich Nhat Hanh, 'we will begin to see what to do and what not to do to bring about a real change.'

AMANDA PARKER IS a teacher in her late forties, an unusually reflective, wise woman who has been suffering for some years from extremely severe health problems. It is her view that most of us have a foundation issue that is aligned to how we think about forgiveness. This might be that we should have been the oldest child instead of the youngest; that we are the wrong gender; that we were overlooked by our parents; that we had to go out to work too early; that a parent died while we were still dependent; that we are gay when we might have preferred to be straight; that we have never married; that we are less beautiful, talented or successful than we might have wished.

It is this grand theme, as well as many minor variations, that reminds us that life does not deliver itself to us in a perfect form. Yet all spiritual teachings point out that it is precisely through the ways in which our life is imperfect that we gain the chance to grow in wisdom. The great Eastern religions of Buddhism and Hinduism especially stress that the life you are living is providing the absolutely ideal lessons for you, if only you can take them up.

Amanda's view is similar: 'Forgiveness in some way *creates* perfection. It makes it all perfect in a larger way. It's a release, an unhooking. Perhaps if one had got what one wanted, one might still be striving. Of course that perfection is not a constant state. It's a momentary thing but it has a lot of power.'

For almost thirty years – all of her adult life – Amanda has struggled with powerful feelings of rage, disappointment and depression for which, she was sure, her selfish, demanding, and often cruel mother was primarily responsible. Yet when her inner work eventually cracked her heart and mind wide open, it was not her mother waiting there for Amanda's forgiveness.

'I had a series of dreams about the love of my life. I had always had ongoing angst about it, about not being able to marry him. I'd stayed faithful to that. I blamed everybody, especially my mother who stopped me from marrying him, but the church too, and all my later boyfriends. Those angry thoughts sustained me.

'Then the dreams showed me different images of me with this great love. This is more than twenty-five years down the track. At about that time, we had a tremendously painful reunion. He hadn't lived his life. I hadn't lived my life. It's so searingly painful I can't bear to think about it. Seeing him again fed my rage, impotence, the feeling that I couldn't have love. I'd rejected love because of the pressure my mother put me under and then unconsciously had set up a whole series of rejections through becoming involved with people who couldn't love me.

'The dreams were so painful I *had* to work with them. I felt I had come totally to the end of something. I had a lot of realisations during that time. All I can talk about is this kind of feeling I got that in the final analysis even though I blamed my mother and I blamed the church and I blamed the list of boyfriends, and my sister for interfering, and so on, I suddenly went back into my twenty-year-old self who I'd had many dreams about and I saw that young self had never been told, "Go for love!" She had never been given the opportunity to think, "When you find love, go for it!" I had no experience of that. And I had no experience of being loved by a man in that way. I realised that something in that twenty-year-old really knew that *this was it*, and that if I had really just said yes to that, my mother's objections, the church's . . . but I didn't say yes. And that was the part I had to forgive. Myself. That I just didn't know, or didn't have enough experience of ever saying yes to anything. And no one had ever really said yes to me, either.

'I knew if I ever really said yes to anything in life, everything that was in the way would fall away. It was just this utter realisation that I had known this was my love . . . But I didn't know how to say yes.

'It was an absolute release to know this. It was forgiveness. I experienced it like a liquid feeling that embalmed me, like grace poured over me. You can't make that happen. I felt like I was being anointed. What I said was: "I did this." And given the same set of circumstances and the same upbringing, I'd do it again. But *now* I wouldn't do it.

'I'm able to see that I have learned a lot – but I don't know that I'll ever have this opportunity again, at that level, but something echoed throughout me. I felt a real advance of my soul and I thought, even if I end up as a bag lady or whatever, I have had this: I have had a great love, and twenty-five years later when we met, we both had the same feeling.

'If I die tomorrow, I have resolved this one and I feel tremendously different towards my mother. I can listen to her constant complaints with genuine kindness. The vicious stuff has gone. But when I am talking to younger women, I urge them to listen to their inner knowing. They must not listen to anything else when they are making a big decision.'

The enormous shift in awareness that preceded her being able to forgive herself, and that moved her into a changed relationship with her mother and with her past, was not possible until Amanda had suffered through most of her adult life, in part through her own undermining feelings of unworthiness and self-destruction.

'For me, being in a state of unforgivingness was very self-destructive. It made me want to destroy my own life. It was a crisis really that threw me head-long into despair and I was in that space for five or six years. I couldn't go on like that. In that time, I got diabetes. I'd given up hope. The opposite of forgiveness for me is self-destructiveness.

'I had to destroy myself over and over and over because I had betrayed the great gift that I had been given. That was what I had to forgive.'

The depth of Amanda's experience of forgiveness is unusual, and so is the protracted period of desolation that preceded it. It has also had a dramatic and largely positive effect on her life in the couple of years since.

Amanda: 'I have become sharper than I was. I can be very analytical, almost harsh. I'm no longer idealising nor am I projecting pain outwards and blaming. The forgiveness I am talking about is the great forgiveness. At a daily level, if something irritates me, I am not as forgiving. Having experienced forgiveness does not mean I have ceased to be judgemental!

'I have had to forgive a couple of terrible betrayals, and have had to see them as awakenings to a deeper purpose in my life. I have learned to look at them in this way – mythologising them and not pathologising them, which is what [writer and social philosopher] Jean Houston suggests. I can see that I was enmeshed with a trail of betrayal. I am not in that now. I am unhooked from it. I haven't betrayed myself, either, since I had this big forgiveness. It's made me far more rational. I am less trapped by my emotions. I feel a bit too tired to enjoy it but it's freed up my creativity as well as my objectivity. In terms of my whole life, it's a freedom.'

MOST OF WHAT we learn that has any value arises out of our own personal experiences. And often what we learn most from, because they are so tenacious and difficult to escape, are our experiences of suffering.

We know this intellectually, yet it remains hard for us to grasp. We want life to be different. We want to believe that we can learn most from books, or from observing other people, or from civilised conversations over glasses of wine. But this is not the case. We do learn from books, observations, arguments, discussions. A great deal of what we learn in this way is invaluable. It may even be what best sharpens our wits. But 'civilised', second-hand learning rarely knocks our corners off, nor saves our souls.

Suffering does that. Through tearing us down, and forcing us to think about what really does matter, it offers an irreplaceable opportunity to see things through the wisdom of the heart as well as of the mind.

WE DO NOT come into this world entitled to anything. If we are exceptionally lucky, we are born where the sun can keep us warm, the water supply is clean, the earth can still yield crops and there are surplus trees to be cut for firewood if we need extra warmth. Everything else is a luxury.

Yet at the heart of so many of our dilemmas is an inability to forgive life itself for not giving us what we believe we deserve.

My dear friend Pam Benton has terminal cancer. This almost certainly means that she will die much sooner than she and those who love her might have hoped. Meantime, she has learned to live. Reflecting on the months that have passed since she discovered that the cancer has metastasised through her bones, she says: 'I guess what has happened is a big shift in my sense of myself as an okay human being and that somehow all that anxiety about not being good enough in a huge variety of ways has gone. I'd accepted this intellectually a long time ago but now emotionally it has also become real. There are times when I feel almost celebratory about my life. This could really be a very limited time now and I must be sure to do what I can with it. And I feel as if I have.'

This relatively new-found peace is not, alas, a constant experience. Like everyone suffering chronic pain, Pam has some days that feel extremely grim: 'Much of my life I have had dreams of being tortured. And I think to live in the twentieth century is to endure being tortured every day vicariously. It's always felt as if I was too lucky to have escaped that main experience of twentieth-century life – which is horrific. It's felt as if some part of me is open to every war, every refugee. The most difficult thing is to remain open to that, not to be inured. The only thing that makes it tolerable – the only way to deal with the pain – is that I have lived my life expecting that I could do some microscopic thing every day that would make a difference.

'Now, with my own pain, I feel as if I can do whatever I need to do – I wish I didn't have to, but I can deal with it. I can find a way to deal with it and to live. At twenty-two I tried to kill myself. I was terrified of pain, terrified of the process of dying. Now I couldn't push a button to end some unendurable end. I don't think in terms of "How can I escape this suffering?", but "How can I embrace this?" There is so much *to* embrace. That's the gift! This is unquestionably the most unproblematically positive period of my life ever. Something shifted within me, and it was there, this capacity to embrace life and possibility and sheer joy in practically every moment of every day. Something shifted in me – and I could embrace it.'

EMBRACING WHAT WE have and cherishing it; relinquishing the fantasy that we can order the world to be as we would like it; finding the means within ourselves to make up for what is lacking, rather than blaming others; opening ourselves to a meaningful engagement with other people's joys and dilemmas: these are all expressions of maturity that we may adopt reluctantly, but they are crucial to forgiveness. Needed with them, however, are discernment, creativity, humour, compassion, love, and a sharp sense of wonder and discovery.

Reflecting on her intermittent outbursts against life, Sally Gillespie said to me: 'What I notice is that when I am not forgiving life [for not giving me what I want] I feel a lot more childish, a lot more petulant and put myself, by focusing on it, into depression. I open up a sense of emptiness, of deprivation, and as I am coming out of the depression again I can feel quite horrified that it's been quite a childish kind of tantrum. I don't give myself too hard a time about it because I do have a dilemma about how much I should try to change things. I need to accept that mood as much as any other. But I am aware that life really doesn't owe us anything. It takes a lot of self-discipline to remember this and to honour the individuality of each of our life patterns.

'We would stay as children if we could just command life around. I think that whole growth movement concept, where you are expected to make life as you want it happen through the power of affirmations and visualisations, is very childish and very egotistic and I think anyone who is pulled to a more spiritual understanding doesn't feel easy putting all their energies into driving things to make them happen in particular ways. As we grow older and see that all kinds of things can happen that we can't foresee or control, we come out of the childish, fairytale vision of life. Life is a tremendous adventure but it can't be that adventure if we have it all controlled.

'The dance of our life is not always gleeful. It has its ecstatic moments, and its peaceful and calm and gentle moments, but it also has those tremendous points of suffering and I am thinking of the Indian sun dancers who pierce themselves with hooks that are attached to strings and they pull against that, which creates the pain that is an initiation for them. It is an acceptance of pain and suffering, and the way that that expands them spiritually in a way that nothing else can.

'The childishness of our view that everything should be lovely – and that life is doing something wrong by us if it is not lovely – is actually working totally against the essence of life, which is to have us do this dance and to be pierced and to live – not to overemphasise suffering – but to know that suffering is part of this existence here that can create these points of opening and expansion, which take us into a larger sense of who we are. We can't come to know the largeness within us, or the points of connection we have with others, without knowing something about suffering.'

I THINK ABOUT my own suffering. Or, to be truthful, I don't think about it. I glance at it, sideways. I can't forget it, but I can't bear either to fully remember it. Yet even looking at it sideways, I am absolutely aware of all that has arisen from it. I have gained gifts of knowledge and experience that will carry me through the writing of this book and into my life beyond it. Had I not been pushed by confusion, rage and feelings of profound inadequacy, I would not have needed to look for help from these virtues; I would not have needed to cry out for help; I may not have discovered how rich the gifts of friendship are when one has long ceased to be amusing; or how infinitely invaluable and restorative love is. I would have understood others' pain less well, and would be less moved by it. I am truly thankful for all of that.

But does that mean I can or should forgive myself for the part I played in my own suffering? Does it mean that I can or should forgive others for the harm I believe their actions did me, and worse, for the hurt I believe those actions caused my children?

I sit with these questions, and become restless. I take them outside with me as I water the garden. I write them on mercilessly blank sheets of paper. They follow me into the shower while I wash my hair. I go to bed with them. I wake up with them.

I reject the feeling that I 'should' do anything. 'Should' sticks in my throat. It reminds me of the hundreds, perhaps the thousands of times I have already berated myself for events over which I could, at best, have had only partial control. I think about how much I have already suffered and that I don't want that suffering any more.

I think about the many people I have talked to about forgiveness. I remember the relief that passes over people's faces and that ripples through their bodies when they talk about the freedom to let go, to put something into the past, to be in the present moment with complete attention. That's not all of what forgiveness is; but it helps.

I remember the passion with which some people say, 'I will never forgive.' The pain in their eyes, their voices; the tension expressed in their bodies speaks of grief as well as the rage that now shapes their lives.

The involuntary intimacy that arises from being locked into a negative relationship with someone feels hideously uncomfortable. Many people can't face it. One woman, now in her mid-fifties, said to me, 'When I perhaps ought to have been thinking about forgiving someone, I would actually just cut them out of my life. I would behave as though they were dead.'

And if someone needed to forgive her for something she had done that was hurtful or wrong? 'I never even thought about other people having to forgive me until I was much older. Well into my forties, probably. I guess I put those people out of my life, had no connection with them or relationship of any kind. I'd cut them out and move on. If that wasn't possible, say if it was a family member or something, I used to drink on the occasions we would meet. I'd put myself right out of it that way.'

Simply contemplating the act of forgiveness may seem to bring us a great deal closer to a person, to events, or to our own most painful and vulnerable feelings, than we want to be. Holding onto our anger, outrage or fantasies of revenge may be immensely harmful for our physical and emotional well-being. But we do it because we believe that it keeps us separate – and safe. Or we do it because we believe we owe it to someone else who has been wronged.

Yet it is one of life's most terrible ironies that betrayal can be as connective as love. It can fill the mind, and colour all your senses. It can keep you tied to that person or to those events as tightly as if you were bound, back to back, or worse, heart to heart. The person you want to think of least may become the person you think of constantly.

'There are many ways and portions to forgiving a person, a community, a nation for an offense,' writes Clarissa Pinkola Estes. 'It is important to remember that a "final" forgiveness is not surrender. It is a conscious decision to cease to harbor resentment.'

It may only be by giving up *while not surrendering* that you catch your first, precious glimpse of freedom. You do this by withdrawing your attention from the person who has hurt you and returning it to yourself and whoever else is in your care; by taking your attention from the past and bringing it into the present moment. You do it by giving up the illusion that your prolonged suffering will ultimately affect that other human being and teach any meaningful lesson. You do it by abandoning them to their own fate, and abandoning the desire to affect that fate.

This can be difficult to achieve. It involves stepping back, trusting the breadth of your vision will shift and expand. And it assumes that the acts for which you are trying to find forgiveness belong securely in the past. Yet, for many people, this cannot be the case.

The wife who must continue to live with an unfaithful husband because she has no independent means of support; the aged parent whose adult children miss each visiting day at the nursing home; the unemployed worker who must pass his old place of employment each time he goes to the railway station; the mother who has been ordered by the court to allow an abusive parent access to their children; the woman who continues to get frightening midnight calls from an ex-lover years after they parted; the quadraplegic who suffers daily the loss of independence; the child who must return to school each day and face the class bully: these are all situations in which partial forgiveness would be a triumph of the human spirit, and where even the tiniest seed of forgiveness must constantly be nourished and renewed.

In all of these situations of apparent emotional imprisonment, something truly revolutionary must happen in order to effect a positive change.

TEACHER AND WRITER Brian Keenan was a prisoner of a small group of terrorists in Beirut from the mid-1980s. He was held in monstrous circumstances for four and a half years, during which time his life was continually under threat. In his book, *An Evil Cradling*, he describes how he moved beyond self-pity, beyond the judgement of his captors and beyond his own need to judge them, through his rare, salutary recognition that 'we are all creatures in need of love'.

'Each morning I awoke to find again the reserves of imagination and reflection to buoy me up from the murk in which memory's hot pinpoints scalded me. At times I would feel overwhelmed by shame or guilt. It was always necessary to face such feelings and question why such emotional turmoil accompanied my memories. The habit I had formed of observing myself allowed me to distance myself from these emotional assaults.

'My father, who had died a few years before, was frequently in my thoughts. At first there were simple incidents from the family history. Certain moments seemed to become more complete and more filled with meaning. I seemed to understand more about each incident in the history than I did when the event occurred. These memories became less and less a recording of the past. My father became not just simply a memory but more a real presence; a presence I could feel more than see, a comforting reassurance that eased the hurt into a deeply filled sadness, yet that same sadness, as it became reflective, lifted me. I began to understand the hurt that was in me. We are all creatures in need of love. My pity moved beyond myself. I wanted to reach out and embrace life . . .

'I was no longer afraid of my guards' violence, nor did I seek to judge them.'

APPROACHING FORGIVENESS, IT is easy to begin to feel that one is returning constantly to the same place. The stairs encircling the inside of a lighthouse come to mind; or friends' descriptions of trekking in the mountains of Nepal or Tibet where you can frequently walk five miles over the most rugged and perilous terrain, only to find that you have progressed less than half a mile in 'real terms' – whatever those may be. In much the same way, hanging in there as you move across emotional terrain that can be just as stark, dangerous and unyielding as those mountains, you may find that whatever lies at the heart of forgiveness is discovered only through years of patient endurance.

When matters are serious – life-shakingly serious – they can rarely be forgiven either directly or conclusively. Such events may take most of a lifetime to assimilate and most of a lifetime to forgive.

During this prolonged period of assimilation and reflection, as you contemplate what forgiveness means to you and those with whom you share your life, sometimes the emphasis will be on yourself: on the part you have played; on the need you may have to forgive yourself for those events, however involuntarily you were involved; on your own capacity to find the distance that forgiveness requires, as well as confronting the profound intimacy that it demands.

Sometimes the emphasis will need to be on the person with whom you are bound through negativity: the person who has wounded, humiliated or betrayed you. Perhaps the person who has hurt you will be courageous and loving enough to acknowledge what they have done. This will demand from you a different level of response from the more common situation where the person denies their involvement, trivialises it, or attacks you. And it may equally be that there is no 'someone' to blame or forgive. Impersonal events happen; or events so massive in their scale that one looks around helplessly to find the source.

For many people who have been wounded, battered and abused over a prolonged period, there may need to be some equally prolonged and effective 'forgetting' *before* there can be 'forgiving'. 'Forgetting' does not mean never remembering or pretending something hasn't happened. On the contrary. It simply means living without those events being in your mind almost every second of the day. It means occasionally waking up without them being the first thoughts to come into your mind; sometimes going for an hour, or a day or a week without thinking about them at all; it may mean feeling relatively secure that painful memories or fears won't intrude whenever you begin to enjoy yourself or relax; it may mean feeling safe to go to sleep and not wake up with a start at 3 a.m. as your mind reruns those same distressing movies.

This is the kind of forgetting that allows a psychological scab to form over an open emotional wound. It is the kind of forgetting that allows you to experience that the world is never reduced to a single series of events. Terrible things happen: yet a chocolate may still taste good; your voice can still rise in prayer or song; a friend's arm around you will continue to feel comforting; lying in a warm, scented bath is as much of a luxury as it ever was.

As often as you are letting your need to forgive lapse (or your need not to forgive), you are also moving away from what happened then, to pay attention to what is happening now.

Attention to *now* is absolutely precious. It does more than liberate us from past events; it delivers to us our life in the present.

Zen teacher Charlotte Joko Beck points to this when she says: 'There is a place of rest in our lives, a place where we must be if we are to function well. This place of resting – the arms of God, if you will – is simply here and now: *seeing, hearing, touching, smelling, tasting our life as it is* [my italics]. We can even add thinking to the list, if we understand thinking as simply functional thinking rather than ego thinking based on fear and attachment. Just thinking in the functional sense includes abstract thinking, creative thinking or planning what we have to do today. Too often, however, we add nonfunctional, ego-based thinking, which gets us in trouble and takes us from the arms of God.'

Let me share a very simple example from my own life. My daughter is talking to me. My son is playing music loudly in his room. I am chopping vegetables. The cats need feeding. The phone rings. At the same time, I look outside and see that rain has already started to fall and I have not yet brought in the washing from the line. As though this was not enough to pay attention to, right now in the present, I am painfully distracted by an unpleasant conversation I had earlier in the day. It made me anxious then, and even though all these other demands are there to be met in the present, it is still my feeling of anxiety from earlier in the day that asks most of me. Following Joko Beck's advice, I need to see my daughter and listen to her; hear the cats, touch them, feed them; touch the washing as I get it in off the line; feel the rain on my body as I do so; smell the vegetables, and chop them with care; and maybe answer the phone with a little spontaneous functional thinking.

If I could do that, with awareness and close attention, the anxiety from earlier in the day would have little room in my mind. It would have to fade away until I am ready to recall it. This doesn't mean that I would have less chance to find a solution for what is worrying me. On the contrary, allowing my anxiety to pollute the present moment is wearing me down and reducing my chances of making a clear-headed decision. It is also making me feel distracted, divided, harassed, and self-pitying. I feel as if I have far too much to cope with, and it's true. While I am coping with the past as well as with everything that is happening in the present, it is too much. Way too much.

I don't need to blame myself that my feelings of anxiety are so bad. I don't even need to forgive myself. I certainly don't need to go to my room and sit on my meditation cushions and hope that the tasks in the kitchen will get done by themselves. All I need do is to switch my attention to what is actually present: music, son, daughter, cats, food, rain, washing, phone.

When it is left alone, even through the maddening itchy stages, your emotional wound can begin to close. Closed, this allows the scab to form, to dry, and eventually to fall off as new skin forms. That new skin will not be like the skin around it. It will be taut and shiny and vulnerable. It will stand out from the skin around it, although in time it will become less different, less obvious. You grow into all your scars, and they grow into you. What is also interesting is that they will have a character of their own. My scars are raised, lumpy and red. Yours may be white, like threads of silk woven into the surrounding skin. These differences say nothing about the wounds that once lay beneath them.

The process of assimilating our scars may take months, years, decades. The original events will not have changed, but you will.

SELF-FORGIVENESS AND the forgiveness of others seem inextricably intertwined. *We move through life hurting others*, as well as being hurt. *We move through life hurting ourselves*, as well as being hurt. Eventually some of these events will fade, and be entirely forgotten. With others, anger will soften to annoyance, irritation, sadness. Grief may blend into sorrow. Lessons will be learned. Distances maintained. Warning signs observed. The cycle of redemption continues: openness, truthfulness, a willingness to be changed, a willingness to make amends; action that removes us from the place of suffering; action that relieves the pain of others; a willingness to learn.

In the concentration camp of Ravensbruck, this extraordinary prayer was left by the body of a dead child: 'Oh Lord, remember not only the men and women of good will, but also those of ill will. But do not remember all the suffering they have inflicted on us; *remember the fruits we have bought, thanks to this suffering* – our comradeship, our loyalty, our humility, our courage, our generosity, the greatness of heart which has grown out of all this, and when they come to judgement *let all the fruits which we have borne be their forgiveness*.'

This radical request – that their murderers should benefit from the gifts retrieved from the suffering that they themselves had caused – is a startling example of compassion at its most profound and unitive levels. At just the moment when feelings of revenge, hatred and contempt would seem not just natural, but inevitable, this prayer is drawing our attention to love.

'Would you still further weaken and break apart what is already broken and hopeless?' asks the Course in Miracles. And, if most of us were truthful, in the face of wounding and betrayal we would have to answer yes. We would like to weaken it. Break it apart. Trample on it. Turn it into dust. Grind it into the ground. Scream at it. Scatter it with our tears and our blood. End it.

The teaching goes on, still challenging us: 'Or would you not prefer to heal what has been broken, and join in making whole what has been ravaged by separation [from God, or perhaps from one's own goodness] and disease?'

In all the mystical traditions there are stories of people who have been tortured and killed and have suffered those fates willingly and even joyously for the chance that it has given them to take on the suffering of others. This depth of connection with life is foreign to most of us. We neither live that intensely, nor could die that gloriously. But we can learn something from it.

I am speaking to a young Chinese poet who is visiting Australia for a year on a writer's fellowship. We have met at the writers' retreat where I am working on this book. He used to be a Zen Buddhist, but a few years ago became a Christian. It's not easy to be a Christian in China. It puts you at risk, politically and socially. Nevertheless, his faith in Christ fills him with joy. The joy spreads right across his face when he speaks of it.

Later in the evening we are talking about his son. The poet tells me what a fine teacher to him his son is. The boy is almost seven. With his mother, the poet's wife, the child had arrived in Australia just a few weeks earlier. He was invited to take part in a children's choir. Unfortunately he was highly praised by the choirmaster, and the choirmaster's son, who was also in the choir, resented this and literally pushed the poet's son out. The poet was angry. Telling me, I can see his offence. The boy, however, was not angry. Instead, he said to the poet: 'I prayed to the Lord to love this boy more. And I prayed that the Lord would keep on allowing me to forgive. Why should I be angry?'

The poet reflects on his son's beauty and wisdom and says to me: 'This boy is filled with the Holy Spirit. This is the Lord's work. He is a very unusual boy.'

I PASS YOU a sheet of paper. It is blue. You asked me for red paper, but I was only half-listening. You are annoyed. You don't like having to ask twice. You frown and sigh. I am annoyed, too. Annoyed with you that you couldn't fetch your own damned sheet of paper, and a little ashamed of myself that I was caught with my mind elsewhere. I don't like this feeling of shame. It adds to my feelings of annoyance with you. But the moment passes. Something else grabs your attention, then mine. After lunch you come back with a large slice of cake. Carefully, you cut it in two. I know that I am forgiven. I smile.

I forgive you, too.

I AM STANDING next to a child at a bus stop. You walk by, dressed in a dark business suit. Suddenly you notice the child and begin to scream a volley of abuse. The child cringes and tries to hide. Your hand goes up to hit the child. You are still screaming. I try to place myself between you and the child. Suddenly you are hitting me, as well as the child. There is an incredible cracking sound as you throw me against the wall of the bus shelter. I have hit my head. Where is the child? Passers-by intervene. There is the noise of a siren. The police arrive, then an ambulance. Two men hold you while you struggle, still screaming. What you are saying is incomprehensible. Anyway, I don't care. The child is standing off to one side, white and silent. My head throbs. Blood pours from my nose and from a wound on my head. I want to be sick. You are a total stranger but I hate you even more than I am afraid of you. I hate what you have done. I hate what you must have been doing to that child to make him cringe just at the sight of you. I hate you. I will never forget you. I will never forgive you.

FORGIVENESS IS THE means to release yourself and perhaps others, too, from an experience of hurt, injury, wounding, suffering, humiliation or pain that has already passed. It is what allows you at least some separation from that experience so that you can be fresh to what is present in this moment.

It is the means to let go not only what was done to you, but *how you were then*, so that you can experience yourself *as you are now*. When it is appropriate, it is also the means to move on from an old version of another person to who that person is now.

In some instances – as when I hand you the incorrect sheet of paper – this process is easy. It may even be fairly automatic. To hang onto that trivial incident and allow it to be present every time we meet would seem unnecessary or even neurotic.

In other instances – as when you injure and terrify me, and have been seriously harming a child – the past is much more difficult to forget. I continue to be reminded of it, voluntarily and often involuntarily. Perhaps I can no longer bear to travel on buses. When I hear someone begin to scream, perhaps I shake and feel ill. When I least want to remember it, perhaps I find myself shuddering and crying.

'It's the shock,' I tell myself. 'It will pass.' But I know it is something worse than that. You personified the violence and lack of control that I anyway fear is all around me. You have made that real and, doing that, you have robbed me of my safety. This may not pass.

The past feels uncomfortably present. I would like to forget you. I would like you to be absolutely outside my mind. I would be glad never to think about you again. But I don't know how to do that. Nor do I know how to forgive you.

THERE IS AN unhelpful lack of balance in how carelessly we use the same word – forgiveness – to restore peace and feelings of comfort and safety between people for the most banal events as well as the most grave.

We sometimes use the word *forgiveness* when we are more accurately *excusing* someone for something they have done to us; or excusing ourselves for something we have done or failed to do. *Excusing* doesn't mean condoning what has been done or not done, or making excuses. It simply means that someone regrets what they have done; probably wishes events could have been different; is at least reasonably optimistic that it won't happen again; says so – and the matter can be dropped. When I am late for our dinner date, pass you the wrong sheet of paper, or buy too many books despite my resolutions not to, it should be quite comfortable for you to excuse me or for me to excuse myself without loss of truth, or permanent injury.

Forgiveness is quite a different matter. It arises to enlighten and lighten another realm of experience altogether: a place that is grimmer, more shadowy, deeper, potentially much more confusing; a place where there is at least some element of fear, cruelty, betrayal or breach of trust.

To forgive may be an act of supreme love and gentleness, but it is also tough. It demands that at least one party faces the truth – and learns something of value from it. It does not involve condoning, trivialising, minimising, excusing, ignoring or pretending to forget what has been done. It does not withdraw blame. Yet it may ask you to be careful how you apportion blame; whether you absent yourself from events, or remain present.

'Hate is not conquered by hate,' the Dhammapada teaches. 'Hate is conquered by love. This is a law eternal.'

Even under the most dire circumstances, long before any version of forgiveness itself becomes possible, impersonal love – the love that makes no distinction between you and all other living creatures – demands that you give up notions of vengeance. This may not mean ceasing to be angry, if angry is what you feel. Forgiveness certainly does not mean pretending

that things are fine when they are not. Nor does it mean refusing to take whatever action is needed to redress past wrongs,
or to protect you in the future.

We often talk about forgiveness in a context that suggests
we are giving something away when we forgive. Or that we are
accepting something in return when others forgive us. This is
illusory. Offering our forgiveness, or allowing forgiveness to
arise in whatever nascent forms within us, takes nothing away
from us. It restores us to something that is always within us but
from which we have become unbound: a sense of unity
expressed through the qualities of trust, faith, hope and love.

That subtle, profound relationship between unity and love
is captured perfectly for me by Gabrielle Lord when she
writes: '[This] is where real love starts to grow, in the dawn-
ing truth that *you are the same* as me. Not the same *person*, as
in obsessive and destructive Heathcliff–Cathy coupling, but
the same in your unchanging spirit – having the same need
for respect, the same longing for peace, the same yearning for
acceptance and love, and having the same fears of suffering
and loss. Once a person has come to comprehend these huge
and over-riding points of similarity, it becomes impossible to
see the differences – of appearance, income, social status – as
having much substance at all any more. People start to be seen
more like the flowers, shrubs and trees of a garden; all entirely
different in appearance, yet all needing the same care to keep
them alive: sunlight, water and sustenance.'

FORGIVENESS NEITHER BEGINS nor ends with words. Words can, in fact, stand in for forgiveness, as poor substitutes for something that actually requires intense reflection, contemplation, resolution and action. Far more important than words are the shifts in attitude those words accompany, the changed actions they allow, the compassion they elicit, and, ideally, the love they free to flow.

'Forgiveness,' teaches the Course in Miracles, 'paints a picture of a world where suffering is over, loss becomes impossible and anger makes no sense. Attack is gone, and madness has an end.'

For anyone enduring the anguish that arouses the desire to retaliate, punish, take revenge, or kill, this picture may seem impossibly rosy. It depends on and also brings together all the virtues that we have been considering: courage, fidelity, restraint, generosity, tolerance. Forgiveness calls on wisdom and calls out to love, and forges them into something strong enough not to wipe out what has been, but to transform the way that one views what has been, and currently experiences it:

> Friend, it's time to make an effort,
> So you become a grown human being,
> And go out picking jewels
> Of feeling for others.

ON THE WAY to becoming a grown human being we need to accept and understand that we are not of a single piece. Within each Mary or John Smith are some very surprising Mary and John Smiths. Within each of us, too, are diverse inner elements, some of which we are proud to call our own, others of which are less encouraging. It is a tremendous challenge of maturity to accept this somewhat confronting reality, and to use our awareness gradually to bring those elements into a synthesis, a whole, so that they can work together rather than against each other, and so that we can enjoy the ease and vitality of being truly awake and at home within our own life.

There may be aspects of ourselves that we need to forgive and transform before we can integrate them. But this can't be done as long as we fail even to recognise them. There may also be aspects of other people that we are loathe to recognise in ourselves. It can seem so much simpler and even more satisfying to see someone as wholly good or bad, but this rarely reflects what is true.

Individually and collectively we are astonished when a pillar of society is caught shoplifting, or having sex in a public toilet, or running off with other people's funds. Nor do we expect a murderer to appreciate Brahms, or a terrorist to cultivate roses. It rocks us to discover that a sex worker could be a highly successful investor on the stock exchange, that an ethereal dancer could be a bully, or that the quiet child we adore could be the bane of her teachers.

Some of these inconsistencies may emerge from the shadow or repressed side of the personality. However, they are more likely to reflect the varying constellations of attitude, behaviour and feelings that exist within every person and that emerge as confusing and sometimes conflicting aspects of a single personality.

The outer self we present to others might be highly consistent. I am always calm, well-groomed, well-organised and distant; you are always rumpled, vague and memorably amusing. This does not mean that either of us is an integrated, synthesised whole within. It may simply mean that we have learned to behave in public in certain proscribed ways that have their specific function and meaning for each of us, and so far nothing has arisen from the outside or within ourselves to disrupt that. The person who is highly consistent (or rigid) in their outer persona may present a very different 'self' to their family, or perhaps only to their lover, or when they are with strangers. None of that is self-evidently wrong. Yet it is also true to say that the person who has brought their disparate fragments more or less into a whole, and can be open and feel real in virtually all situations, is likely to have far more emotional energy at their disposal, arising from a greater sense of authenticity and the wellbeing that goes with it.

HERE IS A description written by a journalist about a public figure, the feminist anti-pornography crusader Catherine MacKinnon. These observations are the journalist's and it is quite possible that some of them are her own projections and that MacKinnon experiences herself quite differently. Yet the range of 'selves' she notes is fascinating, not least because it is unlikely to be any greater or more extreme than you could begin to observe within your own self.

'Interviewing MacKinnon is not like questioning just one person, it's strangely like encountering a whole host of personalities: a fussy Jesuit, a cranky despot, a stroppy schoolgirl, an

irascible tutor, a ferocious aunt, and an adroit legal wrangler –
which, of course, she is.

'The Jesuit quibbled and disputed . . . The despot made
lurid claims . . . The tutor reprimanded me . . . The aunt said,
"Well, I will decide when you can have it and when you can't."
The lawyer kept the grounds of our argument shifting so fast
that it was almost impossible to keep a foothold . . .'

IF WE ARE lucky, we come to understand that we can have
increasing choice about who we are and how we will
behave. We learn this by being observant, open, reflective,
discerning, self-responsible, and forgiving.

Through understanding that we ourselves are not the uni-
fied person we long to be, we may come to view others' weak-
nesses, inconsistencies, failings and insufficiencies differently
also. This does not mean making excuses for actions that are
inexcusable, or pathologising behaviour that is irresponsible,
careless or selfish, or retreating into cynicism or indifference.
But it may involve surrendering the temporary satisfactions of
ignorance, smugness, divisiveness and self-righteousness.

Incorporating what we have disowned, bringing the fragments of our disunited selves home to become part of the solid
ground within, we become more alive, more attuned – not to
ourselves only, but to life in its infinite brilliant and mysterious
forms outside ourselves.

IN THE FINAL months of more than four years of captivity and
extreme deprivation, Brian Keenan grasped what he had
learned from ants: 'Hundreds and hundreds seasonally invaded

the cells in which we were kept. Like the giant Gulliver in a rage of frustration and cold sweat I would stamp and slap and crush them without mercy, without any thought of their separate existence. But after days of this I got tired of my anger. It exhausted me. The ants were inexhaustible . . . As I watched them pour into the cell through so many different places they became for me a form of entertainment. I watched them work. I watched how they would search out a crumb of bread four or five times their own size. They would trail and pull or push this piece of bread the full length of my tiny cell, scale a vertical wall, crawl along ridges until they found an exit point and take with them what they had found.

'My fascination made friends of them. I was grateful for their fortitude, for their strength, for their resilience and instead of raging at them I would sit awaiting their return. I watched how they worked together. And how, if I had crushed one in the night by accident, the others would gather around and if there was life in it still, a comrade would lift this wounded companion and carry it across what for these tiny creatures must have seemed like miles, crawl up the vertical wall and search out an escape point through which they could take this maimed insect to be amongst its own. This incident became a symbol for me in this blank room with its three chained creatures [prisoners]. We cannot abandon the injured or the maimed, thinking to ensure our own safety and sanity. We must reclaim them, as they are part of ourselves.'

TO CLAIM THE wholeness of our lives, and to release the compassion that only such wholeness can allow, we need to free ourselves from the prison of indifference, from the chains of cynicism, from the manacles of false innocence. We need to step into the open air, feeling the earth that's beneath our feet and being thankful for that, and looking up at the sky.

There is such fierce and free beauty in any rare moment in which we stand upright between earth and sky, conscious of the blessings of existence. 'We and nature are one,' sings the poet Andrew Harvey. 'One dance, one feast, one radiance . . .'

It is easy to complain that the dance is not to our liking, that the feast has turned sour, that the radiance has dimmed.

We can rage against that, and beat against our fate with our tiny hands. We can shout that life is unfair; that we deserve better; that suffering's long stick should tap some other shoulder.

Or we can look around us.

Looking around us, we can see how others also suffer – and may need our help. We can see that the seasons of suffering are often and quite incredibly followed by seasons of insight, increased wisdom and even joy. We can see that sometimes the suffering is of our own making – and it is we who must most urgently and humbly make amends. We can see that help comes when we ask for it – but sometimes wearing strange disguises.

A new heart I will give you,
And a new spirit I will put within you:
And I will take out of your flesh,
the heart of stone;
And give you a heart of flesh.

ROBERTO ASSAGIOLI TELLS this old story of three stone-
cutters, all employed on the building of a cathedral in medieval
times. When the first was asked what he was doing he said,
angrily, 'As you see, I am cutting stones.' The second replied,
pragmatically, 'I am earning a living for my family.' The third
said, joyfully, 'I am building a great cathedral.'

Forgiveness lives or dies not on what has been done to us,
and how we feel about that, but on the deepest and most
telling attitudes that we bring to our own stone-cutting, to the
meaning we find in existence. At the heart of forgiveness lies
a bewitching paradox that echoes in all the virtues: that the
more openly and truthfully we experience our connection
with others, the less personal and conditional this connection
needs to be. In bowing deeply to the heart of the person you
have injured, or feel injured by, you acknowledge what you
share; yet this knowledge can set you free. For only when we
understand what we share will we also understand how compassion emerges from truth and love and wholeness – and
changes everything.

Notes

Full publishing details for the works mentioned below are given in the Bibliography, which follows. Page numbers refer to Australian editions when they are listed.

Introduction

Page

viii   'Cultivate Virtue . . .': *Tao Teh Ching*, trans. John C. H. Wu, v. 54, p. 111.

5   'You can consciously . . .': Deepak Chopra, *The Seven Spiritual Laws of Success*, pp. 69–70.

8   'My heart, my . . .': quoted by Nor Hall, *The Moon and the Virgin*, p. 187.

Courage

Page

12   'It isn't for . . .': Anne Morrow Lindbergh, *Hours of Gold, Hours of Lead*.

16   'The purpose of life . . .': Foreword by His Holiness the Dalai Lama, in Mark Epstein, *Thoughts Without a Thinker*, p. ix.

19   'Existence cannot be postponed . . .': Irvin D. Yalom, *Existential Psychotherapy*, p. 161.

20   'Life is, if anything . . .': James Hall, quoted by Dee Wedemeyer, 'His life is his mind', *New York Times Magazine*, 18 August 1996.

22   'It is a great event . . .': *The Dhammapada*, ch. 14, v. 182, p. 62. In 1973 Juan Mascaro translated the line as: 'It is a great event to be born a man.' Times change.

26   'The soul of Nietzsche . . .': Rudolf Steiner, quoted by Piero Ferrucci, *Inevitable Grace*, p. 144.

27   'Give justice to . . .': Psalms (Revised Standard version) 82:3–6.

28   'Courage is two French words . . .': Matthew Fox interviewed by Samantha Trenoweth in her excellent book *The Future of God*, p. 240.

28   'We need tremendous courage . . .': Jack Kornfield, *A Path with Heart*, p. 8.

29   'The eye goes blind . . .': from 'Someone digging in the ground', brilliantly translated by Coleman Barks and included in Robert Bly's glorious, sensual collection of sacred poetry *The Soul Is Here for Its Own Joy*, p. 166.

31   'My child . . .': Proverbs 3:11–12. The original King James version reads: 'My son . . . even as a father the son in whom he delighteth.'

32   'The discontent . . .': Polly Young-Eisendrath, *The Gifts of Suffering*, p. 27.

32   'Buddhists talk . . .': ibid., p. 30.

33   'Over the years . . .': Elisabeth Kübler-Ross, in Richard Carlson and Benjamin Shield (eds), *Handbook for the Soul*, p. 131.

34   'I have found . . .': Elisabeth Kübler-Ross interviewed by Samantha Trenoweth in *The Future of God*, p. 57.

34   'An opportunity . . .': Elisabeth Kübler-Ross, in Carlson and Shield, p. 132.

34   'Perhaps one of the . . .': ibid., p. 133.

36   'Fear of fate . . .': Carl Gustav Jung, *Collected Works*, vol. 5.

37   'Nothing in the world . . .': *Tao Teh Ching*, v. 78, p. 159.

39   'The more and more . . .': quoted by Sogyal Rinpoche, *The Tibetan Book of Living and Dying*, p. 122.

40   'During that half . . .': Frankie Armstrong with Jenny Pearson, *As Far as the Eye Can Sing*, pp. 75–6.

41   'When you are no longer . . .': Ken Wilber, *No Boundary*, p. 158. Wilber is also the author of *Grace and Grit*, the story of the journey of his wife, Treya Killam Wilber, towards death from breast cancer. Their insight, openness and love – and their 'failures' and failings – exemplify all that I have been trying to learn about courage.

42   'I somehow managed . . .': Nini Herman, *My Kleinian Home*, p. 112.

42   I owe a great deal of inspiration and pleasure to the poetry of Lauris Edmond. 'Hymn to the body' can be found in *A Matter of Timing*, p. 17. *New and Selected Poems* offers more.

45   For a longer description of that trip see Stephanie Dowrick, 'Saving grace', *Sydney Morning Herald*, 11 November 1995.

47   'Suffering that is not understood . . .': Jung, *Collected Works*, vol. 18. This is an exceptionally important point, which I have made in different ways throughout this book. For readers who wish to take it further, I cannot recommend too highly Viktor E. Frankl, *Man's Search for Meaning*.

48   'Swami [Sai Baba] . . .': Kanya Stewart, private communication, 1996.

50   'Genuine breakdown . . .': Jim Glennon in conversation with Caroline Jones on ABC Radio, in Caroline Jones, *Search for Meaning*, 1989, p. 108.

51   'I'm not someone . . .': ibid.

52   'One should not . . .': Jung, quoted in G. Young, *Doctors Without Drugs*.

52   'What it meant for me . . .': Jones, *The Search for Meaning*, 1989, p. 108.

53   'Whenever one is . . .': Frankl, p. 178. See also my note for p. 47.

54   'My God . . .': Psalms (King James version) 22:1–2, 14, 19.

55   'The Lord is my Shepherd . . .': Psalms (King James version) 23:1–6.

57   'If one can conceive . . .': D. W. Winnicott, *Home Is Where the Heart Is*, p. 82. This vital point – which proceeds from self-responsibility and which allows the re-owning of projections – is most usefully developed by Jungian analyst James Hollis in his book about mid-life, *The Middle Passage*.

58   'There in the lucky dark . . .': both these lines and the anecdote about St John of the Cross can be found in Matthew Fox, *The Coming of the Cosmic Christ*, p. 54. There is great vitality, beauty and *inclusiveness* in Matthew Fox's Christian teachings. See also his *Original Blessing*.

59   'My son had died . . .': this story arose in private conversation. Anne Deveson's unforgettable account of her son's illness and death can be found in *Tell Me I'm Here*.

63   'The shattering of . . .': Andrew Harvey and Mark Matousek, *Dialogues with a Modern Mystic*, p. 58.

63   'Separation of the Creator . . .': ibid., pp. 58–9.

63   'I see a light . . .': Rabindranath Tagore, from 'Gitanjali', v. xxvii, in Bly, *The Soul Is Here for Its Own Joy*, p. 150. See also my note for p. 29.

66   'When someone has . . .': *The Dhammapada*, v. 22, l. 313, p. 79. Published as: 'When a man has something to do, let him do it with all his might.'

Fidelity

Page
70   'To be faithful to . . .': Ferrucci, *Inevitable Grace*, p. 253.
72   'This above all . . .': William Shakespeare, *Hamlet*, Act I, Scene 3.
73   'We were all narcissistic . . .': see also Stephanie Dowrick, *Intimacy and Solitude*, especially pp. 45–51.
76   'Much of the self-esteem . . .': Stephen R. Covey, in Carlson and Shield, pp. 143–4.
76   'He that is faithful . . .': Luke 16:10.
79   'There is the one . . .': Sri Sathya Sai Baba, quoted in Phyllis Krystal, *Sai Baba*, p. 133.
81   'Solid ground inside . . .': Dowrick, *Intimacy and Solitude*, p. 8; Marie-Louise von Franz, *Carl Gustav Jung*, p. 73. See also Fraser Boa, *The Way of the Dream*, which shows through conversations with Marie-Louise von Franz how, from the 'ether' of dream work, 'solid ground' evolves.
82   'Ego urges you . . .': for an arguably more positive and certainly credible view of the ego see Carol S. Pearson, *Awakening the Heroes Within*, pp. 32–7.
86   'Why do we . . .': James Hillman, *Inter Views*, p. 180.
87   'You may not . . .': for further reading on sub-personalities see Ferrucci, *What We May Be*, pp. 47–59. For active explorations of the complexity and creativity of the 'self', see Stephanie Dowrick, *The Intimacy and Solitude Self-Therapy Book*, pp. 37–88.
90   'While maintaining fidelity . . .': Hollis, p. 98.
91   'Everyone's task is. . .': Frankl, p. 172.
92   'A couple of years ago . . .': Stephanie Dowrick's interviews on change with Jean Shinoda Bolen and David K. Reynolds, *Living with Change*, audiotape.
107   'A spiritual life . . .': Thomas Moore, *Care of the Soul*, p. xii.
107   'Each promotes . . .': Robin Skynner and John Cleese, *Life and How to Survive It*, pp. 306–7.
108   'When a person . . .': Hazrat Inayat Khan, *The Art of Being and Becoming*, p. 189.
110   'Darkness within darkness . . .': Lao Tzu, quoted by Andrew Harvey, *The Return of the Mother*, p. 304.
111   'As the body . . .': *Meditations with Julian of Norwich*, trans. Brendan Doyle, p. 29.
114   'Blonde, great build . . .': Isabel Miller, *Side by Side*, p. 108.
115   'Lovemaking is . . .': Matthew Fox, interview in Trenoweth, p. 252.
118   'Human love is . . .': Dom Bede Griffiths, teaching in Australia, 1992.
119   'We've neglected . . .': ibid.
120   'A sexual relationship . . .': Thich Nhat Hanh, *Living Buddha, Living Christ*, pp. 97–8.
127   'Lust by itself . . .': Matthew Fox, interview in Trenoweth, p. 253.
128   'The flowers appear . . .': Song of Solomon (King James version) 2:12–16.
129   'The chief aim . . .': Frances G. Wickes, *The Inner World of Choice*, p. 138.
129   'For we are family . . .': Ephesians 4:25.

Restraint

Page
138   'I arise about. . . .': Robert Fulghum, in Carlson and Shield, pp. 10–11. See also Robert Fulghum, *All I Really Need to Know I Learned in Kindergarten*.
139   'Understanding that we can . . .': Kornfield, p. 114.

143 'God said . . .': Genesis 1: 26.
144 'The highest form . . .': *Tao Teh Ching*, v. 8, p. 17.
145 'We will establish . . .': William Johnston, *Letters to Contemplatives*, p. 103.
147 'The one corner-stone . . .': Caroline Stephen, quoted in Edward Cell (ed.), *Daily Readings from Quaker Spirituality*, p. 44.
147 'Recognizing a feeling . . .': Daniel Goleman, *Emotional Intelligence*, p. 43.
147 'At its best . . .': ibid., p. 47.
150 'Well, are you . . .': Jane Smiley, *The Age of Grief*, p. 181.
152 'My uniform experience . . .': M. K. Gandhi, *An Autobiography*, p. 452.
152 'Healthies have a . . .': Skynner and Cleese, p. 256.
153 'It's more difficult . . .': ibid.
153 'Warm and genuine . . .': Alice Miller, *For Your Own Good*, p. 32.
154 'Completely desist . . .': Chopra, *The Seven Spiritual Laws of Success*, p. 61. Such an expression of restraint need not be confused with either cynicism or passivity. It actually demands and develops a high level of active self-awareness and compassion.
158 'We are our own . . .': oral teachings of His Holiness the Dalai Lama, Sydney, December 1996.
159 'What power is it . . .': *The Bhagavad Gita*, ch. 3, vv. 36–8, 40, p. 59.
159 'They say that . . .': ibid., ch. 3, vv. 42–3, p. 60.
169 'Suffering completely fills . . .': Frankl, pp. 69–70.
170 An accessible introduction to thinking about archetypes is provided by Pearson, *Awakening the Heroes Within*. See also my note above for p. 87 re sub-personalities, which provides a complementary way of puzzling through the complexity and paradoxes within each human nature.
173 'In order to have . . .': Ferrucci, *Inevitable Grace*, p. 204.
173 'Science seems to . . .': ibid., p. 210.
176 'The best thing . . .': Nancy Friday, *Jealousy*, p. 576. This book provides stimulating access to the ideas and work of the psychoanalyst Melanie Klein.
176 'Once an elderly . . .': Frankl, pp. 178–9.
178 'In the community . . .': Winnicott, p. 34.
179 'We're not instructed . . .': Mark Matousek, in Harvey and Matousek, p. 97.

Generosity
Page
186 'From the conception . . .': Antony Alpers, *Legends of the South Sea*, pp. 55–6. In his notes Alpers explains that this chant was 'freely translated by the Reverend Richard Taylor, who collected it in the North Island of New Zealand around 1850' (p. 369).
187 'In the beginning . . .': Genesis (King James version) 1:1–31.
190 'How simple life is . . .': Isabel Allende, *Paula*, p. 327.
193 'An individual can . . .': James J. Lynch, *The Broken Heart*, p. 224.
194 'In the most ironic . . .': ibid., p. 225.
197 'The relationship wasn't . . .': Lisa Alther, *Other Women*, p. 16.
198 'Consumer capitalism's dependence . . .': Robert Bly, *The Sibling Society*, p. xiii.
200 'A gift is pure . . .': *The Bhagavad Gita*, ch. 17, vv. 20–2, pp. 113–14.

202 'The one principle . . .': Hazrat Inayat Khan, *Smiling*, pp. 44–5.

203 'When it comes . . .': Swami Chidvilasananda (Gurumayi), *My Lord Loves a Pure Heart*, p. 88.

204 'And Jesus sat . . .': Mark (King James version) 12:41–4.

204 'Her mite contributed . . .': William Johnston, *The Inner Eye of Love*, p. 171.

205 'What am I here to give? . . .': see Chopra, *The Seven Spiritual Laws of Success*, pp. 96–7. See also Deepak Chopra, *Return of the Rishi*.

205 'Service to humanity . . .': Chopra, *The Seven Spiritual Laws of Success*, p. 99.

207 'Everyone knows about . . .': Skynner and Cleese, pp. 106, 108.

211 'Ye have heard . . .': Matthew (King James version) 5:38–41.

211 'A young teenager . . .': David K. Reynolds, *Constructive Living*, pp. 76–7.

212 'Servitude and subjugation . . .': ibid., p. 77.

214 'When you hammer . . .': Hanh, *Living Buddha, Living Christ*, p. 66.

215 'It is my growing . . .': Henri J. M. Nouwen, *Reaching Out*, p. 16. See also Henri Nouwen's *The Road to Daybreak*.

216 'Our work . . .': Leonard Cheshire in conversation with Caroline Jones on ABC Radio, *Search for Meaning*, audiotape.

217 'In the Tonglen . . .': Sogyal Rinpoche, p. 205.

218 'The one thing . . .': ibid., p. 207.

220 'The law of love . . .': Gerald G. Jampolsky, *Goodbye to Guilt*, p. 184.

224 'In all the years . . .': Mary Pipher, *Reviving Ophelia*, p. 184.

226 'Eight million women . . .': ibid., p. 185.

227 'In 1996, an international declaration . . .': from *Sydney Morning Herald*, December 1996, reporting from Reuter, Agence France-Press.

227 'The United States believes . . .': ibid.

228 'Seriously undermine . . .': Pamela Bone, 'Poor excuses', *Sydney Morning Herald*, 18 October 1996.

232 'The reward of life . . .': Khan, *Smiling*, p. 45.

233 'Love deeply and strongly . . .': Ferrucci, *Inevitable Grace*, p. 264.

233 'It is in giving . . .': Prayer of St Francis.

Tolerance
Page
241 'In a famous . . .': Susan Griffin, *A Chorus of Stones*, p. 98.

243 'People cannot think . . .': Anonymous, presented to the Soviet Peace Committee, Moscow, 1951, by the Religious Society of Friends, London, reprinted in Cell, p. 76.

244 'People have asked . . .': Nancy Mairs, in Susan Wadia-Ells (ed.), *The Adoption Reader*, p. 150.

245 'When I recall . . .': Abraham H. Biderman, *The World of My Past*, p. 305.

247 'When we were . . .': Robert Bly, *A Little Book on the Human Shadow*, p. 17.

248 'Bly suggests . . .': ibid., p. 18.

248 'Whenever we are . . .': Marie-Louise von Franz, talking to Boa, *The Way of the Dream*, pp. 80–1.

250 'When people learn. . . .': ibid., pp. 82–3.

253   'Most people feel . . .': June Singer, *Boundaries of the Soul*, p. 226. Singer (p. 224) also
      usefully describes the person who projects his own shadow: 'This means that he
      will not see his own weaknesses, but will find causes everywhere else for his
      inability to accomplish more of what he sets out to do. Always there will be
      an unfortunate combination of events which works against him, or there will
      be somebody who is out to get him. That somebody will inevitably be described
      with great vehemence as having just those despicable qualities which he fails
      to see in himself, but which dog his every step.' This human capacity to project
      one's own shadow is so widespread and so damaging it is impossible to
      overemphasise how important it is that we come to recognise it, not least
      within ourselves.

253   'The person who. . . .': ibid., p. 227.

256   'The psychology of war . . .': ibid., p. 226.

260   'I first met him . . .': Robert Dessaix, *A Mother's Disgrace*, p. 187.

260   'In saying that . . .': ibid., pp. 187–8.

265   'It's really interesting . . .': for more information on Sally Gillespie's accessible,
      rewarding way of working with dreams see Sally Gillespie, *Living the Dream*.

266   'A life of ease . . .': Jung, *Collected Works*, vol. 18.

267   'We imagine that . . .': Charlotte Joko Beck with Steve Smith, *Nothing Special*,
      p. 57.

267   'In her novel . . .': Rosellen Brown, *Before and After*.

269   'The secret, immortal centre . . .': Heita Copony, *Mystery of Mandalas*, p. 19.

269   'When we see . . .': ibid., p. 20.

270   'Hilarious comedy . . .': see John Cleese's pertinent comments in Skynner and Cleese,
      p. 82.

276   'We use our parents . . .': Doris Lessing, in Ursula Owen (ed.), *Fathers*, p. 80.

276   'Successful artistic parents . . .': John Fowles, in John Hoyland (ed.), *Fathers and Sons*,
      p. 44.

277   'I realise now . . .': ibid., p. 46.

277   'Over twenty years ago . . .': ibid., p. 47.

279   'Directly one looked up . . .': Virginia Woolf, *To the Lighthouse*, p. 16.

280   'We have to understand . . .': Hanh, *Living Buddha, Living Christ*, p. 84.

281   'Love your enemies . . .': Matthew 5:44–5. This exquisite passage, which is at the
      heart of Christian teaching, is exactly what is ignored and insulted when,
      tragically, in the name of Christianity, people practise intolerance, divisiveness
      and hatred.

281   'There are four kinds . . .': *The Bhagavad Gita*, ch. 7, vv. 16–18, p. 75. Published as
      'There are four kinds of men . . .'

282   'In the early stages . . .': Garry Lynch, speaking to Gina Lennox, *Struck by Lightning*,
      p. 143.

283   'I remember this . . .': ibid., p. 91.

283   'If we visualize . . .': Hanh, *Living Buddha, Living Christ*, p. 83.

284   'Whatever acts . . .': Sri Sathya Sai Baba, quoted in Don Mario Mazzoleni, *A Catholic
      Priest Meets Sai Baba*, p. 126.

285   'Here is Kabir's . . .': Kabir, 'Why should we part?', in Bly, *The Soul Is Here for Its Own
      Joy*, p. 93.

Forgiveness

Page

288 'The holiest . . .': *A Course in Miracles*, vol. 1, p. 522.

292 'The works of a . . .': *The Bhagavad Gita*, ch. 18, v. 42, p. 119.

293 'Forgiveness in no way . . .': Dawna Markova, *No Enemies Within*, p. 291.

294 'When I look back . . .': Young-Eisendrath, p. 18.

295 'When suffering leads . . .': ibid., p. 22.

295 I have made free use of the myth of Demeter and Persephone. In Greek mythology
     there was no concept of hell in the Judaic-Christian meaning of that word.

299 'We must be quite . . .': Hillman, 'Betrayal', p. 78.

302 'I got terribly . . .': Michael Leunig in conversation with Caroline Jones on ABC
     Radio, in Caroline Jones, *The Search for Meaning*, 1992, p. 160.

305 'I find that . . .': ibid, p. 161.

306 'Our enemy is . . .': Hanh, *Living Buddha, Living Christ*, pp. 75–6.

312 'And the Lord God said . . .': Genesis (King James version) 3:22–3.

312 'Do not what is . . .': *The Dhammapada*, ch. 14, v. 183, p. 62.

312 'Desire has found . . .': *The Bhagavad Gita*, ch. 3, vv. 40–2, pp. 59–60.

314 'For us to achieve . . .': Hanh, *Living Buddha, Living Christ*, p. 76.

315 'Only an exceedingly . . .': Jung, *Collected Works*, vol. 10, p. 220.

316 'Looking deeply . . .': Hanh, *Living Buddha, Living Christ*, p. 76.

327 'There are many ways . . .': Clarissa Pinkola Estes, *Women Who Run with the Wolves*,
     p. 372.

329 'We are all creatures . . .': Brian Keenan, *An Evil Cradling*, p. 85. I am immensely
     grateful to Jo Upham for bringing this remarkable book to my attention.

329 'Each morning I . . .': ibid.

332 'There is a place of rest . . .': Beck, pp. 160–1.

334 'Oh Lord, remember . . .': G. Appleton (ed.), *The Pocket Oxford Book of Prayer*, p. 25.

335 'Would you still weaken . . .': *A Course in Miracles*, vol. 1, p. 349.

339 'Hate is not conquered . . .': *The Dhammapada*, ch. 1, v. 5, p. 35.

340 '[This] is where . . .': Gabrielle Lord, 'Love and alcohol', in Jean Bedford (ed.), *Loves*,
     pp. 169–70.

341 'Forgiveness paints . . .': *A Course in Miracles*, vol. 2, p. 408.

341 'Friend, it's time . . .': Ansari, 'Friend, it's time', in Bly, *The Soul Is Here for Its Own Joy*,
     p. 13.

343 'Interviewing MacKinnon . . .': Catherine Bennett, 'God is a woman', *HQ Magazine*,
     November 1994.

344 'Hundreds and hundreds . . .': Keenan, pp. 287–8.

346 'We and nature . . .': Harvey and Matousek, p. 67.

347 'A new heart . . .': Ezekiel 36:26.

347 'Roberto Assagioli tells . . .': Roberto Assagioli, *The Act of Will*, p. 110.

Bibliography

Printed Works

Allende, Isabel. *Paula*. HarperCollins, London, 1995; New York, 1995.

Alpers, Antony. *Legends of the South Sea*. John Murray, London, 1970.

Alther, Lisa. *Other Women*. Knopf, New York, 1984.

Appleton, G. (ed.). *The Pocket Oxford Book of Prayer*. Oxford University Press, Oxford, 1989.

Armstrong, Frankie, with Pearson, Jenny. *As Far as the Eye Can Sing*. The Women's Press, London, 1992.

Assagioli, Roberto. *The Act of Will*. Viking, New York, 1973.

____. *Psychosynthesis*. Penguin Books, New York, 1976.

The Bhagavad Gita. Trans. Juan Mascaro. Penguin, Harmondsworth, 1962; Viking Penguin, New York.

The Bhagavadgita. Trans. S. Radhakrishnan. George Allen & Unwin, London, 1948; Harper San Francisco, 1994.

Beck, Charlotte Joko, with Smith, Steve. *Nothing Special: Living Zen*. Harper SanFrancisco, San Francisco, 1993.

Bedford, Jean (ed.). *Loves*. Angus & Robertson, Sydney, 1995.

Biderman, Abraham H. *The World of My Past*. Random, Sydney, 1996.

Bly, Robert. *A Little Book on the Human Shadow*. Harper & Row, New York, 1988.

____. *The Sibling Society*. Addison-Wesley, Reading, 1996.

____ (ed.). *The Soul Is Here for Its Own Joy: Sacred Poems from Many Cultures*. Ecco Press, New Jersey, 1995.

Boa, Fraser. *The Way of the Dream: Conversations on Jungian Dream Interpretation with Marie-Louise von Franz*. Shambhala, Boston, 1994.

Brown, Rosellen. *Before and After*. Farrar, Straus & Giroux, New York, 1992.

Carlson, Richard, and Shield, Benjamin. *Handbook for the Soul*. Doubleday, New York, 1996.

Cell, Edward (ed.). *Daily Readings from Quaker Spirituality*. Templegate, Springfield, 1987.

Swami Chidvilasananda (Gurumayi). *My Lord Loves a Pure Heart: The Yoga of Divine Virtues*. Syda Foundation, South Fallsburg, 1994. Available from Syda Foundation, 371 Brickman Road, PO Box 600, South Fallsburg, New York, NY 12779–0600.

Chopra, Deepak. *Return of the Rishi: A Doctor's Search for the Ultimate Healer*. Houghton Mifflin, Boston, 1988.

____. *The Seven Spiritual Laws of Success*. Amber-Allen, San Rafael, 1994.

Copony, Heita. *Mystery of Mandalas*. Theosophical Publishing House, Wheaton, 1989.

A Course in Miracles, 3 vols. Foundation for Inner Peace, Farmingdale, 1975; Viking Penguin, New York, 1996.

The Dhammapada. Trans. Juan Mascaro. Penguin, Harmondsworth, 1973; Viking Penguin, New York.

Dessaix, Robert. *A Mother's Disgrace*. HarperCollins, Sydney, 1994.

Deveson, Anne. *Tell Me I'm Here*. Penguin, Melbourne, 1993; Viking Penguin, New York, 1992.

Dowrick, Stephanie. *Running Backwards Over Sand*. Viking, Harmondsworth and Melbourne, 1985.

———. *Intimacy and Solitude*. Heinemann, Melbourne, 1991; The Women's Press, London, 1992; W. W. Norton, New York, 1994.

———. *The Intimacy and Solitude Self-Therapy Book*. Heinemann, Melbourne, 1993; The Women's Press, London, 1993; published as *The Intimacy and Solitude Workbook*, W. W. Norton, New York, 1994.

Edmond, Lauris. *A Matter of Timing*. Auckland University Press, Auckland, 1996.

———. *New and Selected Poems*. Oxford University Press, Auckland, 1992; Dufour Editions, Chester Springs, 1993.

Epstein, Mark. *Thoughts Without a Thinker*. Basic Books, New York, 1996.

Estes, Clarissa Pinkola. *Women Who Run with the Wolves: Contacting the Power of the Wild Woman*. Rider, London, 1992; Ballantine, New York, 1992.

Ferrucci, Piero. *What We May Be: The Visions and Techniques of Psychosynthesis*. Turnstone, Wellingborough, 1982; Jeremy P. Tarcher, New York, 1983.

———. *Inevitable Grace*. Crucible, Wellingborough, 1990; Jeremy P. Tarcher, New York, 1990.

Fox, Matthew. *Original Blessing*. Bear & Co, Santa Fe, 1983.

———. *The Coming of the Cosmic Christ*. Harper & Row, New York, 1988.

Frankl, Viktor E. *Man's Search for Meaning*. Beacon, Boston, 1962.

Franz, Marie-Louise von. *Carl Gustav Jung: His Myth in Our Time*. G. P. Putnam's Sons, New York, 1975.

Friday, Nancy. *Jealousy*. Perigord, New York, 1985.

Fulghum, Robert. *All I Really Need to Know I Learned in Kindergarten*. Grafton, London, 1989; Random House, New York, 1988.

Gandhi, M.K. *An Autobiography: Or the Story of My Experiments with Truth*. Penguin, Harmondsworth, 1982.

Gillespie, Sally. *Living the Dream*. Transworld, Sydney, 1996.

Goleman, Daniel. *Emotional Intelligence*. Bantam, New York, 1996.

Griffin, Susan. *A Chorus of Stones: The Private Life of War*. Doubleday, New York, 1992; The Women's Press, London, 1994.

Hall, Nor. *The Moon and the Virgin: Reflections on the Archetypal Feminine*. The Women's Press, London, 1980; Harper Collins, New York, 1980.

Hanh, Thich Nhat. *Peace Is Every Step: The Path of Mindfulness in Everyday Life*. Bantam, New York, 1991.

———. *Living Buddha, Living Christ*. G. P. Putnam's Sons, New York, 1995.

Harvey, Andrew. *The Way of Passion: A Celebration of Rumi*. Frog, Berkeley, 1994.

———. *The Return of the Mother*. Frog, Berkeley, 1995.

———, and Matousek, Mark. *Dialogues with a Modern Mystic*. Theosophical Publishing House, Wheaton, 1994.

Herman, Nini. *My Kleinian Home: A Journey Through Four Psychotherapies*. Quartet, London, 1985.

Hillman, James. Betrayal. Lecture 128, Guild of Pastoral Psychology, London, 1964. Published in *Spring*, 1965, pp. 57–76.

———. *Inter Views*. Harper & Row, New York, 1983.

———. *A Blue Fire*. Ed. Thomas Moore. Harper & Row, New York, 1989.

Hollis, James. *The Middle Passage: From Misery to Meaning in Mid-Life*. Inner City Books,

Toronto, 1993; Lothrop, Lee & Shepard Books, New York.

Hoyland, John (ed.). *Fathers and Sons*. Serpent's Tail, London and New York, 1992.

Jampolsky, Gerald G. *Goodbye to Guilt*. Bantam, New York, 1985.

Johnston, William. *The Inner Eye of Love: Mysticism and Religion*. Harper & Row, New York, 1978.

_____. *Letters to Contemplatives*. HarperCollins, London, 1991; Orbis Books, Maryknoll, 1992.

Jones, Caroline. *The Search for Meaning*. ABC/Collins Dove, Melbourne, 1989.

_____. *The Search for Meaning: Conversations with Caroline Jones*. ABC/Collins Dove, Melbourne, 1992.

Julian of Norwich. *Revelations of Divine Love*. Trans. Clifton Walters. Penguin Books, Harmondsworth, 1966; Viking Penguin, New York, 1992.

Jung, Carl Gustav. *Psychological Reflections*. Princeton University Press, Princeton, 1970.

_____. *Collected Works*, vols 5, 10, 18. Princeton University Press, Princeton, 1952, 1964, 1976.

Keenan, Brian. *An Evil Cradling*. Hutchinson, London, 1992; Viking Penguin, New York, 1993.

Khan, Hazrat Inayat. *The Art of Being and Becoming*. Omega, New Lebanon, New York, 1989.

_____. *Smiling*. Sufi Movement of India, New Delhi, 1995. Available from Sufi Movement of India, 129 Basti Hazrat Nizamuddin, New Delhi 110013.

Kornfield, Jack. *A Path with Heart*. Bantam, New York, 1993.

Krystal, Phyllis. *Sai Baba: The Ultimate Experience*. Samuel Weiser, York Beach, 1985.

Lennox, Gina. *Struck by Lightning: The Story of Garry Lynch*. Allen & Unwin, Sydney, 1996.

Lynch, James J. *The Broken Heart: The Medical Consequences of Loneliness*. Basic, New York, 1979.

Markova, Dawna. *No Enemies Within*. Conari, Berkeley, 1994.

Mazzoleni, Don Mario. *A Catholic Priest Meets Sai Baba*. Leela Press, Faber, 1994.

Meditations with Julian of Norwich. Trans. Brendan Doyle. Bear & Co., Santa Fe, 1983.

Miller, Alice. *For Your Own Good: Hidden Cruelty in Childrearing*. Faber & Faber, London, 1983; Farrar, Straus & Giroux, New York, 1983.

Miller, Isabel. *Side by Side*. The Women's Press, London, 1996; Naiad Press, Tallahasse, 1990.

Moore, Thomas. *Care of the Soul: A Guide for Cultivating Depth and Sacredness in Everyday Life*. HarperCollins, New York, 1992.

Nouwen, Henri J. M. *Reaching Out: The Three Movements of the Spiritual Life*. Fount, London, 1976; Doubleday, New York, 1975.

_____. *The Road to Daybreak: A Spiritual Journey*. Doubleday, New York, 1988.

Owen, Ursula (ed.). *Fathers: Reflections by Daughters*. Virago, London, 1983; Pantheon Books, New York, 1985.

Pearson, Carol S. *Awakening the Heroes Within: Twelve Archetypes to Help Us Find Ourselves and Transform the World*. Harper SanFrancisco, San Francisco, 1991.

Pipher, Mary. *Reviving Ophelia: Saving the Selves of Adolescent Girls*. Ballantine, New York, 1995.

Reynolds, David K. *Constructive Living*. University Press of Hawaii, Honolulu, 1984.

_____. *Playing Ball on Running Water*. William Morrow, New York, 1984.

Singer, June. *Boundaries of the Soul: The Practice of Jung's Psychology*. Anchor, New York, 1973.

Skynner, Robin, and Cleese, John. *Life and How to Survive It*. Methuen, London, 1993; W. W. Norton, 1995.

Smiley, Jane. *The Age of Grief*. Knopf, New York, 1987.

Sogyal Rinpoche. *The Tibetan Book of Living and Dying*. Harper SanFrancisco, San Francisco, 1992.

Tagore, Rabindranath. *Collected Poems and Plays*. Macmillan, London, 1958; New York, 1993.

Tao Teh Ching (by Lao Tzu). Trans. John C. H. Wu. St John's University Press, New York, 1961; Shambhala, Boston, 1989.

Trenoweth, Samantha. *The Future of God: Personal Adventures in Spirituality with Thirteen of Today's Eminent Thinkers*. Millennium, Sydney, 1995; Morehouse, Ridgefield, 1995.

Yalom, Irvin D. *Existential Psychotherapy*. Basic, New York, 1980.

Young, G. *Doctors Without Drugs*. London, 1962.

Young-Eisendrath, Polly. *The Gifts of Suffering*. Addison-Wesley, Reading, 1996; republished as *The Resilient Spirit: Transforming Suffering into Insight, Compassion and Renewal*, Allen & Unwin, Sydney, 1997.

Wadia-Ells, Susan (ed.). *The Adoption Reader*. The Women's Press, London, 1996; Seal Press, Seattle, 1995.

Wickes, Frances G. *The Inner World of Choice*. Coventure, London, 1963; Sigo, Boston, 1988.

Wilber, Ken. *No Boundary: Eastern and Western Approaches to Personal Growth*. New Science Library, Shambhala, Boston, 1979.

_____. *Grace and Grit: Spirituality and Healing in the Life and Death of Treya Killam Wilber*. Shambhala, Boston, 1991.

Winnicott, D. W. *Home Is Where the Heart Is: Essays by a Psychoanalyst*. The Hogarth Press, London, 1972, 1986; published as *Home is Where We Start From*, W. W. Norton, New York, 1986.

Woolf, Virginia. *To the Lighthouse*. The Hogarth Press, London, 1927; Harcourt Brace, New York, 1927.

Audiotapes

Dowrick, Stephanie. *The Intimacy and Solitude Tapes*. Reed, Melbourne, 1995.

_____. *Living with Change: Interviews with Jean Shinoda Bolen and David K. Reynolds*. ABC Audio Tapes, Sydney, 1995. Tape available from ABC Audio, GPO Box 9994, Sydney 2001.

_____, with Geraldine Doogue. *The Humane Virtues*. ABC Audio Tapes, Sydney, 1996. Tape available from ABC Audio, GPO Box 9994, Sydney 2001.

Jones, Caroline. *Search for Meaning*. Tapes available from ABC Audio, GPO Box 9994, Sydney 2001.

Acknowledgements

I have many people to acknowledge, and I do so with the deepest gratitude: Jocelyn Krygier, for her exceptional loyalty and friendship; Gabriel and Kezia Dowrick, for never failing to illuminate every aspect of my life; Geraldine Doogue, Jo Upham and Eurydice Aroney, for the stimulating, sustaining work we have done together for ABC Radio National's 'Life Matters', and especially for the series I recorded with Geraldine on the Humane Virtues, which was the essential springboard for this book; Bernadette Neubecker at ABC Audio, who produced the audiotape of those talks; the Soul Travellers, and especially Tony Backhouse, Liz Strickland and Jane McLean, for the amazing grace of shared singing; Caroline Jones, for her inspirational work on radio; Wendy Ashton, Pam Benton, Chris Burvill and Greg Andrews, Mary Helen Dowrick, Peter East, Sally Gillespie, Margaret Gottlieb, Niki Honore, Robyn Ianssen, Caroline Josephs, Susanne Kahn-Ackermann, Geraldine Killalea, Drusilla Modjeska, Neil Philips, Hanan al-Shayk, Melissa Shannon, Elizabeth Stead, Erika Villaneuva, for invaluable support during the time of writing this book or the several years that preceded it.

The people who told me their stories of how the virtues play through their lives have made an invaluable contribution. Some of them are named, most are not. All bring the richness of real life to these pages. Thank you.

I have drawn from other writers in developing my ideas, and have been moved and inspired as I did so. For permission to use their work I thank most sincerely: Isabel Allende, Lisa Alther, Frankie Armstrong, Charlotte Joko Beck, Abraham H. Biderman, Robert Bly, Robert Dessaix, Lauris Edmond, Piero Ferrucci, Caroline Jones and ABC Enterprises, Brian Keenan, Gabrielle Lord, Garry Lynch, Mary Pipher, David K. Reynolds, Samantha Trenoweth, and The Women's Press on behalf of Susan Griffin.

The publication of this book has been exceptionally happy. For that I need to thank most warmly my agent, Barbara Mobbs; four publishers: Kathy Gale at The Women's Press, London; Amy Cherry at W. W. Norton & Co, New York; Geoff Walker at Penguin New Zealand; and especially Julie Gibbs at Penguin Australia who has unstintingly offered a level of attention and enthusiasm that would match any writer's dream. I am delighted also to thank Lesley Dunt, for exemplary editorial and personal support, and Sandy Cull, for designing this book with such subtle, intelligent care for beauty.

Finally, I want to acknowledge that I would not have been able to complete this book without the support of Jane Moore. With pleasure and love, she looked after my children when I needed to give this book the attention it deserved. She read early drafts. She directed me to Sufi teachings, and renewed my faith in countless ways. I hope that my appreciation is adequately expressed through the shared dedication of this book to her.